Y0-AFV-817

Faith Born in the Struggle for Life

A Re-reading of Protestant Faith
in Latin America Today

Edited by
DOW KIRKPATRICK

Translated by
LEWISTINE MCCOY

WILLIAM B. EERDMANS PUBLISHING COMPANY
GRAND RAPIDS, MICHIGAN

Copyright © 1988 by William B. Eerdmans Publishing Co.
255 Jefferson Ave. S.E., Grand Rapids, Michigan 49503

All rights reserved
Printed in the United States of America

Library of Congress Cataloging-in-Publication Data

Faith born in the struggle for life.

   1. Theology, Doctrinal—Latin America. 2. Protestant churches—Latin
America—Doctrines. 3. Latin America—Church history—20th century.
I. Kirkpatrick, Dow.
BT30.L37F34   1988   280'.4'098   88-16364
ISBN 0-8028-0355-5

Contents

PART II: THE ORIGINAL LEGACY—DISTORTIONS IN ITS TRANSMISSION

PART III: EVANGELIZATION AND ECUMENICAL VISION

Contributors

Altmann, Walter. A Lutheran theologian, he is president of Lutheran Theological Seminary, São Leopoldo, Brazil.

Alves, Rubem. A Presbyterian sociologist/theologian at the University of Campinas, Brazil.

Araya, Victorio. A Methodist theologian at Biblical Seminary, San José, Costa Rica.

Arias, Mortimer. President of Biblical Seminary, San José, Costa Rica. He is also a professor at Claremont, Calif., and a former bishop of the Methodist Church in Bolivia.

Assmann, Hugo. A Catholic theologian at the Graduate Department, the Methodist University, Piracicaba, Brazil.

Batista Guerra, Israel. A Methodist theologian in Cuba.

Bingemer, Maria Clara. A Catholic theologian in Brazil.

Boff, Leonardo. A Catholic theologian in Brazil.

César, Ely Éser Barreto. New Testament professor and academic dean, the Methodist University, Brazil; he is Methodist.

de Santa Ana, Julio. An educator with Base Christian Communities in Brazil, he is a Methodist from Uruguay.

de Araújo, João Dias. A Presbyterian pastoral theologian in Brazil.

Dias, Zwinglio M. A Presbyterian pastoral theologian in Brazil.

Etchegoyen, Aldo. President of the Council of Latin American Methodist Churches, he is a Methodist pastor in Buenos Aires, Argentina.

Maciel, Lysâneas. A lawyer and member of Congress, he is a Presbyterian layman in Brazil.

Míguez Bonino, José. A Methodist theologian at the Institute for Graduate Studies, Buenos Aires, Argentina. He is a former president of the World Council of Churches.

Pagura, Federico. Bishop of the Methodist Church of Argentina, he is the president of the Latin American Council of Churches.

Pereira, Nancy Cardoso. A Methodist pastor in Brazil.

Pixley, Jorge. A biblicist at Baptist Seminary, Managua, Nicaragua.

Ritchie, Nelly. A Methodist pastor in Argentina.

Rivera Pagán, Luis N. A Baptist theologian in Puerto Rico.

Ruiz, Jerjes. A Baptist theologian in Nicaragua.

Schwantes, Milton. A Lutheran biblicist in Brazil.

Sepúlveda, Juan. A Pentecostal theologian in Chile.

Tamez, Elsa. A Methodist biblicist in Costa Rica.

Is Latin American Protestant Theology Relevant for Us?

The Protestant churches of Latin America show striking vigor in their efforts to commit themselves to a renovated spirituality. It is a spirituality arising out of the gospel announcement that God has taken an option for the oppressed poor. This option must define the mission of the church today.

Since 1975 I have been privileged to witness this struggle for a new spirituality at close range. As a missionary-in-reverse for the United Methodist Church, my vocation has been to bring the gospel from Latin America to North America.

Protestantism entered Latin America largely through North American missions, to provide a necessary alternative to Catholicism. The prevailing Catholicism, overwhelmingly dominant in the culture, had a history of linking itself with the controlling classes. This self-definition was challenged by the Latin American Catholic Bishops' Conference in Medellín, Colombia, in 1968. Forces very like those of the sixteenth-century Protestant Reformation began to reshape the theology and practice of the Roman Catholic church in Latin America—not, of course, without struggles with the traditional definitions.

While this reformation was good for the Catholic church, it was a principal cause of a growing Protestant identity crisis. It was no longer clear why a minority Protestantism was necessary. For example, in the past various Latin American cities jailed early Protestant missionaries, at the instigation of the Catholic bishop, for distributing Bibles; now there is more Bible study among Catholics than among Protestants.

Even before Medellín the Protestant crisis was already in motion. Two other factors were operating: second- and third-generation Protestants were dissatisfied with their churches' ghetto mentality. They began to claim a place in the Latin American society, with its problems and struggles. They were no longer willing to be a foreign "colony." This awareness came together with the social crisis of the fifties and sixties with its "irruption of the poor," which revealed the injustice and oppression in society. Long before Vatican II, an awakened Christian conscience among Protestants was expressing itself in a variety of ecumenical organizations, as they began the search for a renewed spirituality.

This critique is not meant to depreciate the work of the missionary. It attempts, rather, to discover an authentic strategy for a new generation. This analysis becomes the starting point for the creation of a newly relevant theology for today. For the deepening of our own spirituality, we need this resource from the faith experience of others whose life context is very different from ours. Thus, this developing body of theology must be made accessible to an English-speaking public.

In Part I ("Recreating the Fidelity") the basic themes of Christian faith are given a new reading. Each one makes evident to us how the context of struggle for life—survival and dignity—changes the shape of every facet of our Christian faith. In Part II the authors detail some of the distortions in theology that resulted from the transmission of the original legacy from its source in Europe via the United States.

Permit me to introduce to you twenty-four persons with whom you may not be familiar, but whose names are widely known throughout Latin America, in both Catholic and Protestant circles. They represent five branches of Protestantism: Methodist (eleven), Baptist (three), Presbyterian (four), Lutheran (two), and Pentecostal (one). Three Catholic theologians are included for very specific reasons. Hugo Assmann, from the Methodist University in Brazil, offers a Catholic evaluation of Wesleyan holiness. Maria Clara Bingemer's treatment of the Trinity is evidence that a feminine perspective is neither Catholic nor Protestant. Leonardo Boff is widely known for his theological production and his resulting censure by the Vatican. Here he contributes a most valuable critique of Luther and the Reformation from a liberation standpoint. Four of the group are laypersons, four are women.

INTRODUCTION

Lewistine McCoy's translation of this material is indispensable in making it accessible to an English-speaking audience. His lifetime of missionary service has given him a facility of language, theological understanding, and a personal commitment to the oppressed that make him an invaluable companion.

Our search for this developing theology has been continent wide. The geographical sweep of those included here covers nine countries of Central and South America. The available materials are prolific; more has been omitted than could be included.[1] Most encouraging is the rapid increase of published materials by women theologians. Those included here are only a small sample of perhaps the most significant factor in current Latin American theologizing.

Another important characteristic of the theological process in Latin America, in contrast to North America, is the community context in which it is done. Two centers of reflection have taken leadership in sponsoring consultations and publishing results: Departamento Ecuménico de Investigaciones (Center for Ecumenical Research, San José, Costa Rica), and UNIMEP (the Methodist University, Piracicaba, Brazil).

The current essays have been selected from a series of consultations related to each other. DEI in Costa Rica is facilitating Encounters on Protestant Theology under the title *La Tradición Protestante en La Teología Latinoamericana* (The Protestant Theological Tradition in Latin America). The results of the Methodist and Baptist studies are now available. In 1984 the Methodists of Brazil continued the Costa Rican dialogue under the title *Luta Pela Vida e Evangelização* (The Struggle for Life and Evangelization). This volume also contains essays taken from other sources.[2]

1. See Dow Kirkpatrick, *Human Rights in Central America: An Annotated Bibliography* (Nashville: Curriculum Resources Committee, 1988). This bibliography lists other publications in English of many of these authors, and also lists other Latin American authors not a part of this volume.
2. Milton Schwantes, "Dize Que És Minha Irmã!" *Meditações sobre Alguns Temas de Gênesis 12-25* (Belo Horizonte, Brazil: Centro de Estudoes Biblicos, 1987), pp. 14-20; Nelly Ritchie, *Cuadernos de Teologia*, VII, 3 (Buenos Aires: ISEDET, 1986), pp. 141-51; Walter Altmann, *Confrontacion y Liberacion: Una Perspectiva Latinoamericana sobre Martin Lutero* (Buenos Aires:

Introduction

Latin American Methodists are leading in the construction of an ecumenism committed to social justice and the primacy of the kingdom of God. The central question for them is: Do Wesley's theology and the Methodist tradition have any relevance for Latin American Methodists today? If so, what should be appropriated and adapted to the current scene? Comparable questions are being asked by other denominations about the relevance of their own historic theology and traditions. Knowing them as they know themselves will greatly enhance our experience of global ecumenism.

Much more is offered the world community by this phenomenon. Here are unique, highly significant impulses, which should change the direction of theologizing, both academic and popular, in the English-speaking world.

The process of "doing theology" in the context of oppression moves in a direction the reverse of that familiar in our Western culture. Latin American theologians begin with the "struggle for life" and move to its articulation; we begin with concepts that we then seek to "apply" to life. Since the directions are different, the results are different. To change from our elitism to a popular origin for theology would radically transform our experience of the faith.

In addition, the Latin American Protestant experience may have more to teach us than does the Catholic experience. The renewal of the Catholic church did not happen at Medellín in 1968; it was announced and given the episcopal imprimatur at that time and place by the Bishops' Conference. Over an earlier period God had spoken to the oppressed poor. The hierarchy had channels that connected them with the poor. So when God spoke to the oppressed, the gospel of God's option for the poor "trickled up" to the bishops.

Latin American Protestantism was born of a North

ISEDET, 1987), pp. 95-109; Leonardo Boff, *Revista Eclesiastica Brasileira*, 43 (Petrópolis: Vozes, 1983), pp. 714-36; Rubem Alves, *Dogmatismo e Tolerância* (São Paulo: Edições Paulinas, 1982), pp. 149-72; Israel Batista, *International Review of Mission*, LXXIV, 295 (Geneva: WCC, 1985). The chapters by Maria Clara Bingemer and Elsa Tamez are found in *El Rostro Femenino de la Teologia* (San José: DEI, 1986), pp. 135-65, 189-203. Other essays (Zwinglio Dias, Lysâneas Maciel, João Dias de Araújo, Juan Sepúlveda, Nancy Cardoso Pereira) were provided directly to the editor by the author.

American mentality brought by the missionaries. They went to the poor. Their witness was planted largely among peasants, workers, and Indians. The ideology of this message, however, was individualistic. Upward social mobility toward middle-class goals was the expected result of conversion and faithful Christian living. It left behind, unliberated, the masses of the oppressed poor. So their connection with the poor has been much like ours in Western Europe and the United States. If God chose to speak a new word to "our" poor, our middle-class mentality would make it difficult for North American Protestantism to hear that word.

Since Latin American Protestants have the same problem, their discovery of ways to hear the gospel offers us a way out of our "captivity." For this reason, the title of the Brazilian Methodist study is instructive: *The Struggle for Life—Evangelization*. The operative word is *evangelization*, not *evangelism*. Its definition is in terms of "struggle for life"—not institutional expansion, nor a privatized experience.

The ecumenical nature of this evangelization is essential to the definitions of both "ecumenism" and "evangelization." This new ecumenism is not based on achieving doctrinal agreements nor structural mergers. It forms around commitment— to the liberation of the oppressed. All who have taken that option are the one true church.

This is made evident by the chapters in Part III. Zwinglio Dias shows us ecumenism going beyond disunity within a denomination, made possible by a rereading of Calvin. The magnet that draws us to one another, says Victório Araya, is the poor. Lysâneas Maciel embodies in his person human rights as an ecumenical event. At the height of the repressive dictatorship, he said on the floor of the Brazilian Congress what he says to us in these pages. In the intervening years, he was expelled from his elected congressional seat. After years of exile, he is again an elected representative in the Brazilian Congress.

The Afro-Brazilian religious phenomenon is in every country of Latin America and the Caribbean, in the Indian as well as African cultures. The revised effort to understand it is so recent that documents of theological analysis have yet to be written. The changing attitude toward this widespread syncretism revolves around three foci:

1. Afro-Brazilian religion is a way the blacks have to express their black identity.
2. Afro-Brazilian religion offers white Christians the opportunity to declare solidarity with the black identity movement.
3. Affirmation of Afro-Brazilian popular religiosity links Christians of all colors and classes with popular movements and the religiosity of all marginalized peoples.

João Dias de Araújo's brief chapter is offered as an ecumenical agenda for developing a theology to address these foci. Readers familiar with Spanish will find a useful resource in the results of the Consultation on Black Culture and Theology in Latin America (1984).[3]

Evaluation of the rapid growth in Latin America of sects based in the U.S. and of the impact of the "electronic church" has enormous implications for North American religiosity. Even more significant is the critique of conventional Christianity practiced in the mainline Protestant churches of the United States. Like Latin American popular religiosity, much of U.S. Protestantism addresses the immediate pain of the individual while ignoring the societal causes of the pain.

The attentive reader will easily perceive the presence of many more critical themes in Latin America that concern Christians and theologians everywhere.

The volume closes with a sermon. The preacher is an ordained Protestant woman ministering in a *favela* (slum) in Rio. The gospel is good news because it announces God's option for the poor which, she tells us, points immediately and ultimately to the child. The end-point of the search for spirituality and the design for the theological task is the child.

So we are enabled, by our Latin American sisters and brothers, to become aware of the ideological filters on our spirituality and with them discover a renovated experience of God.

DOW KIRKPATRICK

---

3. *Cultura Negra Y Teologia* (San José: DEI, 1986).

PART I
RECREATING THE FIDELITY

Conversion: A Latin American Rereading

JOSÉ MÍGUEZ BONINO   (*Methodist, Argentina*)

The Latin American commitment to the history of our people, according to our faith, raises the perennial question of the relationship between the action of God and human responsibility.

If faith is to be lived out in history, we cannot imagine a "transcendental" human subject who has a relationship with God apart from the historic human subject who acts within the world. Neither can we imagine a transcendental action of God in the empty spaces outside of the chain of processes to which human beings are subject.

Traditional Protestant theology has been so concerned to avoid any temptation to sacralize human works at the expense of divine transcendence that it runs the risk of emptying human action of any theological significance. Reference to God is invoked only to relativize and to limit every human project, restricting the significance of all human action to the penultimate. This makes it dispensable, optional, and, in the end, something without significance.

*   *   *

Wesley introduced a new element into the history of Protestantism in his doctrine and practice of conversion and sanctification. The lively discussion about this has habitually turned around the question of whether Wesley was truly Protestant or whether his doctrine of grace and sanctification was "contaminated" by Catholicism. Yet I believe this has limited the subject to a confessional question. For us it is more important to try to understand the contribution Wesley can make to the theological question we propose, whatever may be its relationship to the Protestant or Catholic "orthodoxies."

What Did Wesley Seek?

Wesley's biographers have passionately debated the relationship between his struggles and "resolutions" in 1725 and the Aldersgate experience of 1738.[1] I believe the key to Wesley's ministry and theology is found more in the unity and convergence of these two experiences than in their contrast and discontinuity.

Until 1725, Wesley agonized over the question of the *active Christian subject*—the authentic and genuine "partner" with God in the covenant. What is a true Christian, a serious and committed Christian? In terms of the specific content of an active Christian life, it does not appear that he brought anything very new. Rather, he synthesized the ascetic, philanthropic, and devotional practice that the best religious literature of his time offered. He did not greatly change this content, which he willed to future Methodist generations—for their benefit . . . and many times for their disgrace!

But in 1738 he discovered a deeper and more decisive existential response. In the Pauline and Protestant perception it is God who creates this authentic subject, the true "partner" of the covenant. The Christian as active subject is a gift.

This is without doubt Luther's response. But Wesley is not primarily concerned with "placating an offended God." Rather, he is uneasy about how to serve God fully. Consequently—if I may be permitted a theological license—Wesley received from Luther a doctrine "of sanctification by grace through faith." Sanctification continues to be for Wesley the goal of redemption and of the Christian life. He has to preach faith because it is the only means of access into the ambit of sanctification.

I believe that this progression is seen in all of his great sermons. Beginning with this interpretation, then, I would like to consider first the theme of conversion and then the theme of sanctification (although it is evident that as far as Wesley is con-

1. Maximin Piette considered the resolutions of 1725 as the true conversion of Wesley, related to his discovery of Taylor and Thomas à Kempis and his decision to dedicate his whole life to God (*John Wesley in the Evolution of Protestantism* [New York: Sheed & Ward, 1937], pp. 305-12). Also see A. Léger, *La jeunesse de Wesley* (Paris: Hachette, n.d.), pp. 77-82. An opposing view is in the works of Cell, Cannon, etc.

cerned this separation is artificial and can be done only for didactic purposes).

What we have in biographical terms called the unity and convergence of the experiences of 1725 and 1738 can be transposed into the theological key as the integration of grace and love. In this sense all of Wesley's theology appears to be a soteriology, within the classic Protestant framework, without servile submission to it, which tries to articulate justification and sanctification in such a way that the victory of grace is revealed and realized in the operation of love.[2]

The Wesleyan Formulation of Conversion

God proposes to create a holy people. This purpose becomes present experience, visible when men and women turn to God with faith. Perhaps that is the way we can sum up Wesley's message. This is the good news.

It is truly good news for the poor of the earth, for the miserable masses of disinherited herded into the new industrial and mining centers, absorbed by the birth of modern industrial capitalism, impotent victims of social anomie.

They were not only accepted by God, but they could also be "made new"—could receive effective, visible, inherent, measurable power and dignity. They could become conscious and active subjects of a new life. Their works were worth something. Their will was free. Entrance into this reality is "conversion."

Most Wesley scholars agree that he identified conversion with regeneration even though some passages justify a certain distinction.[3] The most characteristic Wesleyan discussions of re-

2. Evidence of the centrality of this unity for Wesley is seen in a study of his controversies. In effect, his general "latitudinarian" attitude in theological disputes became combative when he thought this relation of grace-love was threatened, whether by a grace "which closes in on itself" without making morality inherently necessary (Calvinism, quietism, antinomianism), or because it belittled grace, excessively exalting the power of the ethical life (moralism, legalism).

3. In this section I have abstained from giving bibliographical references that would be incomplete or involve considerable work. I recommend to the reader the classic works of Cannon, Lindstrom, etc., which offer abundant bibliographies.

generation may be legitimately taken to present his concept of conversion. In general we can situate it within the classic Protestant doctrinal structure of the *ordo salutis*.

The distinctive emphases of Wesley seem to me to be grouped around the question of continuity and singularity and the question of the "consciousness" or "experience" of regeneration. Wesley likes to explain regeneration by using the analogy of "birth."[4] Two facts stand out: the first is the decisive character of regeneration. There is a "before" and an "after." Conversion marks a decisive about-face (*conversio* in the original sense) from sin to God. We know that for some time Wesley embraced the idea (which Peter Böhler had taught him) of the instantaneous character of this change but he later vacillated about it to admit a variety of possibilities. He never doubted, however, that there would be a change, a decisive about-face, a qualitative difference, created by this act of God and of the human person, called conversion or regeneration. But the analogy also underlines continuity: it is the same person. There is life before birth—with the same organs of perception and feeling—which now has become actual and operative by the power of the Spirit. More important, the analogy is amplified by reference to permanent growth to full maturity.

Conversion, then, looks backward to a humanity that is real, though powerless, and forward to a human maturity, still imperfect, but increasingly full (until one receives a total perfection, the complete reality of love, given in this life or in the life to come).

Wesley himself did not develop in a consistent manner the relationship of conversion to the Augustinian doctrine of prevenient grace. But William B. Pope—without doubt the most consistent systematic theologian in the Wesleyan tradition until the present century—does it in such a way as to give conversion its own distinctive place. Pope locates it on the doorstep of the new life as a movement by which persons in the power of this prevenient grace cooperate with the salvific grace of God. Prevenient grace is accessible to all by virtue of the expiation that "surrounds and embraces" all of humanity.

---

4. See, among other references, the notes on John 3; sermon XLV: II, 2 or sermon XIX: I, 8-10.

In this sense conversion is the meeting point of the human search and the grace of God, "the outer court of the Christian temple." However, Pope does not limit his interpretation strictly to the religious sphere. Looking at conversion also from the ethical perspective he affirms a continuity between the operation of love, under prevenient grace, and the transformation that raises it to the level of sanctification.

Certainly we are here near to one of the possible—and recently dominant—interpretations of Roman Catholic doctrine. But this should not inhibit us from paying attention to this significant continuity.

For both Wesley and Pope, conversion corresponds more strictly to the beginning of the Christian life as a decisive initial "leap." We would say "qualitative." But both admit a more general use of the term to refer to the "crises of growth" in the Christian life. This vacillation appears to me to document once more the double emphasis on singularity and continuity. In both the religious and the ethical spheres it characterizes the Wesleyan doctrine of conversion.

The other distinctive aspect is the well-known emphasis on "experience." One is aware of the new situation in which one finds oneself. The new birth gives its own witness with a self-evidence that does not need external proof. In the same way, it is not necessary to prove which is the light of the sun and which is the light of the stars.

However, this is not merely a subjective sentiment. It must be substantiated by the quality of life. In concrete realization of acts of love, the Spirit witnesses to its presence and operation. Thus regeneration is verified on a conscious level in both its religious and ethical dimensions, in which there is novelty and continuity.

In my opinion the central point is found, after all, in the moral conscience that is elevated to a new level of self-understanding and realization. If these observations are valid, we can sum up the Wesleyan doctrine of conversion as inclusive of the following elements:

1. It is situated in the perspective of the human search for moral excellence.
2. It turns around the enabling power of grace.

3. It culminates in the perfection of the human moral struggle, not through a mere quantitative growth, but through a qualitative change produced by the grace of God.
4. It links the previous ethical human experience to a subsequent growth *in* grace, so that the new person (regenerated) is at the same time the fulfillment and the reinstallation of the old person (not regenerated).
5. It invokes the subjective consciousness—substantiated by the corresponding action—of this fundamental transformation.

Conditions for Rethinking Wesleyan Doctrine

In my view it would be a serious error, fraught with negative consequences, to try to transfer directly to our situation the Wesleyan point of view of conversion. In fact, when this attempt is made, as in some evangelistic "campaigns," the outcome is a caricature of the original. Yet it could not be otherwise, because present conditions impose a very different connotation on previous concepts and formulations. Thus it is necessary to reconceptualize conversion. This should be done giving attention to at least three groups of factors.

On the theological level, it is necessary to go beyond the formal character of Wesley's doctrinal articulations in regard to Christology, love, and the concept of God. In a serious and thoughtful study, John Deschner has tried to read Wesley's Christology in "the best possible light." Despite this he has to recognize several serious shortcomings. Of particular interest to us here is Wesley's lack of interest in the humanity of Jesus Christ as a concrete historical reality. This omission is aggravated by an abstract emphasis on law in relationship to the prophetic office and by his difficulty in recognizing fully the reality of humiliation.

As we will see, these deficiencies are reflected in that which is central in the Wesleyan doctrine of sanctification, the idea of love. It is possible to point out the reason for these deficiencies. Wesley was able to presuppose the content of these doctrines. Therefore what appeared to be urgent was to vitalize and give effectiveness to a "plan of salvation," the theological substance of which could be taken for granted.

The biblical and theological renewal of the last fifty years obliges us to take a decisively different perspective. What has to be revised profoundly is the content of the vision with which these theological schemes operated; the God of the Scriptures, the Jesus Christ of the Gospels, the meaning of salvation, the context of the biblical understanding of love—all these are far from coinciding with the meanings "received" from the eighteenth century.

The central theme of the renewal is: In *which* God do we believe? *Who* is Christ the Redeemer? *What* love is offered us and required as the substance of the kingdom? In other words, we have to rethink *from what* and *to what* we are converted.

The simple fact is that we have to formulate these contents in terms of the kingdom and the history of salvation, of the proclamation of the jubilee of the grace of Jesus, of the hope for new heavens and a new earth—more than in the ecstatic and metaphysical terms characteristic of much tradition. Such a reformulation introduces a decisive change in the concept of conversion.

The second group of factors has to do with the philosophical, psychological, and sociological presuppositions of eighteenth-century formulations. We must take into account how the social conditions of the era affected the Methodism that was coming to birth. The vision of life, the ethos, the human model that arose with the modern world, made possible and demanded by new economic and social conditions—all of these things channeled the energies of the religious awakening.

In saying this, we do not ignore the prophetic element of the Methodist message. It is necessary to recognize that the human model, in terms of which the experience of conversion and new life is lived, corresponds to the efficient and productive individual of an industrial society. The economic and social upward movement of Methodism witnesses to this symbiosis.

Despite the powerful philosophical movements that took place in Great Britain in the eighteenth century, theological conceptualization moved principally in the Aristotelian metaphysical perspective of Scholasticism (Catholic or Protestant). Here I am only interested in pointing out the peculiar relationship, which can be seen in this perspective, between being and doing. In both God and the human there is a positive "being" in itself that subsequently "acts" or "is made manifest."

The ethos of Wesley's evangelization seems to challenge this concept, but his theology is still its prisoner. Consequently it became possible to conceive of a conversion or regeneration that takes place on a metaphysical plane. Only afterward is it "reflected" or "acted out" in history—in a kind of "second moment."

It is not my purpose here to raise a polemic against this concept. It is enough to point out that whatever may have been its value in interpreting the gospel in dialogue with a certain philosophical concept, it is neither radically biblical nor adequate to our situation.

Not even the Bible appears to be interested in a "being" of God that would be beyond or separated from action. Nor does it conceive—as modern thought does not conceive—of a human person constituted apart from the actions and relationships of historic existence.

This observation must be amplified in relation to the idea of interiority and subjectivity. In the traditional Methodist idea of conversion, the subjective conscience is defined individualistically. The religious change takes place in an "inner sanctuary," "alone with God."

This criticism may appear arbitrary in the light of Wesley's repeated affirmations of a "social holiness," his rejection of a "solitary religion," and the practical measures he took to assure a communitarian growth in faith and holiness. But I believe that a careful exegesis of the contexts in which such expressions appear shows that society, for Wesley, is not an anthropological concept but only a convenient arrangement for the growth of the individual.

Finally, it is the individual's soul that is saved, sanctified, perfected. Communion is in the last analysis an *externum subsidium*. Such ideas are, to say the least, fictional in the light of what we know today of human psychology—of the subconscious, of symbols, of ideological mechanisms. Conscience is not a "private" area, but the focus of a complex process that includes historical relationships in time and space. Our awareness of ourselves (self-consciousness) is shaped by social representations and the dominant symbols of a society (or of groups within it).

Our "hearing" of a message is mediated by the prevalent "code" around us. Any concrete "conversion" is a reply to a *mediated* challenge in which a certain form of consciousness and praxis is already presupposed. Unless this challenge deals explicitly with such forms of awareness and conduct, it will only succeed in unconsciously reenforcing them. There is no conversion in a vacuum.

These critical observations are not intended to belittle conversion. Quite the contrary, they take seriously the manner in which all experience is shaped, in any era, by prevailing conditions. Such awareness assists the search for the way in which conversion can reacquire its central place and significance in the evangelizing responsibility of today's church. That appears to me to be urgent and decisive for Christianity in the present moment.

Notes for a Rereading

From the *phenomenological* point of view, I would like to define conversion as the encounter between the call of the Christian message and a personal response. Conversion is characterized, then, by an awareness—as Methodist tradition affirms—both in relationship to the content of the message and as a self-awareness of commitment in a new relationship.

Ontologically conversion is the process by which God incorporates the human being as active and conscious partner into God's covenant with humankind, a covenant witnessed to, renewed, and assured in Jesus Christ.

For this call to be significant it must be articulated in terms that correspond to the needs and hopes of the human being of today, personally and collectively. This does not mean, however, that the message must accept the validity or adopt the content and characteristics of such hopes and expectations.

A simple observation of the New Testament will show that the centrality of Jesus Christ and the call to faith in him are expressed in terms of reference substantially different and at times apparently contradictory (e.g., the synoptics, the Fourth Gospel, Paul, Hebrews). Jesus Christ is always the same but not with the static identity of "final" objectives or events. His sameness is in the dynamic identity of the Spirit—as the history of the church gives witness.

In our own particular Latin American situation (though not only here) we experience, individually and collectively, human existence as artificially blocked. Ideological and structural imprisonment holds persons back from material and spiritual realization.

The Christian message cannot respond to this situation by evading the central point of the problem and offering some substitute or escapist solution. Christ would become a *soter* of a mystery cult or an *eon* of a Gnostic sect. (This is something the New Testament radically rejects, but more than once it has come back to infiltrate the announcement of the message.)

On the contrary, an authentic message must relate the totality of the Christian message to the objective and subjective conditions of our world. Jesus Christ is the archetype and mediator of a true human life—personal and collective—not a means to achieve some subjective superhuman exaltation!

The goal of conversion is not the mere assimilation of a message or the formal acceptance of a doctrine, but the "creation of a new creature." This is a commonplace few will deny. It is, however, constantly contradicted in the evangelizing process. People are expected to respond by accepting a verbal formulation. What happens (sociologically and psychologically speaking) in these cases is simply that a person accepts, for a variety of reasons, incorporation into a religious community. In other words, the community reproduces itself through evangelization.

In the New Testament, on the other hand, if I am not mistaken, the call to conversion is an invitation to discipleship, whether it be the call of Jesus himself to follow him or the apostolic form of participation through faith in the messianic community (those who announce the coming kingdom).

Evangelization cannot rotate around itself as self-reproduction. Its center cannot be anywhere other than the kingdom itself. Consequently it involves a community committed to an active discipleship in the world.

In primitive Methodism this communitarian commitment to the gospel in the midst of concrete conditions of its world is clearly perceptible. The call had a concrete content witnessed to in the "General Rules." This is what it meant concretely "to follow Christ" for the community. It was what men and women were invited to do in the power of the Spirit. It was the present and discernible face of the "new creature." Clearly this was an image tied to an era, and as such cannot and should not be reproduced outside that era. Yet such a historical location is not a defect: it gave it its value and importance.

In contrast, our so-called evangelizing is often empty. Persons are filled, perhaps unconsciously, with the dominant stereotypes of what it means to be "religious"—the accepted, standardized images of piety ideologically loaded. As such they can be accepted or rejected.

Unless the evangelizing community faces the challenge of a specific witness relevant to present conditions, evangelization is condemned to be a mere instrument for the reproduction and sacralization of the dehumanizing conditions in which people live. In very simple terms, evangelization ought to deal with the question: What does it mean concretely and specifically to follow Christ in thought and action in today's world?

The awakening of self-awareness in a new situation is a sociopersonal, active-reflective process. Modern psychology and sociology have demonstrated this clearly. There is no purely individual consciousness nor one void of the content of action.

Evangelization, then, has to be related to the way in which human groups situate themselves in the world, their worldviews, their forms of social representation, their consciousness of class and group, their modes of action. This means conversion can come about in reply to a verbally articulated message or to a given communitarian praxis of believers. After all, both things have to happen. But the awareness can move from the recognition of a conceptual content to a form of life, or from an assumed commitment to a communitarian praxis, to the acceptance of the self-understanding implicit in the message.

We are again confronted with the centrality of a practicing community, a community committed to a specific action in the world, as the "form of Christ" in which the verbal articulation and the "acted out" articulation come together, thus allowing the process of conversion to take place.

This affirmation does not lessen the centrality of the action of the Holy Spirit, because, it appears to me, what distinguishes the Holy Spirit from the magic "spirits" is that it acts through historic mediations. This seems to be the significance of the incarnation and of the church. I agree completely with the following statement made by the neoevangelical journalist and theologian Jim Wallis.

> I have steadily become more convinced that understanding conversion is truly the central question for today's churches. Conversion understood apart from or outside of history must be reappropriated and understood in direct relationship to that history.[5]

The critical observations we have formulated have as their precise purpose to clarify the way to an evangelization worthy of the radical nature of the gospel and of the urgency of our times. To quote Wallis again:

> Evangelism is to this end. The purpose of evangelism is to call for conversion and to call for it in its wholeness. The most controversial question at stake in the world, and even in the church, is whether we will follow Jesus and live under the banner of his kingdom. The evangelist asks that question and aims it right at the heart of each individual and at the heartbeat of our society. Evangelism confronts each person with the decisive choice about Jesus and the kingdom, and it challenges the oppression of the old order with the freeing power of a new one. The gospel of the kingdom sparks a fundamental change in every life and is an intrusion into any social order, be it first-century or our twentieth-century world.[6]

---

5. Jim Wallis, *The Call to Conversion* (San Francisco: Harper & Row, 1981), p. xvi.

6. Ibid., p. 16.

Sanctification:
A Latin American Rereading

JOSÉ MÍGUEZ BONINO (*Methodist, Argentina*)

For Wesley, holiness continues to be the goal of redemption and of the Christian life. It is therefore necessary to maintain a strict unity between justification and sanctification.

This is also, surely, the intention of the Reformers. Calvin says, "Just as Christ cannot be divided into parts, these two things are also inseparable, justice and sanctification, since we receive them together."[1]

In the dialectic of Wesley's piety and preaching, the concern which most involved him was "the grand design." Here sanctification has an undisputed primacy. God proposes to create a holy people, "and this intention becomes a present, visible, experienced reality when men and women turn to God in faith."

It is not difficult to sum up briefly the central elements of Wesleyan teaching about this. The fall corrupted the whole human race, erasing the moral image of God in the human being, corrupting the totality of that being, and making humans incapable of correcting themselves and returning to God. Sin not only caused the corruption of the human species but it also disfigured nature itself. The ultimate consequence is the physical and spiritual death of the human.

However, humanity did not remain in the state of total moral impotence. Prevenient grace, the universal consequence of expiation, gave back a certain moral discernment, the possibility of recognizing the law of God (even while breaking it) and of responding to the invitation of the gospel. In other words, God restores to sinful humanity, by grace, some free will. The

---

1. Calvin, *Institutes*, 3.11.6.

15

good works carried out in this freedom are therefore fruits of grace and do not carry within themselves any merit.

Justification means the forgiveness of sins—original and present—and regeneration, a change in our soul by which we pass from sin to a life of justice. Sanctification begins immediately after justification and brings about a transformation by which our carnal mind is changed into the likeness "of the mind which was in Christ Jesus." Motivations, thoughts, and actions become inspired by love.

Normally this experience of justification (forgiveness) is accompanied by an awareness of having been "reborn," of being a "child by adoption." The Holy Spirit witnesses to and with our spirit. One who has been reborn still retains remnants of sin which sanctification gradually overcomes until arriving at "perfection" ("full sanctification" or "the great salvation").

Perfection can be achieved in this life, either progressively or instantaneously, or it can be received in the moment of death. In any case perfection is always an aspiration and a hope that is expected from divine grace. It does not mean absolute perfection in the sense of moral infallibility but that all actions and thoughts are born of the love of God "shed abroad in our hearts by the Spirit."

Good Works

We must understand the importance for our purposes of the idea of "double" justification: the first entirely by faith in the moment of conversion, the second "not without works," in the final judgment. This idea of a "double justification"—an expression itself suspect since the time of the Reformation—seems to place Wesley decidedly outside the Protestant camp.

I believe the problem should be put in other terms. Wesley never imagined an autonomous human operation apart from the grace of God. Consequently, he totally excludes the idea of merit. At this point there is no discrepancy with the Reformers: neither with Luther who insisted that true faith is an active principle that "must do good works" nor with Calvin, for whom faith includes us "in Christ" not only in a forensic sense but in an active and effective manner by the work of the Holy Spirit.

We may say, perhaps too simply, that the Reformers insist "without Christ there cannot be good works." Wesley formulates it positively: "In Christ *there are* good works." The distinction is important. It has to do, on the one hand, with two distinct "states" of spirit that respond to two different spiritual and historic situations.

The Reformers, especially Luther, lived in the medieval search for salvation from the power of the devil, from wrath, and from death. Wesley, on the other hand, feels the modern necessity of finding himself as a "person"—new, useful, active.

In the crisis of the ecclesiastical institution and the medieval sacramental system, the Reformers found in God the assurance of salvation. God chose to be on our side in Jesus Christ (Luther), who from all eternity destined us to be God's own (Calvin). It is God, and not our vacillating conscience or the ecclesiastical institution, who is the sure support of our life. Consequently it is necessary to exclude any other "mediation" that can reintroduce our salvation into the swampy terrain of human ambiguity. In the beginning, during, and at the end of life's journey, there is no other security except divine grace.

What the Reformers did not see was that by proceeding in this way they introduced a dangerous dichotomy whose serious consequences were soon felt. On one side the action of God and human action were placed as "symmetrical," and on the other, as opposites. To affirm the first it is necessary to disqualify the second. Thus, every affirmation of the second results in a detriment to the first. So what was meant to be an affirmation of salvation, "not by works," came to be "without works."

This lapse is what horrified Wesley in the Moravian quietism and scandalized him when he read, in Luther's commentary on Galatians, language he considered a "blasphemy with respect to good works and the law of God" (*Journal*, June 15, 1741 [*sic*]).

On the other hand, good works appear later in certain Protestant orthodoxies as separate from the concrete human will, attributed to the Holy Spirit who then comes to be not the incarnate power and divine initiative but a "substitute subject" for the human in historical reality. With good reason the Reformed theologian Otto Weber said that, in this orientation,

> works were to be taken in isolation from the person doing them, and it would not be true that "a good and religious man does good and religious works." Instead, he would wait passively to see if the Spirit does them through him or upon him. As a person he would not be involved. This would produce what we call pneumatological docetism.[2]

How can the subject of works be expressed without compromising the priority of divine action or annulling the human subject? In a sharp criticism of Protestant theology, Juan Luis Segundo reminds us that "the disappearance of the notion of merit from Protestant theology, since the Reformation, seems to have undermined the possibility of a theology of history." The reason is that the notion of merit ("that is to say, the eternal value of effort and righteous intention") is the only thing that gives historic action a value related to the kingdom. With its disappearance, "this last bond of union between the two is cut by the theology of salvation by faith alone, by the exclusive merits of Christ."[3]

One can say that with his notion of "calling," Luther adds a new link, or that the value of Calvin's "third use of the law" fulfills this same purpose. Nevertheless there is no doubt that historically Protestantism was defenseless against this religiosity of "cheap grace" that Bonhoeffer had to denounce.

Certainly Juan Luis Segundo does not intend to return to the notion of merit and recognizes fully the importance of the gracious nature of salvation the Reformers defended. But the problem persists and Segundo invokes the possibility of overcoming it in "a fruitful and liberating synthesis."

> Faith frees us from preoccupation with the law so that one can launch oneself into a creative love and not be paralyzed by the problem of individual certainty and salvation, whose only static criterion can be the law. However, this surrender of our destiny to God should not lead us to think that God

---

2. Otto Weber, *Foundations of Dogmatics*, trans. Darrell L. Guder, 2 vols. (Grand Rapids: Eerdmans, 1981-82), 2:322.

3. Carlos Lohlé, *Liberación de la Teología* (Buenos Aires, 1975), pp. 160-61.

wants us to leave God to work alone as if all collaboration on our part would be a disrespect of God's glory. To the contrary, the Christian God is a God who loves and needs to be loved.

God needs our creativity for the Divine task and therefore asks that we surrender to God our destiny by faith.[4]

I believe that the modern notion of "alienated work" can help us to see this problem more clearly. It is easier to understand the Pauline-Lutheran polemic against "works" and "merits" when we observe that what they attack is a "use" of works as a human product that is converted into a thing, a "coin" for transactions with God and neighbor. Such changing of works into things depersonalizes relationships with God and neighbor. "Works" are interposed between the human and the Divine. By them it is possible to establish a pact with God in which we are not personally involved—that is to say, where faith in its personal character of "faithfulness" is absent. It is absent precisely because the "work" is separated from its author and becomes a religious or moral "installment payment" objectified in relationship to a law.[5] On the contrary, both Paul and Luther recognized a "work of love" or "works of faith" that are the person as a subject actively involved in a personal relationship of surrender to God and neighbor.

The notion of merit, as if the works had an "exchange value," is not appropriate in this case. Rather, the notion of "significance" or "validity" of the works as inseparable from the person who carries them out and as incorporated in the purposes and actions of God is appropriate. If they are considered as "the person uniquely in the character of active subject," works are the only historic manifestation of the person. They are the witness to the concrete historicity of the work of God, as in the

---

4. Lohlé, *Liberación de Teología*, p. 172.

5. This parallel between the idea of "works" and "alienated work" was first called to my attention by K. Lenkensdorf in an unpublished thesis about the theology of St. Paul submitted to the University of Mexico. See my *Ama e faze o que quiseres* (Buenos Aires: La Aurora, 1971), pp. 41ff.; *Doing Theology in a Revolutionary Situation* (Philadelphia: Fortress, 1975), pp. 110-11. Recently T. Runyon, ed., *Sanctification and Liberation: Liberation Theologies in the Light of the Wesleyan Tradition* (Nashville: Abingdon, 1981), pp. 22-30, elaborates the same analogy.

affirmation of the Johannine Christ, "Believe me for the very works themselves" (John 10:38; cf. 5:31-36 et passim), or the polemic affirmation of James, "I by my works will show you my faith" (Jas. 2:18).

Wesley's struggle in defense of sanctification has, in my opinion, the value of recovering this active character of the believing person and of rejecting all separation between faith and love. However, the theological framework of *ordo salutis* is a straitjacket from which Wesley could not free himself. It became in the hands of Protestant scholasticism a rigid sequence of moments that, instead of unlocking the richness of the unique and multiple grace of God, forced the Christian experience into preestablished molds.

Very soon the *ordo* was psychologized in a series of "spiritual awakenings, actions, and states of a religious and moral type."[6] Wesley was caught in this net. Since he abandoned justification as a "moment," it was inevitable that he would fall into the trap of double justification—making a distinction between a "provisional" salvation and a "final" salvation—therefore putting in peril the very heart of faith. Justification and also sanctification come to be, then, a series of moments almost disconnected, always precarious, and threatened by sin. The unity of the human subject is obscured and distorted, as well as the unity and faithfulness of the grace of God.

Thus, the Wesleyan formulation of sanctification and perfection becomes psychologically untenable. Besides this, spiritually, it opens the door to a sick scrupulosity or a pernicious arrogance. The fact that Wesley did not become a victim of either of these in his own spiritual life only proves—as in the case of many other saints—that his piety is much better than his theology.

---

6. Runyon, *Sanctification and Liberation,* pp. 36-37, maintains that Wesley did not fall into the trap of fixing the *ordo* into a sequence, and that this permitted him to maintain the priority of grace along with the significance of works. Justification by faith was not for him "a point of departure which marked the course of the future to be constructed," but the center around which "the dance of life" turned. The figure of speech seems very meaningful for me as the correct understanding of the unity of justification and sanctification. But I doubt it is possible to affirm that Wesley consciously maintained this unity in very clear terms.

The Specter of Synergism

Positions such as Wesley's have been stigmatized by Protestant theologians with the belittling epithet of "synergism," and condemned to the trash heap of the "heresies" of Protestantism (in this case, "Arminianism" in "separation" from Calvinism).

Albert Outler shows very clearly that the Wesleyan concept continues a traditional theological affirmation that in the West suffered the consequences of the Augustinian polemic. The concept of "synergism," perfectly orthodox in the Eastern tradition, comes to be identified as a "Pelagian" version of the same, by which all human "cooperation" takes away from the action and glory of God.[7]

This outright exclusion of all synergism, of all active human participation in the work of God, has been tragic for Protestantism. As Juan Luis Segundo has so well emphasized in the above-mentioned article, it has made it impossible to give an intrinsic place to human action in God's work in bringing about the kingdom.

Translated into contemporary theological discussion as "eschatological reserve," this ultra-monergism not only relativizes but trivializes historic action for justice and peace. It does so by transforming it into a transitory act of derived value. This is the creation of a mere scenario, destined to disappear, where the truly important act is the salvation of "the soul."

Is it possible to affirm a "synergism" that does not deny the permanent priority of grace? The question is, as we have suggested, of crucial importance for Latin American theology.

Albert Outler points out one direction that I believe is correct and fruitful, when he distinguishes between a "contractual synergism" Wesley had inherited in the tradition of "facere

---

7. See Albert Outler, "Methodist Theological Heritage: A Study in Perspective," in *Methodist Destiny in an Ecumenical Age*, ed. Paul Minus (Nashville: Abingdon, 1969), pp. 49-66. Outler gives a significant history of the problem, underlining Ambrosiaster's definition, "Facienti quod in se est, Deus non denegat gratiam," to show that there is a theological and anthropological affirmation asserted in these terms which should be related to the Augustinian-Reformed emphasis. "It is hard to deny that Wesley was a *synergist*, unless "synergism" is defined in exclusively Pelagian terms" (p. 58).

quod in se est" ("if a person behaves according to his or her understanding, access to salvation of that person has the status of
a *right*") and a "synergism of the covenant" (*covenantal* synergism) "in which *both* prevenient and saving grace are recognized
as the coordinated actions of the one true God of love" who established the covenant.

It is possible to talk about whether Wesley really perceived and clearly established the difference between both
forms of collaboration between God and human beings. What
is important is to point out that this second concept represents
the legitimate possibility of a positive opening of a theological
problem of decisive importance for praxis.

On an anthropological level, the theme becomes a problem of the constitution of the subject-human. But, in Latin America, the anthropological question must be raised beginning with
the condition of nonperson, that is, of those who have been
stripped—objectively and subjectively, individually and collectively—of the character of subject of their own existence, as
makers of their own history.

Consequently, the meaning of the grace of God must
speak explicitly to this question: How does God reconstitute the
human subject? How does grace bring about a de-alienation of
this subject—also objective and subjective, individual and collective?

One of the elements of this response has to be a de-
alienation of the concept of grace itself. In other words, the forms
of "religious aid" (sacramental or evangelistic) very often assist
in the reduction to "nonperson," taking away even the possibility of being a "subject" in relation to the Divine.

Reflection that tries to respond to these questions must
be set in the broadest theological context of the relationship between God and human beings. This relationship, which God
wishes and has offered since creation, is "covenant." When God
created the human being, a "partner" (minor) was raised up,
making God a "partner" (major) with a purpose—which is the
content of the partnership. This purpose can be defined in terms
of its outer manifestation—the reconstruction of the world—or
in its inner and motivating dynamic—the exercise of *agape*.

Redemption must be seen, then, against this horizon.
Within it must be situated the great deeds of reconciliation, justi-

fication, and sanctification. The breaking of this covenant is the fundamental alienation. It is simultaneously the destruction of its dynamic and motivation *(agape)*, and of its project (the construction of the world). The human renounces the role of subject in relation to God, to the world, and to neighbor.

The Totality of the Human Race

In speaking of the "discontent" with the present that Wesley's idea of "perfection" introduces, Runyon adds: "this holy dissatisfaction is readily transferable from the realm of the individual to that of society . . . where it provides a persistent motivation for reform in the light of 'a more perfect way' that transcends any *status quo*."[8]

Such a widening of the concept of perfection is required, according to Runyon, by the very concept of the kingdom of God in Wesley's thought. In effect, he insists that the kingdom has already begun to be realized on earth. Two quotations confirm this. The first comes from his *Notes on the New Testament* (commenting on Matt. 3:2, "the kingdom of heaven is near"):

A society has to be formed . . . to subsist, first on earth, and later with God in glory.

In some passages of scripture the expression is applied more particularly to the earthly state of the kingdom; others refer only to the glorious state, but most references include both.

A second citation comments on the petition in the Lord's Prayer: "Thy kingdom come, thy will be done":

the meaning is that all of the inhabitants of the earth, the whole human race, ought to do the will of the Father who is in heaven as voluntarily as do the holy angels; that they do it continually . . . and perfectly. . . . In other words, we pray that we and all humanity may do the will of God in all things.[9]

8. Runyon, *Sanctification and Liberation*, p. 10.
9. Wesley, *The Works of John Wesley* (Grand Rapids: Zondervan, 1958), 5:337.

Christian perfection is thought of in active terms: not merely to abstain from evil, but to be committed to the good. Therefore, Methodists should not isolate themselves from the world (as the mystics or quietists would do) but "leaven everything around them."

The doctrine of perfection is tied to a vision of the renovation of all creation. The following quotation describes this vision of the "grand plan"—the triumph of full love:

> Suppose now the fulness of time to be come. . . . What a prospect is this! . . . Wars are ceased from the earth . . . no brother rising up against brother; no country or city divided against itself and tearing out its own bowels. . . . Here is no oppression to "make" even "the wise man mad"; no extortion to "grind the face of the poor"; no robbery or wrong; no rapine or injustice; for all are "content with such things as they possess." Thus "righteousness and peace have kissed each other"; . . . "Neither saith any of them, that aught of the things which he possesseth is his own." There is none among them that lacketh; for every man loveth his neighbour as himself.[10]

Runyon himself deplores the fact that this vision did not come to fruition in the Methodist movement. He attributes this, in part, to the lack of consistency in Wesley himself, who, in other articulations of the doctrine of perfection, especially in the well-known "A Plain Account of Christian Perfection," gives a much more individualistic and moralistic vision of perfection. This led to legalism and the "spiritual pride" that is often tied to this doctrine.

On the other hand, given Wesley's conservative political position, all social progress is thought of as a mere extension and correction of existing institutions and structures. Even the paragraph we quoted above shows in its "utopian vision" conservative and theocratic traces.

Perhaps the criticism should go deeper. It seems to me, despite these affirmations, that Wesley did not overcome an individualistic anthropology. Such a view conceives of human relationships as extrinsic to the person, as the field where the person exercises virtue. This is consistent, as we have said before,

10. Wesley, *Works*, 5:46.

with Wesley's lack of understanding of the structural character of human life.

Given the historic circumstances and the ideological and theological limitations themselves, it is difficult to imagine that Methodism could have fulfilled a role very different from the one it did in the Great Britain of the eighteenth and nineteenth centuries.

It is not a matter, then, of claiming some supposed "revolutionary" role for Methodism or a "liberating" role for its theology. What is of interest to us is to observe a particularly significant theological thematic in the face of the problems of a liberating historic praxis today in Latin America. More precisely, Wesley posits, within Protestant theology, while trying to maintain fidelity to its theocentric Christology, an inescapable problematic for a theology that seeks to assume a serious commitment to a historical project of liberation.

What freedom for fruitful action on the historical level has the human, individually or collectively? What transcendent value, what eschatological significance, does a human project have? What possibility for progress toward justice and love within the kingdom can we hope for in history?

What relationship can there be between the kingdom of God as divine eschatological act and human action—between salvation as a gift or salvation as an undertaking, a vocation? Wesley refused to give a unilateral reply that would exclude the second term of these questions and condemn the human to a lack of transcendence in real, historic existence. Such anthropology seemed to him to be unworthy of the universality of grace and the power of divine love.

The articulation of his replies within the framework of the theological categories and the ideological conditionings of his time are far from satisfying to us. The historic project with which Methodism in its origins entwined its spirituality, which is quite similar to our own Latin American Protestant origins, no longer represents for us a liberating possibility. But the questions Wesley dared to pose to his theological tradition continue to be fruitful for our theological and pastoral agenda today in Latin America.

Is "Social Holiness" Enough?— A Catholic Reading

HUGO ASSMANN   *(Catholic, Brazil)*

"The gospel of Christ knows no religion which is not social religion; it knows no holiness which is not social holiness."

—John Wesley (1703–1791), Works, 8:593

Introit and Penitential Act

Let us begin liturgically. For some time now out of sinful curiosity I have read a lot about Methodism, especially from John Wesley himself. Don't think I went to the exaggerated point of reading everything Wesley wrote. After all, as everyone knows, the man perpetrated about two hundred writings.

Wesley was also a biographical subject from many angles. The quantity of books written about him is impressive. A number qualify as "immoderately reverential." Others arouse the suspicion that they have been put together with the hidden agenda of facilitating a moving away from the "Wesleyan heritage." They pride themselves in bringing to light his weak (or strong?) side—the tragedies in his love life, his irascibility, his mistakes in personal relationships, and that authoritarian streak in him which near the end of his life earned him the nickname "Pope John."

Two impressions at which I arrived through these readings are important here. First: Wesley's written work is not just vast and complex; it is quite confused and contains more than a few contradictions. Although it is possible to distinguish a clear emphasis on certain themes, it is not easy to describe clearly in systematic form the logical structure of each theme. Therefore it seems evident that the subject to be studied, above all, is the socioreligious phenomenon of Methodism.

Second: it is strange that having so much written by and about Wesley, practically none of it has come to the heart and hand of Latin American Methodists. This fact raises the questions: What are the reasons for such distance from Wesley? What is the doctrinal and theological continuity of Methodists?

Can it be that the propagation of Methodism was due more to institutional forms and channels than to the clarity of its religious message? I confess to a certain perplexity when I look at the possibility of invoking a consistent, original "Wesleyan heritage" that could afford a "re-sourcing" and consequent renewal of the peculiar identity of Methodism. At this point, then, not having discovered what I was sure I would be able to prove, I am obligated to a penitential act.

I confess to an exaggerated anxiety to find in Wesley a firm support for the deepening of a series of theological themes which today's reality imposes on us.

Little by little I came to the impression that some themes have less emphasis in Wesley than I expected and that other themes are confused beyond hope of clarity. If this were confirmed by people who understand the subject better, it would have an important implication. Wesley cannot be invoked, then, for everything Methodism needs for a fruitful incarnation in the Latin American reality.

On the other hand, even if there is no fidelity to the origins which can be invoked as "fecundating orthodoxy" in the face of the distorting (North Americanizing) transmissions of later Methodism, there does exist the right to creative innovation, since there are other arguments for moving away from these mediations.

Whatever was the force of the original Wesleyan legacy, there is no doubt there has been a moving away from it. Whatever may have been the later distortions, there is no doubt that it is also necessary to move away from them. Likewise there is also no doubt that the present task is to "construct a new identity in a new originating context (Latin America)."

Since every penitential act must culminate in a willingness to be open to grace, I declare that I am conscious of the abundance of the gifts I have already enjoyed in living together with Methodists in Latin America. Their ecumenical openness, their theological flexibility, and their human warmth have for me a meaning I did not perceive earlier.

The absence of sectarianism may very well be, I now see, a characteristic note of Methodism, but something more important will be the central theme of this chapter. It no longer seems to me a casual fact that many Methodists on the world level have a progressive social mentality. I believe it can be shown that in Wesley and in the origins of Methodism there is much which should disturb reactionary Methodists.

Distrust of Roman Catholic Versions of Wesley

There really are not very many Catholic readings of Wesley, who still has not merited much attention on the part of Catholic theologians. I do not recall having seen him mentioned in the famous lists of "adversaries" always present in the "thesis" of classic manuals of Catholic theology.

In 1925 the French priest Maximin Piette published his famous book, *John Wesley in the Evolution of Protestantism*. The English translation apppeared twelve years later, done by a Catholic and edited by a press linked to the Catholic church.[1] The work is not explicitly polemic and anti-Protestant. It does, however, make an enormous effort to "deprotestantize" Wesley. Piette's thesis is that Wesley is more in discontinuity than continuity with the Protestant Reformation. He is a clear case of "reaction in the evolution of Protestantism." His concept of faith would be closer to the Council of Trent than to that of Luther and Calvin. Furthermore, Wesley's "social religion" would be more Catholic than Protestant. In doctrinal terms he would have very few points of friction with Roman Catholicism, given his "doctrinal vacuum." Piette sees Wesleyan Methodism as "a religion of common sense." The social dimension of Wesley's preaching—a point of special interest to us here—is reduced to generosity in works of charity. Piette does not perceive in Wes-

1. Maximin Piette, *John Wesley in the Evolution of Protestantism* (New York: Sheed & Ward, 1937).

ley an ethical appeal that, although primarily incarnated in works of assistance, would have a social meaning beyond mere philanthropy.

My readings have left me with a suspicion, the extent of which I am not able to evaluate. In various cases the following tendencies seem to have been repeated: Whenever there is the attempt to transconfessionalize or universalize Wesley's religious significance, two strangely related elements come into play. They are the approach to Roman Catholicism and the reduction of the social message to the philanthropy of relief assistance.

Published three years after Piette's work is that of J. Ernest Rattenbury.[2] Rattenbury accepts many of Piette's theses, just as on the social plane he agrees with Elie Halévy, to whom we shall refer later.

A second example of a Catholic version of Wesley's views with questionable aspects is the ecumenical edition of "John Wesley's Letter to a Roman Catholic" with a long introduction by the Jesuit editor Michael Hurley, and prefaces by Bishop Odd Hagen, at that time president of the World Methodist Council, and Cardinal A. Bea, former president of the Secretariat for Christian Unity of the Vatican. Such a "sacramented" publication should be a positive factor, and indeed there are undeniable positive aspects in the introduction with regard to the historical context in which Wesley's letter originated: strong opposition to Methodist preachers in Ireland, where riots and physical aggression by popular groups were manipulated by leaders who were not very open to ecumenical dialogue.

For this reason it seems an exaggeration to elevate the document, which had very little circulation at the time, to the plane of a Magna Carta of the ecumenical openness of Wesley. Everything indicates that it was an appeal to mutual tolerance in an emergency situation. As to content, the letter contains a pietistic theology of grace and Christology, which Wesley supposed to be the common doctrinal patrimony between Methodists and Catholics. The editor doesn't even touch on the ques-

2. J. Ernest Rattenbury, *Wesley's Legacy to the World* (Nashville: Cokesbury, 1928).

tionable points of the common content of the letter. Once again Wesley is presented with Catholicizing traces at a distance from the extreme of other lines of Protestantism.

As the founder of a "religious society within the (Anglican) Church,"[3] Wesley is compared with the great founders of religious orders, in particular with St. Francis of Assisi. His religious reform is presented as "emphatically sacramental and eucharistic," which is quite questionable. "A Methodist is a follower of Wesley . . . attached to him in a way no Lutheran is attached to Luther, or Presbyterian to Calvin."[4]

Cardinal Bea himself reinforces the colors of ecumenical diplomacy when he says, "From the historic point of view Wesley's 'Letter to a Roman Catholic' . . . anticipates by more than a century and a half many of the insights and ideals of the modern ecumenical movement"; and "John Wesley's *Letter* is remarkable also for the reason that it anticipates many aspects of the mind and mood of the Roman Catholic Church as expressed in the documents of the Second Vatican Council and in the addresses of Pope Paul VI."[5]

The Controversy over the Social Weight of Methodism in England

The few observations I shall make about this controversy are necessary to the central hypothesis of this chapter. A deeper study would demand more research into the authors cited. A synthesized and balanced appreciation of the subject is found in other chapters of this volume, especially those of José Míguez Bonino.

A first group of social and political analysts, some influenced by Marxism, agree with the characterization of Methodism as the castrator of the working classes and the popular conscience in general, and as a reactionary and repressive religion.

3. Michael Hurley, SJ, ed., *John Wesley's Letter to a Roman Catholic* (New York: Abingdon, 1968), p. 26.

4. Ibid., p. 22.

5. Ibid., pp. 15-16.

Some who stand out in this group are E. P. Thompson, Leslie Stephen, the Hammonds, and E. J. Hobsbawm.[6]

Unlike the focus of Max Weber, whose sociological analyses include theological hypotheses, none of the cited authors attributes much importance to "Methodist theology" as an element to be taken into consideration in the analysis. Rather, they concentrate directly on the economic, social, and political elements in the formation of the social classes in eighteenth-century England.

Since they see the theological thought of Wesley and his early followers as "confused beyond rescue and intellectually inadequate," one must ask whether an analysis that does not take into consideration the specifically religious elements is capable of explaining the socioreligious ethos unleashed by Methodism. The institutional forms and model of the exercise of power the Methodist movement took on, although inevitably leading to a privileged linkage with certain social classes, cannot be explained without analyzing the motivations that led to these class commitments.

My question is this: Is not the Methodist movement a distinctly peculiar case and, therefore, highly interesting as a case study of subtle, slow, surreptitious but inevitable perversion of the noblest ideals of service to neighbor? And if such a thing has already happened, let us understand that it can happen again, perhaps even to the famous "preferential option for the poor."

A second group is made up of two slightly different positions, each depending on and complementing the other. In 1906 the French historian Elie Halévy (1870–1938) in his book, *History of the English People in the Eighteenth Century*, set forth the following thesis: "England was spared the revolution toward which the contradictions of her polity and economy might otherwise have led her, through the stabilizing influence of evangelical religion, particularly of Methodism."[7] The book was revived in 1971 in an English version under historic circum-

---

6. See the full bibliography of these authors at the end of *Sanctification and Liberation: Liberation Theologies in the Light of the Wesleyan Tradition*, ed. Theodore Runyon (Nashville: Abingdon, 1981).

7. Elie Halévy, *The Birth of Methodism in England* (Chicago: University of Chicago Press, 1971), p. 1.

stances in which Halévy's affirmation was finally elevated to an important question for many.

Bernard Semmel, in a book that has already become a classic, *The Methodist Revolution*,[8] takes up again Halévy's thesis and formulates it positively: Methodism did not "prevent" the revolution, but gave positive support to a revolution, the modernization of capitalism. In his words, it *"might* have helped— that is all we can safely say—to bridge the gap between the traditional and the modern orders without tumultuous upheaval, while at the same time promoting the ideals which would be most useful to the new society."[9]

The new contribution of Semmel consists in a more detailed research into the slow formation of the synthesis or the behavioral code of the "basic personality" given impulse by Methodism. The study seems to me to be very rich in several aspects, although one can disagree in part with the basic thesis. José Míguez Bonino accepts it in principle. The richness is, among other things, in Semmel's peculiar method of analysis, quite Weberian in background.

It is useless to look for explicit semantic formulations of a liberal creed in Wesley. One must penetrate into the details of the mediations, including the doctrinal, for example, to understand Wesley's role against antinomianism (i.e., the religious-anarchic tendency, a variant of pietism) and in favor of Arminianism (from Arminius, who in the line of Erasmus, opposed a rigid Calvinism). Wesley's "practical faith" would be a form of "Protestant Arminianism." Beyond the explicit semantics, this Arminianism would have generated a behavioral code to be synthesized in such post-Wesleyan terms as *Liberalism, Order,* and the *Mission of the Nation.*

In more recent days other authors, such as R. D. Hughes, P. d'A. Jones, and T. W. Madron,[10] have appeared, dedicated to

8. Bernard Semmel, *The Methodist Revolution* (New York: Basic Books, 1973).

9. Ibid., p. 8.

10. Robert D. Hughes, "Wesleyan Roots of Christian Socialism," *The Ecumenist* 13 (May-June 1975); Peter d'A. Jones, *The Christian Socialist Revival, 1877–1914* (Princeton: Princeton University Press, 1968); Thomas W. Madron, "John Wesley on Economics," in Runyon, ed., *Sanctification and Liberation*, pp. 102-15.

a reexamination of Wesley's economic thought and of the relationships between fragments of the Methodist movement and "Christian socialism." It is undeniable that post-Wesleyan Methodism is more multifaceted, even in the United States and Latin America, than is usually admitted. May the historians have fun with these strands!

The common element in these different approaches to the real social and political significance of the early Methodist movement is this: nobody doubts its social weight, because it was truly relevant. The awareness in relation to the future perspectives of the socioeconomic system (capitalism in the passage from its mercantile to its industrial phase) in the Methodist religious revival was probably rudimentary and fragmentary. One can see this in Wesley himself. Otherwise, there is no explanation for the frequent burial of the political options under the predominant structure, religious semantics. At least one lesson is clear: in the midst of the conflicts of history, innocence is not possible for any religious expression. Neutrality is an ideological subterfuge that may be alleged, but it is always denied by the facts. In other words, there is no religion of the "heart" that does not become religion of the whole body, including the social body of the historical projects.

No "social holiness" can deny that it is "political holiness." The problem of the articulation of the experience of faith, with the mediations of socioeconomic-political power, is at the center of any religious language. This does not empty it of an inner consistency or deprive it of spaces of relative autonomy on the plane of activity. However, expressions of faith in the social realm that are not recognized as religious nonetheless deal furtively with religious elements without making their strength fully felt.

A Balance of Assets and Liabilities

I hope that the obvious statements I dare to make now will not be seen as polemic from a Roman Catholic. They are given in the spirit of fraternal dialogue in search for better common understanding.

I consider it impossible to construct a convincing profile

of a "Wesley of the poor," just as it seems to me the accent on a "Wesley of the rich" is deplorable. Neither can things be forced to the point where one can find in Wesley a forerunner of the "Theology of Liberation."

The concept of "practical faith" in Wesley tied to other themes of his, such as "conversion," "sanctification," and "perfection," do not entirely correspond to the concept of praxis in Latin American theology, although there may be some converging lines. What sets us apart from Wesley is—among various other things—our explicit demand for the inclusion of certain historic mediations, with the perspective of a certain "utopia," in the concept of faith-praxis.

From the theological point of view, there is a series of other central themes where it is impossible to agree with Wesley: his Christology is centered in the "atonement, in "substitutional expiation." His idea of sin, Augustinian in root but not in elaboration, is practically identical with "guilt" (psychological). Therefore, besides being profoundly interwoven with personal frustration (even in the erotic field), it is basically subjective and private. In consequence, his vision of grace also includes the subjective elements of "assurance" (security of salvation), which goes back to a subjective experience of having been struck by the certainty of justification. This pietist vision of conversion is the problem with which almost all lines of Protestantism are faced.

One question we could all ask ourselves is this: Why did the Reformers and their followers, as had so many mystics and spiritual innovators who preceded them, have to subjectivize so much and express with such intensity the element of "certainty of justification" in conversion? This psychological trivialization of the subject will not get us very far. Even less will it help us understand why the oppressed masses, beginning precisely with the certainty of their impotence (absolutely real and so difficult to destroy), are fascinated by the promise of spiritual "certainty of salvation."

The rigidity of the structures of oppression in society, tied to the "banking" and "commercial" character of the simulation of saving moments in clericalized churches, is the brick wall against which the anguished conversion of pietism is hurled. This gives it at least a hint of a libertarian tendency.

Wesley sought with anguish and lived intensely (with the endocrine accompaniments of the "warm heart" at Aldersgate) this typically intimate, subjective, and pietist conversion. I do not find in him an explicit demystification of the experience, in the tragic facts of the years before 1738, which can stand up to psychological analysis. But Wesley found more indirect ways to relativize the "moment of conversion." Otherwise there is no explanation for his emphasis on "sanctification," "perfection," and similar themes, nor would his polemics with the Calvinists make any sense.

In sum, in an enormous quantity of his letters and in his extensive diary, Wesley exposes without shame his strengths and his weaknesses. It is no service to Methodism to try to justify all his ideas and attitudes. Nor is it possible to forgive everything in the name of "the spirit of the times." I think especially women cannot accept this kind of excuse in the case of the absurdities Wesley practiced and defended in relation to them.

The Demand for "Social Holiness"

On the level of verbal formulations, it is perfectly possible to collect a good quantity of very clear texts from Wesley about the social implications of the process of conversion.[11] I believe it can be shown they are not the casual or marginal explosions of a passionate preacher. They are formulations that, with coherence but not much elaboration, grow out of his central themes: conversion, the new person, justification expressed by an operating faith, sanctification, and the calling of all Christians to perfection.

It probably would be an exaggeration to say that the social aspect of holiness is the most visible in the preaching of Wesley. I dare express the impression that this dimension, although neither marginal nor secondary, is expressed only in some germinal elements.

Wesley was not just a fiery preacher. He was also a man

11. Cf. a selection of texts (in Portuguese) on the social aspects in an edition (off-set) by the Methodist University of Piracicaba in the centennial year of Brazilian Methodism.

full of practical plans and initiatives: an administrator of works and institutions. On this practical level, where ideas take form in the use of power, Wesley consumed much of his energy. Even the doctrinal discussions were debates about things that had to be done, works that had to be carried forward, initiatives that had to be supported or cut off.

It is in this practical terrain that Wesley is, in my opinion, remiss in not taking advantage of occasions to reflect on coherent articulations of a social holiness. On reading parts of his correspondence, especially after 1760, I am often perplexed by the extreme naiveté by which Wesley established alliances with "whoever can help." There were so many projects to be carried forward he did not find time for reflection. He allowed himself to be carried headlong by the avalanche of the growing institutionalization of the movement he had unleashed.

Sometimes I ask myself, why does there not break forth here and now in the heart of this activism some substantial theological nourishment? The administrator did not totally devour the ardent preacher, but appears to have kept the fiery preacher from becoming aware of the theology implied in his attitudes and practices.

One has the impression that for Wesley everything appeared simple, because the essential had already been formulated: to be converted to the depths of the heart, to project this conversion in a "practical faith," to know oneself called to the fullness of perfection in a sanctifying service to neighbor.

Wesley seemed to be profoundly convinced of the permanent nutritional force of a spirituality that is content with these basic elements—in other words, a faith and spirituality that was not aware of its unavoidable immersion in ideology.

We live in a world in which such naiveté would not only be culpable but fatal for the Christian witness. Today we face social conflicts, on both the micro and macro levels of society, which Wesley did not. The historical mediations with which the experience of faith must be articulated form an indispensable part of our reflection about the Christian commitment to certain causes.

History has moved a long way and conflicts have become sharper on all levels. It has been said that at the beginning of this century Christians were about one third of humanity.

Today we represent a fifth. At the end of this century we shall be barely one sixth of the population of the planet. And we are talking about "nominal Christians."

Yet the relevance of Christianity in the world is a quite different situation. If we add to this what we know about hunger, misery, all kinds of oppression in an increasingly divided and threatened world, it is obvious that for us the appeal to "social holiness" is much more challenging, much more demanding, and very much more complex.

But the primacy of conversion remains intact. It is a constant imperative for today's Christian. It is distressing to see how little the churches are concerned with "this conversion," a conversion to social holiness that is given concrete form in the commitment on the side of the poor, the excluded, the threatened of the earth.

We can verify a strong neoconservative current, a tendency to institutional strengthening, and a re-clericalizing in many areas of the church. All of this is accompanied by a call to a conversion of generosity to the neighbor, which declares itself to have an absolutely neutral and nonideological content. To take seriously the historic mediations of effective love and "to get into politics" is to stain the purity of the message. This is seen as a betrayal of the gospel. Let us not delude ourselves; the churches have come to a frightening impasse. Christianity has become more difficult, and, therefore, more necessary than ever.

Yes, there was an intentional irony in the title of this chapter. Let us not deceive ourselves any further. Quotations about "social holiness" taken out of context form the rhetoric of all Christian churches and movements, including the most alienating and reactionary. The verbalizations and proclamations are necessary, but they are not sufficient nor are they immune to ambiguity. "Social holiness" depends on the historic mediations which articulate it. Simply put: **"Social Holiness" is not enough!**

A Reading of the Bible, Beginning with the Poor of Latin America

ELY ÉSER BARRETO CÉSAR   *(Methodist, Brazil)*

Latin America Protestants have not, up to now, faced fundamentally the questions related to a rereading of the Bible which begins with the present reality of our continent.

The biblical hermeneutic of Latin America is basically Catholic. It does not respond to the restrictive questions of the Protestant principle of *Sola Scriptura:* "The Holy Scriptures contain all that is necessary for salvation, so that what is not found in them nor can be proved by them should not be demanded of any person to be believed as an article of faith, nor should be judged necessary to salvation."[1]

Protestants have difficulty with the principle that the only legitimate rereading of the Bible begins with contemporary reality. This hermeneutic seems much more compatible with the Catholic principle of tradition held as a criterion of theological elaboration.

A rereading of the Bible from Protestant inspiration in our new sociohistoric context will follow three guidelines.

1. A recovery of fundamental Protestant principles from the perspective of John Wesley.
2. Possible hermeneutic guidelines beginning with the principle of *Sola Scriptura*, in the context of the Protestant principles revised by Wesley and brought up to date by our reality.
3. The necessity of a Latin American missionary pastoral to sustain a biblical rereading beginning with the poor.

---

1. "25 Articles of Religion of Historic Methodism," art. 5 in *Cánones da Igreja Metodista 1982* (São Paulo: Imprensa Methodista, 1982), p. 24.

Fundamental Protestant Principles from the Perspective of John Wesley

Justification by faith alone *(Sola Fides)* comes exclusively by the merits of Jesus Christ and not through meritorious human works *(Sola Gratia)*. This article, central to Protestant faith, has been understood throughout history as an antithesis to the Roman Catholic principle of good works.

The concentration of the saving act in God and Jesus Christ by Protestants has led to a dehistorization of faith to the point that the historic act has been stripped of theological value. Every political act has been seen as incompatible with any evangelizing act.

Based in a dualism, this principle localizes salvation in a metaphysical sphere. Evangelization is of the "spiritual" soul. The metaphysical basis of these principles seems to explain, on one hand, the difficulty of relating the eschatological idea of the kingdom of God with concrete political projects, and on the other, with the individualistic character of the Protestant ethic.

John Wesley, with his concern for human participation in the process of salvation, a fact expressed in his doctrine of sanctification, opens significant possibilities for a rereading of tradition beginning with history. He criticizes the limitations of the Protestant principle of "justification by faith alone." Listen to this classic quotation:

> To preach salvation, or justification, by faith alone is to preach against holiness and good works. To this assertion a specific reply can be given: "such rupture would take place, if we spoke as some do, of a faith separated from holiness and good works" but we speak of a faith not of this nature, but productive of all good works and holiness.[2]

With his concept of salvation Wesley recovers the Catholic principle of necessary works as a part of faith and an aid toward the "final justification."

Ted Runyon reminds us that the Aldersgate experience, in which Wesley seems to have resolved the problem of the nature of faith and of justification, does not place in question the

2. John Wesley, *The Works of John Wesley*, vol. 5, 3d ed. (Grand Rapids: Baker, 1978), p. 12.

role of works in the Christian life. "The transformation that occurred at Aldersgate is not in Wesley's anthropology (the conviction that human life is fundamentally purposive activity), but in the relational *foundation* that undergirds that activity."[3]

Against the idea of *Sola Gratia,* Wesley elaborated a theology of "sanctification by grace through faith." The process of sanctification is one of human responsibility, but it takes place thanks to the enabling power of the grace of God. The grace of God is, then, the active presence of the love of God in human existence. What Wesley affirms, against the principles of *Sola Gratia,* is that the presence of grace does not eliminate the necessity of the disciplined action of the human person.

Of importance here is that traditional Methodism, in stressing the notion of sanctification, introduced an important anthropological element into Protestant principles with a strong metaphysical content. A contemporary reelaboration of Wesleyan anthropology, beginning with the reality of Latin America, will permit us to establish history as the only possible mediation for making concrete our salvation. By doing so *we still maintain our "Protestantness."*

We can deepen the principle of the Scriptures as the only rule of faith and practice, beginning with the actualization of our concept of sanctification. In fact, the doctrine of sanctification leads Wesley to take seriously facts of concrete individual life. Therefore, experience, alongside Scripture, is one of his criteria for religious knowledge.

If Wesley's formulations of Scripture indicate that he identified them more with the code of metaphysical truths that point the way to heaven, in practice he was influenced by historic contingencies that accompanied the development of his theology. His theology is eminently pastoral. That is, it grows out of his rereading of the Bible, beginning with his reading of the contemporary reality. The scientific-cultural conditions of his time did not allow for a reading of the Bible as a historical process that reflects the revelation of God. In this sense his biblical rereading is basically rationalistic.

3. T. Runyon, ed., *Sanctification and Liberation: Liberation Theologies in the Light of Wesleyan Tradition* (Nashville: Abingdon, 1981), p. 32; cf. pp. 30-35.

For our purposes it is important to point out that, though we are not today able to go along with the rationalistic hermeneutic of Wesley, we still see the Bible as the starting point for Protestant theological concepts. If the hermeneutical guidelines we are seeking in Latin America today are to reach our Protestant community in a significant way, they must be supported by the Scriptures themselves.

Before we attempt such a task, however, we must be aware that even in reviewing the foundations of Protestantism we are within a hermeneutic perspective. That is, we cannot lose sight of the fact that the foundations of Protestantism in its historic origins belong to the history of the Protestant peoples of the northern hemisphere. They were willed to us by a missionary movement that was not exempt from some forms of cultural violence. As Míguez Bonino has already said, "Our identity is not primarily forged in an identification with the past, but in the realization of present tasks and in the commitment to an historic project."[4]

However, the realization of these tasks and this historic project will not take place without the past. The search for our identity can be a "call to a reinterpretation of history which frees us from the blockades and permits us to participate in these changes (historic projects), a memory which evokes a call and a mission."[5]

Possible Hermeneutic Guidelines—from the Principle of *Sola Scriptura*, in the Context of Protestant Principles, Revised by Wesley, Brought Up to Date for Our Reality

The basic principle which this reading of our tradition provides for the biblical rereading is the *principle of historic mediation*. By this principle we can see each period of history as a partial actualization of the saving project of God.

4. *Luta Pela Vida e Evangelização* (São Paulo: Paulinas, 1985). José Míguez Bonino, "Foi O Metodismo Um Movimeinto Libertador?" pp. 22-33. Also in Spanish, "¿Fue el Metodismo un Movimiento Liberador?" in *La Tradición Protestante en la Teología Latinoamericana* (San José: DEI, 1983), pp. 63-73.

5. Ibid.

This leads to our *second hermeneutical guideline*. Concrete manifestations of salvation in the Bible itself become normative for our journey. Our focus will be the modes of relationship of the concrete manifestations of biblical salvation with our contemporary world.

How are the various biblical periods in which the experience of salvation has partial reality related? These relationships of the various biblical historic moments with the biblical past will give us the hermeneutic clue we are seeking. This method of biblical interpretation responds to the Protestant principle of *Sola Scriptura*. This process was suggested by Clodovis Boff[6] and taken up by Elsa Tamez.[7]

Of the various hermeneutic principles that have circulated throughout history, those not based on a historical category and those that search for analogies do not do justice to the historic problematic lived by Latin America. This is true whether based only on the text (as, e.g., Cullmann) or limited to existential, psychological philosophy (Bultmann).

Studies of the Old Testament, especially those begun by Gerhard von Rad, delimit certain periods of the history of Israel that, beginning with their specific historical moment, picked up the same historic events recognized as partial concrete manifestations of salvation (Exodus, Sinai, kingship of David, cultic life in Jerusalem, exile). They brought them up to date to achieve an understanding and recovery of a new present in the face of the challenges and projects it presented.

For example, the historic books of the Deuteronomist (Samuel, Kings, and Judges) took up the entire tradition of Israel from the perspective of the exile. Beginning with the exile, these books review the history of the two kingdoms (Judah and Israel) to understand the reasons for this tragedy. The kings are judged from the point of view of their attitude toward worship in Jerusalem. All the kings of Israel are judged negatively because "they walked in the sins of Jeroboam." That is, they wor-

6. Clodovis Boff, *Theology and Praxis: Epistemological Foundations*, trans. Robert Barr (Maryknoll, N.Y.: Orbis, 1987).
7. Elsa Tamez, "Wesley as Read by the Poor," in *The Future of the Methodist Theological Traditions*, ed. M. Douglas Meeks (Nashville: Abingdon, 1985), pp. 67-84.

shiped nature in the high places (cf. 2 Kings 17:7-8). In the kingdom of Judah only Hezekiah and Josiah escaped this fate. This great historical fact occurs as a confession of sin. Within this perspective King David becomes the focus of hope, characterized as a messianic hope.

From the exile onward, the history of Israel is a history of judgment. The God who judges leads the people to repentance and salvation. The historian covers the same period as the Deuteronomist, but now from a postexilic perspective. In this period it is no longer the "house of David" that supports the faith of the people, but the cult. While in the Deuteronomist's account several generations suffer for the sins of some kings, in the historian's version each individual generation demonstrates the judgment or the salvation of God.

The generation of the historian must maintain hope because its salvation depends entirely on its attitude toward the worship of Yahweh. It will not pay for the sins of past generations. Furthermore, David is completely purified of his errors and weaknesses, coming to be seen as the true founder of the cult, the true priest. The law becomes identified with cultic ritualism; election is no longer that of a people but of the king, of the sanctuary, of the Levites (1 Chron. 15:2; 28:4; 2 Chron. 7:12-16; 12:13; etc.). The concept of the covenant disappears.

To be faithful to Yahweh is to be faithful to the sanctuary in Jerusalem. In the time of the historian, which was the time of the restoration by Ezra and Nehemiah, the telling of the history of Israel passes through a process of shrinking, because the history of the people had shrunk.[8] This simple example indicates that within the Old Testament the necessity for relevance was a valid hermeneutic principle. That is, the necessity of illuminating the new circumstances of a new present determined the criteria for the rereading of past concrete manifestations of salvation.

For the present, the past was not seen as a static reality that transmitted eternal and immutable truths. Even though it contained concrete manifestations of salvation or the judgmental actions of God, it would have meaning for the new present

---

8. G. von Rad, *Theologie de l'AT*, vol. 1 (Geneva: Labor et Fides, 1967), pp. 292-305 (E.T., *Old Testament Theology*, vol.1 [New York: Harper, 1962]).

only if it were revised to the point of affording guidance for a new generation facing new challenges.

An examination of the use of the Old Testament by the authors of the New Testament is suggestive. The author of the Gospel of Matthew corrects, adds to, alters, or eliminates texts that he uses as proof-texts of the fulfillment of prophecy in the life of Jesus Christ. However, it is the history of Jesus or the new missionary challenges of the evangelical community that seem to determine the recovery of the past tradition.

Let us examine a typical example of the way the Apostle Paul makes use of the Old Testament. In the Letter to the Galatians he appeals ten times to explicit Old Testament texts. The context of Galatians is that of the legitimacy of the Gentile mission threatened by a Judaizing preaching that seemed to stimulate the Galatians to the practice of circumcision as one way of guaranteeing access to salvation. In Galatians 4:27 Paul cites Isaiah 54:1 (Septuagint). Here he proposes an allegorical analysis around the figures of Sarah and Hagar, seen as representatives of two opposing ways, that of the promise (Sarah) and that of law (Hagar). As Paul cites the text, he does not alter the Greek text of Isaiah:

> For it is written: rejoice barren one, the one who does not give birth; explode with joy and cry out, the one who has not suffered the birth pangs. Because many shall be the children of the desolate, many more than of those who have a husband.

In the Old Testament text, the bereft woman represents the Jerusalem of the exile, desolate because of the absence of her children. Her joy is tied to the certainty of the return of her children, when her prosperity will be greater than ever.

St. Paul rereads the prophet from the perspective of the mission to the Gentiles in the context of the rejection of Jesus Christ by the official Judaism of Jerusalem. While Isaiah mentions only one Jerusalem, Paul sees two: an earthly Jerusalem enslaved (Gal. 4:25) and one on high, free, the mother of the Galatians (4:26). Jerusalem after the exile, which in the vision of Second Isaiah will have many children, is for Paul the figure of the new Jerusalem. Jerusalem before the exile represents the capital of Judea, in his time captive under the barren law.

The apostle's rereading transforms the captivity of Babylon to the captivity of the law. The promise of Isaiah to the Jews in exile becomes the curse of the Jews in Palestine, Paul's contemporaries. The promise of Isaiah, on the other hand, is applied to the Galatian Gentiles (4:26), now more fruitful than the children of the synagogue. The Jerusalem of Isaiah comes to represent Sarah and Hagar.

What enormous irony! The Jerusalem of the true children of Abraham is represented by Hagar, while the legitimate historic descendants of Isaac are seen by the apostle, in his surprising rereading, as descendants of Ishmael, the son of Hagar.

Why? Because the Galatians, being the children of promise, can be seen only as the descendants of Isaac. What, in the historic circumstances lived by Paul, would give legitimacy to such a rereading? The persecution of the Gentiles by the Jews prefigured in the persecution of Isaac by Ishmael.

Paul understood that the direction of the acts of God in his history had taken a new path. This new path indicated the direction the Galatian community ought to take: freedom from the law! The past must be reorganized in keeping with this new present. This rereading has the purpose of helping the Galatian community to face its complex present and the journey the new circumstances demand.

Another example of how the Old Testament was interpreted by the New Testament church may be seen in the various roles assigned to Jesus in these communities depending on the varied concrete problems facing them at the time. Here we offer only a rapid summary of a broader analysis. The very tradition of Jesus comes to be updated in various moments lived by the primitive church, and this even in the short period covered by the New Testament.

The *Galatian Jesus* responds to the specific circumstances of that community. The major problem for the Galatians was the new Judaizing preaching that sought to subject to circumcision converts from pagan origins. Jesus Christ is received in this context as the one who gives freedom from the curse of the law.

The *Jesus of Matthew,* formulated about thirty years after the Jesus of Galatia, responds to the problems of a mixed Christian community composed of Jews and Gentiles. The break with the synagogue seems to be a marked phenomenon of the community of the years 80-90, many years after the fall of Jerusalem (c. A.D. 70).

As the Matthean community seems to be aware, Jesus is really the Jewish Messiah who fulfills the promises of the Old Testament. The break with the synagogue provoked some kind of identity crisis because Israel's traditions are still cultivated. This best explains a notable fact we see throughout the gospel: it lost the missionary perspective.

In this context Jesus Christ is confessed as the Jewish Messiah who, despite Israel's rejection, brings to the world a new kingdom of justice. But he is the Messiah of the Gentiles, the strange Messiah of Nazareth, Galilee, of the Gentiles! The new life he brings is founded on justice, the justice of the kingdom, the justice of love, superior to that of the Scribes and Pharisees. Besides being the Messiah, he is also the resurrected presence who sends the community out into the world for the grand missionary project and the kingdom of the new life.

The *Jesus of the Apocalypse,* formulated about A.D. 95, responds to the dramatic circumstances of a community threatened and persecuted by the best-organized empire of antiquity. Therefore, Jesus is the Lamb, the faithful martyr who offers life and communion to the disciple who is faithful until death. He is also the warrior Lamb who will avenge himself on those who make martyrs of the Christians.

These three roles of Jesus indicate that, although Jesus was the same historical personage, he was actualized in a specific way according to the circumstances of each community.

What are the *hermeneutical consequences* that come from this analysis? Both the rereading of the Old Testament by the early Christians and the rereading of the tradition about Jesus Christ by different New Testament communities show that each period of history covered by the Bible consists in a partial updating of the saving project of God. What forces directed this updating and can still direct our contemporary hermeneutical process?

1. All biblical periods constituted historical processes that actualized segments of the past tradition into the concrete circumstances of a new present, lived by the community. In this way *dominant character is given to the present*. Past tradition is significant in terms of the present. It is by this process that faith maintains the possibility of continuing to be live faith, signifi-

cant and dynamic today. It should be noted here that in the processes we have examined, the present is not an individual present but one lived and shared by a community.

2. For this process of actualization to take place, *faith must open dialogue with tradition in terms of problems it discerns in the present*. It appears that in the biblical world it was never tradition that defined the agenda for theological elaboration and missionary practice.

This indicates the need for a community to possess mediating elements that permit it to capture the true reality. The author of the Apocalypse, for example, did not slip in the direction of an ingenuous and triumphalist expression of the faith, imagining that the victory of the Lamb would automatically guarantee the victory of the believing community. He sees with great seriousness the power of the Roman Empire, which he identifies with the power of Satan! He can offer Christians only the solution of martyrdom, if they are faced with the extreme option.

3. It is fundamental that *the dialogue of the living community with past tradition be selective*. After all, it takes place as a function of the relevance of the faith. The criterion of selectivity is given by the present agenda. The community must have access to a significant quantity of the tradition so the selection may take place with reasonable adequacy.

4. The criterion for the process of actualization is that of the historic process that the community *is already living*. It is not concerned just about knowledge. This actualization can never be disinterested, "scientific." It is impossible to conceive of the living faith of a community except under the demand for commitment.

5. Does there appear to have been some sense of faithfulness to the Scriptures and to the tradition in the processes we have analyzed? The freedom with which Christians return to tradition can be misunderstood. The faithfulness they expressed was not to a text fixed in the past or to a static tradition. The sense of fidelity, in the cases we have examined, indicates a fidelity to the direction of the acts of God in history.

When the Jews asked Jesus for a sign that he would give salvation concrete form in history, they were wearing the wrong glasses. So much so, that no sign was given them. They did not see what the disciples see, that is, the historic signs of the arrival of salvation in Jesus. This theme of discerning the signs is important in Matthew (11:2-15; 1:18-23; cf. 28:16-20). Paul criticizes the Galatians because they do not discern the history of their own community as the history of the acts of the Spirit (Gal. 3:1-5). The author of the Apocalypse constantly appeals to this historic discernment: "who has ears let him hear what the Spirit says to the churches."

In the three documents we examined, Christians are invited to work always in three horizons: the horizon of the historic Jesus, the horizon of the tradition of Israel, and the horizon of the future. Much of the "theological work" of these documents consists in a controlled dialectic relationship between these three horizons. The starting point for this dialogue is the present.

6. Our analysis of the New Testament indicates that we can posit the hypothesis that the historic practice of faith was the ultimate criterion that confirmed fidelity of the community. If this hypothesis is sustained, then our perception is confirmed that the historic process of sanctification is an open human process. That is, the decisions of the historic journey of a community depend basically on their prophetic clarity and are subject to the vicissitudes of all historic process.

Faithfulness is not defined just in relation to the past, but above all in relation to the present. It is not so much fidelity to the letter, but fidelity that takes place in history! For Matthew, isn't to be a disciple *to do* the will of God? In Galatians, isn't faith demonstrated precisely through the operation of love? Does fidelity to the Apocalyptic Lamb not consist precisely in following wherever he goes? The truth of the hermeneutic process is not in exegetical purity but in the perception, controlled by historic praxis, of the direction of the acts of God in history.

The hermeneutic process that appears to come from this analysis of the partial actualizations of the saving project of God can be summed up in two basic operational criteria, which may be used in our Latin American Protestant hermeneutic:

1. The criterion of relevance.

a. It is only beginning with the present reality, perceived through the mediations of adequately selected analysis of the very nature of reality, that one can go to tradition to find light and impulse for Christian praxis.

b. Tradition will be selected on the basis of the agenda that arises from reality itself.

c. The purpose of this selective process is to reenforce the identity of a community by an orientation of its comtemporary history toward a renewed future.

2. The criterion of fidelity.

a. Only that which effectively belongs to tradition can be brought up to date. Tradition that illuminates the present from the past must always operate dialectically, revealing sin and offering righteousness.

b. Fidelity is measured by the perception of the direction of the historic acts of God. This sense of direction can be controlled by the line projected from the present to Jesus Christ and from him to the Old Testament, and from both of them to the near and far future, by way of the present.

c. The final criterion of the legitimacy of this entire process is the confirmation or correction afforded by the community's praxis.

In our specific situation in the Third World, the decisive fact that defines our search for hermeneutical correction is, on the one hand, that the reality of poverty in the world is provoked by the developed nations. On the other hand is our biblical perception of the direction of the acts of God in history, where we see God's preferential option for the poor. We understand that it is on these two levels that our dialogue must take place with the bourgeois segments of our society or with the dominant societies.

The facts of the world historic reality cannot be indefinitely manipulated. The biblical tradition reveals in a decisive way on which side of history God has placed the Divine. It might be worthwhile to analyze the New Testament, which systematically demonstrates this fact, as we have already done with the Old Testament.

The Latin American *Missionary Pastoral* to Support a Biblical Rereading, Beginning with the Poor

We will not stay long on this topic, only to call attention to the fact that a new rereading of the Bible and the Wesleyan tradition will not take place artificially. It will not take place by altering the teaching materials prepared for Sunday schools or church groups or other steps on this level, although at certain points this could be helpful.

The starting point for our hermeneutic is a commitment to the reconstruction of society beginning with the claims of the poor. Hermeneutic will take place within the context of this commitment.

An effective encounter with the poor results in a conversion from a mentality educated in the context of domination to a mentality that can discover that the building of a new society must begin with the people and with the claims of the poor.

In this way, along with the theoretical instrumentation that supports the new biblical hermeneutic, there is fundamental need for the instrumentation of Protestant communities. Thus, we may truly experience a pastoral that produces a new community structure and a new historic commitment.

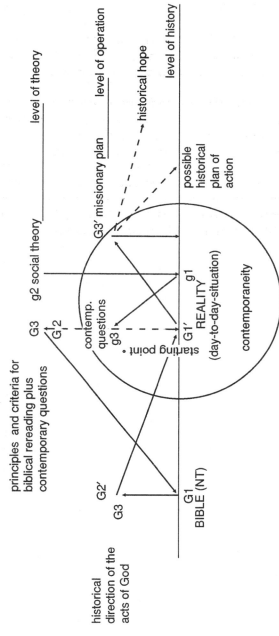

MOVEMENT OF CONTEMPORARY REREADING OF THE BIBLE

the order of the movements:
1. g2→g1→g3→social analysis
2. G2→G1→G3→questioning the Bible from contemporaneity
3. G2'→G1'→G3'→questioning contemporaneity from the Bible

Toward a Theology of Peace: Critical Notes on the Biblical Hermeneutic of Latin American Theology of Liberation

LUIS N. RIVERA PAGÁN   *(Baptist, Puerto Rico)*

The New Latin American Hermeneutic

Contemporary Latin American theology has made a significant contribution in its emphasis on the popular origin of the Bible as a fundamental interpretative axis. It has set the sacred Judeo-Christian Scriptures in the matrix of the historical experiences of Israel, their sufferings as the poor and oppressed, situated under the armies of powerful nations.

The Old Testament knows of enslavement and emancipation in Israel. It is impossible to understand it apart from the polarity of oppression-liberation as the constant factor in the history of the Hebrew nation.[1] The first confession of faith of the Israelites is related to their liberation by God from the slavery of Egypt.

> My ancestor was a wandering Armenian who took his family to Egypt. . . . They were few in number when they went there, but they became a large and powerful nation. The Egyptians treated us harshly and forced us to work as slaves. Then we cried out for help to the Lord, the God of our ancestors. He heard us, saw our suffering, hardship and misery. By his great power and strength, he rescued us from Egypt. He worked miracles and wonders and caused terrifying things to happen. He brought us here and gave us this rich and fertile land. (Deut. 26:5-9)

1. Hugo Assmann, *Opresión—liberación: Desafío a los cristianos* (Montevideo: Editorial Tierra Nueva, 1971).

The New Testament, according to this exegetical line of thought, comes from a people colonized by the force of Roman arms, impoverished by taxes, and spiritually subjugated by its religious authorities. The result was a great number of poor people, suffering illnesses typical of poverty (such as leprosy) and prostitution. There are many evidences of the precarious nature of society found in the Gospels.[2]

The reinterpretation of the Bible by the new Latin American theology, situated in today's context of the struggles and hopes of the poor and oppressed, does not imply the transubstantiation of its original structure of meaning.[3] It does not lead, as some ecclesiastical authorities fear, to the arbitrary substitution of political themes for religious ones.[4] Rather, it has to do with the recovery of the rebel memory that underlies the biblical texts.

The German Marxist, Ernst Bloch, in an excellent criticism of the individualistic hermeneutics of Rudolf Bultmann, insisted that the pristine and original meaning of the Bible is only captured adequately through a perception of the social horizon of the antagonism between oppressors and oppressed, dominators and dominated, expressed in many diverse ways in the biblical texts.[5]

2. Raúl Vidales, "El mundo socio-económico y político de Jesús," in *Desde la tradición de los pobres* (Mexico: Centro de Reflexión Teológica, 1978), pp. 61-114.

3. The poor people and poverty have motivated a rich and provocative reflection by contemporary Latin American theology. Outstanding examples are Jon Sobrino, *The True Church and the Poor*, trans. Matthew J. O'Connell (Maryknoll, N.Y.: Orbis, 1984); Gustavo Gutiérrez, *The Power of the Poor in History* (Maryknoll, N.Y.: Orbis, 1983); Leonardo Boff, *La fe en la periferia del mundo: El caminar de la iglesia con los oprimidos* (Santander: Editorial Sal Terrae, 1981); and Thomas Hanks, *God So Loved the Third World: The Bible, the Reformation, and Liberation Theologies* (Maryknoll, N.Y.: Orbis, 1983). About the significance of this reflection for the development of a new theological sensitivity, see Luis N. Rivera Pagán, "Christliche Neuorientierung in Lateinamerika und in det Karibik," *Standpunkt—Evangelische Monatschrift* (July 1982): 190-91.

4. See the "Instrucción de la Sagrada Congregación para la Doctrina de la Fe sobre algunos aspectos de la teología de la liberación," signed by Cardinal Joseph Ratzinger, prefect of the Sacred Congregation, and by Archbishop Alberto Bovone, its secretary, published by *L'Osservatore Romano*, Spanish language edition, September 9, 1984.

5. *Atheism in Christianity: The Religion of the Exodus and the Kingdom*, trans. J. T. Swann (New York: Herder & Herder, 1972).

LUIS N. RIVERA PAGÁN

This exegetical intuition, however, was not developed until Latin American theology took it up again and applied it globally to the biblical texts, forcing an authentic hermeneutic revolution.

This historic-social interpretation, which places the biblical text with its sagas and narratives, confessions and hymns, in correlation with the history of the people, their oppressions, and liberations, is no doubt an exceptional contribution to the universal biblical hermeneutic.[6] Its definitive contribution has been documented and analyzed by a number of authors, among whom is the Puerto Rican Baptist, Samuel Silva Gotay, in his very useful work, *El pensamiento cristiano revolucionario en América Latina*.[7] Silva Gotay carefully analyzes the origin of the Latin American theology of liberation and reproduces the consensus at which many of its authors arrive on biblical hermeneutics and exegesis.

In my opinion, this Latin American biblical hermeneutic can be of great value to us to give precise definitions to the visions of peace that are found in the Bible, and to their theological implications in our dilemma with the new technology of nuclear war and destruction. To achieve this end, however, we must make some critical observations about Latin American exegesis. We will use the work of Silva Gotay as our guide in this critical dialogue.

First Critical Note: Historicity or Liberation

Some Latin American theologians have put too much emphasis on the historic matrix of hermeneutics, insisting on a supposed recovery of the primacy of history as the significant, particular, and proper ambience of the Bible. Silva Gotay has written:

6. See, e.g., the influence of Latin American exegesis in the collection of North American hermeneutic essays *The Bible and Liberation: Political and Social Hermeneutics*, ed. Norman K. Gottwald (Maryknoll, N.Y.: Orbis, 1983).
7. *El pensamiento cristiano revolucionario en América Latina: Implicaciones de la teología de la liberación para la sociología de la religión* (Salamanca: Ediciones Sigueme, 1981).

The reply of Latin American theologians is that salvation, in biblical religion . . . takes place in the only history which exists, not in "the beyond" of Platonism; that salvation is a historic process which takes place in real, material and objective history.[8]

It is not enough, however, to insist on the fully historic character of the soteriological events of the Bible. The same could be said of Herodotus and Thucydides, or even of the great pedagogue of Greek youth, Homer. A concern for history is neither peculiar nor exclusive to the biblical texts.

The special and exceptional in the Judeo-Christian Scriptures, compared with similar works of antiquity, rests in the emphasis on the enslavement of the people and their hopes of liberation. In reporting the deeds of the monarchs and their dynasties, the narration does not reproduce the stereotyped glorification of the prowess and feats of the kings generally found in Egyptian, Persian, and Chaldean parallels. On the contrary, there is a very critical and condemning accent. It censures the oppressive character of the princes and the royal court, which was the final cause of the nation's ruin. Among many others, the second chapter of Ezekiel constitutes a dramatic example in which there is a violent diatribe of the prophet against the court, landholders, priests, and prophets in the service of the court.

> In you the princes of Israel, one and all, have used their power to shed blood; men have treated their fathers and mothers with contempt, they have oppressed the alien and ill-treated the orphan and the widow. . . . The princes within her are like lions growling as they tear their prey. They have devoured men, and seized their treasure and all their wealth; they have widowed many women within her walls. Her priests have done violence to my law and profaned what is sacred to me. . . . Her officers within her are like wolves tearing their prey, shedding blood and destroying men's lives to acquire ill-gotten gains. . . . The common people are bullies and robbers; they ill-treat the unfortunate and the poor, they are unjust and cruel to the alien. (Ezek. 22:6, 7, 25-27, 29)

This text from Ezekiel is typical of the dominant biblical perspective. It is not a telling of history in terms of an excessive

8. Silva Gotay, *El pensamiento cristiano revolucionario*, p. 97.

spiritualized soteriology. Ezekiel rather emphasizes the conflictive nature of history. There are poor people, oppressed by the powerful, who moan and call out to God for liberation.

This polarity between oppression and liberation is expressed in prophetic-utopian symbols: the land that flows with milk and honey, the mountain of God, the new heavens and new earth, the kingdom of God. It is the history of those who have no history, an exploited people who cry out for and dream of liberty. The definitive particularity of the Bible rests at this point: it arises from a reversal of history, of the "defeated."

Second Critical Note: Plato and Hellenism

The Latin American hermeneutic has been contaminated by a marked anti-Hellenism, and, especially, by its criticism of Plato. He has been made into the new Lucifer who supposedly introduces into the West "abstract," "speculative," "idealistic," "metaphysical," "spiritualistic," and "ahistorical" ways of thinking. The Hellenization of Christian thought, according to this view, is the theological original sin of the church fathers. This, allegedly, has led to a confusion between "nature" and "history" and to a "dehistorization" of theology and a "dogmatization" of Christian faith. For example, Silva Gotay says,

> When Constantine converted the Christian faith into an ideology which legitimated imperial power and the dominating classes, to the point of sacralizing them . . . , they had already been ideologically undermined by the Hellenist "spiritualism" of Platonic rootage.[9]

With this type of analysis, so common in contemporary Latin American theology, in my opinion, a number of very serious errors are committed.

1. The enormous richness and variety of Hellenic thought and Greek culture is lost. Its gifts and contributions to the history of literature, philosophy, art, politics, science, and even physical education are extraordinary and cannot be reduced to the Procrustean bed of a petty interpretation of late Pla-

---

9. Silva Gotay, *El pensamiento cristiano revolucionario*, p. 76.

tonism. For one thing, the Renaissance thinkers instituted the dialogue with classic Greek culture as a historic, renewing project.

José Porfirio Miranda reflects this fear of Hellenic culture and thought. "The question of the de-hellenization of Christianity . . . is much deeper than the scholastics believed. . . . Greek philosophy was born to neutralize reality and keep it from disturbing us; to reduce it to a cosmos in which everything goes well."[10] This description is a caricature incapable of explaining the unease Greek philosophy has provoked in more than two thousand years. It is true that Greek philosophy tries to understand reality as *cosmos,* ruled by reason *(logos),* not a *chaos,* but why should this be carried to "neutralization," pretending that everything is going well? In Plato, on the other hand, there is a pessimistic, not illusory, vision of the historical process.

2. Plato is confused with later Hellenistic Platonism. From the works and letters of Plato we can capture the primary political character of his thought.[11] The government of the polis was by far the principal problem for the great Athenian philosopher, as it was in general for the young aristocrats of his city. Socratic pedagogy, dialectically systematized in the Academy and its dialogues, is directed neither exclusively nor primarily to the purification of the individual soul, but to the political and social reconstruction of Athens.

There is in Plato a profound political intentionality.[12] This is seen chiefly, but not exclusively, in his political works, such as *Laws* and *The Republic,* the latter being the most extensive and perhaps most important of his dialogues. It is true that the key concept of his writing, justice, is examined from a dual perspective: the political—referring to an adequate social order—and the psychological—the harmony of the soul. But it is significant that the work is called "The Republic" not "The Soul," which re-

10. José Porfirio Miranda, *Marx and the Bible,* trans. John Eagleson (Maryknoll, N.Y.: Orbis, 1974), pp. xvi and xx.
11. See the seventh letter of Plato about the political character of his philosophic intent; a useful book is Paul Friedlander, *Plato: An Introduction* (New York: Harper, 1958), pp. 3-31.
12. Werner Jaeger, *Paideia: Los ideales de la cultura griega* (Mexico: Fondo de Cultura Economica, 1985), pp. 458-66, 999-1014.

flects the predominance of political considerations over the psychic. The primary pole of analogical thought is political. The work begins and ends with the ideal society and its governance.[13]

It was the Platonism of the later period of the dissolution of the Greek city-state of the polis that transformed the Platonic *paideia*, which depoliticized it and made of its idealist metaphysics and its rememorative psychology the exclusive hermeneutic keys of the master. The metaphysic is converted into the refuge of political impotence. It is, as Jaeger says, "Plato as seen through the eyes of Plotinus."[14] This spiritualist evolution of Platonism does not justify the mutilated and partial interpretation of Plato by a large part of present-day Latin American theology.[15]

3. It is relevant, in the face of such interpretation of Plato, to point out that *The Republic* outlines a utopian, revolutionary scheme of the best possible social order, including a strong critique of discrimination against women, and arguments for the abolition of private property (at least for the governing classes), and the elimination of the family and of wars of conquest. Few works in the history of Western thought are so provokingly subversive.

It is Aristotle, Plato's disciple, who assumes in his work *Politics* the defense of the classic institutions of the polis—slavery, the inferiority of women, private property, the legiti-

---

13. Friedlander, *Plato*, pp. 9ff.: "*The Republic* and *The Laws* surpass in size any other work of Plato. A revision of the totality of his writings should place *The Republic* at the center of his entire literary production. In fact, it would be legitimate to consider the majority of his previous dialogues as direct preparation for *The Republic*. The internal structure of *The Republic* on its part is determined by the thesis that the true governors and the true philosophers should be identical."

14. Jaeger, *Paideia*, p. 458.

15. It is true that in such works as *The Banquet*, Plato develops a theory of the hierarchy of being (the true/beautiful/good) through affirmations that are very useful to later idealism ("eternal beauty, uncreated and imperishable, which has nothing of the bodily"). This subordination of the body to the spirit does not lead, however, to an ascetic negation. Otherwise the festive, *erotic*, character of *The Banquet* could not be explained.

macy of war against the "barbarians"—protecting them from the innovations proposed by his master.

Every later revolutionary and utopian movement feeds on *The Republic*, picking up its themes and reflecting on the ways opened by Plato—including such subjects as the division of classes.[16] All reform movements that try to avoid revolutionary excesses appeal to Aristotle's *Politics*.

Werner Jaeger's evaluation of the great Hellenic philosopher deals more fairly with the political nature of Platonic thought:

> The political for the one whose fundamental works are *The Republic* and *Laws* is not only the content of certain stages of his life, . . . but the very foundation of all his cultural existence. It was the object of his thought which included all the others. . . . So for Plato to know, *gnosis*, is not a mere contemplation disconnected from life, but becomes a *techné*, an art, and *frónesis*, reflection on the true pathway, the correct decision, the proper goal, the real good.[17]

Silva Gotay, Miranda, and other Latin American theologians are in error in not giving a reasonable explanation for the appearance of the concept of unity between Platonistic Hellenism and Christianity. Platonism is not replaced by Christianity. The ideal of a renewed society is frustrated, but the doctrine of the soul remains. As it is developed in *Meno, Phaedrus,* and *The Republic*, the soul—immortal, true subject of the good and the true, immutable substance that represents the maximum of interiority and transcendence—stripped of the necessity of reforming the polis and material reality, seeks its eternal salvation in the world of ideas and forms. Therefore, the *psyche* and not the *polis*, the doctrine of the immortality of the soul and not social transformation, remains as the imperishable legacy of Platonism.

Platonism, as a philosophy of the doctrine of the soul which seeks the eternal truth and good, can be wedded to patristic Christianity because it too has seen the frustration of the hope

---

16. This seems to me to be evident in the Renaissance utopias such as Thomas More's *Utopia* and Tommaso Campanella's *The City of the Sun,* and in the Marxist utopias of the nineteenth century.

17. Jaeger, *Paideia*, pp. 464, 999.

of the prompt return of Jesus Christ and the earthly and global transformation it will bring about.[18]

The *eschaton* is postponed indefinitely, millennialism is repressed, and Christianity is transformed into a religion of the salvation of the soul beyond history, *post mortem.* The doctrine of the resurrection of the body and its implications for the rebuilding of a new Jerusalem remains. But it loses its centrality and emphasis before the immortality of the soul.

Christianity devoid of its eschatological expectations finds in the Platonic doctrine of the soul, in Jaeger's words, "a prepared bed."[19] It takes from it the philosophical conceptualization and presents it not as its theoretical but its soteriological culmination. It is a synthesis of extraordinary historical significance, as can be seen in the works of St. Augustine.

4. Through the reduction of all Hellenic culture to a narrow interpretation of later Platonism, the intellectual anti-Semitism of a good part of German philosophy of the nineteenth century, which would have served propaedeutically the fascist anti-Semitism of the Third Reich, becomes the anti-Hellenism that is a sizeable part of the theology of the twentieth century. This creates difficulties both in theological reflection on Hellenic culture and in understanding its assimilation by patristic Christian thinkers.

St. Augustine, to take an important and often cited example, does not justify slavery on the basis of his Platonic metaphysics and epistemology but on the necessity of assuring the Romans the preservation of the "order of peace," which includes slave labor as the basis of production.[20] (In fact, the references to slavery in *The Republic* are scarce and of little importance, giving the impression that it is not essential to a just social order.)

In this way, Christianity gives full guarantees to the

18. The expectation of the imminent return of the Resurrected One is expressed in numerous passages of the New Testament, among them Mark 13:30 (and his synoptic parallels, Matt. 24:34 and Luke 21:32); John 21:22; Phil. 4:5; 1 Thess. 4:13-18; Jas. 5:8; Rev. 22:6-7, 12, 20. The indefinite delay in the event set the bases for theoretical readjustments in Christianity, among them its conversion into a religion of the salvation of the soul.

19. Jaeger, *Paideia,* p. 152.

20. *The City of God,* chaps. 15-16 (Everyman's Library [New York: E. P. Dutton, 1947], pp. 252-54).

dominant Roman classes that it will not conspire against their social and economic interests. The right to slavery is relativized in referring it to the order of sin, not of creation, and at the same time preserving and legitimizing it. Slavery is converted into a consequence of human sin. It is a clever theological manipulation through which the material and temporal well-being of the masters is made to coincide with the spiritual and eternal happiness of their servants.[21]

The same thing happens with the doctrine called "just war." Christianity as an imperial religion is forced to relegate the pacifism of the primitive apostolic community to the monastic orders, and to bless the use of the sword against foreign enemies (especially if they are pagans or, like the Arian barbarians, are heretics).[22] The Christian faith becomes the defender, not the adversary, of the *pax romana*.

The anti-Hellenism and anti-Platonism so common in the theology and hermeneutics of Latin America create enormous difficulties for understanding the crucial eras of the history of theology (e.g., the second to the fifth centuries, and the thirteenth), and substitute a specific type of metaphysics—the worst, a priori antimetaphysics—for concrete historic exegesis.

Third Critical Note: The Captivity of Israel

Latin American exegesis has excessively taken the Exodus as the exclusive hermeneutic key to the Bible. Silva Gotay writes:

> The new hermeneutic . . . has succeeded in playing out how Israel's faith . . . is articulated around the historic and sociopolitical event of the liberation of Israel from Egypt. . . . The term "salvation" is rediscovered as interchangeable with

21. In the same way seventeenth-century English treatises justify the slavery of Negroes, arguing that it contributes to the civilizing and Christianizing of the Africans, without necessarily assuming any Platonic metaphysics.

22. For the Augustinian doctrine on a just war see Roland H. Bainton, *Christian Attitudes toward War and Peace: A Historical Survey and Critical Reevaluation* (Nashville: Abingdon, 1960), pp. 91-100.

"liberation" and "justice" beginning with the rediscovery of the Exodus as "paradigm" for the interpretation of all space and all time in the Bible.[23]

In this context Silva Gotay cites Rubem Alves, the Brazilian Calvinist theologian:

> The Exodus was the awareness-generating experience for the people of Israel. It became the structural center which determined the manner of organizing time and space. . . . It determines the logic of integration, the principle of organization and interpretation of the facts of historic experience. It becomes the paradigm for the interpretation of all space and all time.[24]

The insistence of Latin American theology on the Exodus as the matrix experience that forges the national conscience of Israel and its vision of God and history is an important contribution to hermeneutics. The Exodus from Egypt, liberation of the Hebrew people from slavery under the Pharaoh, is the foundation event, according to the Old Testament, of the nation of Israel. Israel becomes a nation thanks to its liberation from Egyptian oppression. This redeeming action determines its national historic memory—the Hebraic interpretation of its special relationship with God and other nations. It also defines the egalitarian nature of its internal social order.[25]

Through a historical-critical analysis of the Old Testament texts, however, we discover the impossibility of attributing the origin of all of that exclusively to the experience of the Exodus. Another event is seen as decisive, the basic axis that forges the biblical consciousness: the *captivity*, the *exile*. The tragic drama of a devastated nation, the destroyed kingdom,

23. Silva Gotay, *El pensamiento cristiano revolucionario*, pp. 141ff.

24. "El pueblo de Dio y la liberación del hombre," *Fichas de ISAL* 3/26 (1970): 9. Cited by Silva Gotay in ibid., p. 143.

25. Severino Croatto, *Exodus: A Hermeneutics of Freedom* (Maryknoll, N.Y.: Orbis, 1981), and Jorge Pixley, *On Exodus: A Liberation Perspective* (Maryknoll, N.Y.: Orbis, 1987). For Pixley, "the Exodus is the basic story of the Old Testament because the liberation narrated in it is the fundamental fact of the people of God which will be the subject of all the books of the Bible" (p. 8).

and the captive people awakens terrible questions: Why does God permit his people, whom he had already liberated from the Egyptian oppression, to be destroyed? What does this say about God and sovereignty? What are the implications of the captivity for the destiny of the nation and its government? Does it lead to a definitive frustration with divine promises and the hopes of the people?

A good part of the Old Testament has as its purpose the answering of these questions. The recounting of the deeds of the monarchs (1 and 2 Chronicles and 1 and 2 Kings) conclude with the sentence that the royal house of Israel and of Judah "have done that which is evil in the eyes of God." This is declared to be the cause of the national desolation.

> Zedekiah was twenty-one years old when he came to the throne. . . . He did what was wrong in the eyes of the Lord his God. . . . All the chiefs of Judah and the priests and the people became more and more unfaithful, following all the abominable practices of the other nations; and they defiled the house of the Lord which he had hallowed in Jerusalem . . . until the anger of the Lord burst out against his people and could not be appeased. So he brought against them the king of the Chaldaeans, who put their young men to the sword . . . and spared neither young man nor maiden, neither the old nor the weak. . . . Those who escaped the sword he took captive to Babylon. (2 Chron. 36:11-20)

Much of the hymnology and confessional literature begins with the lamentations of national captivity. "If only Israel's deliverance might come out of Zion! When God restores his people's fortunes, let Jacob rejoice, let Israel be glad" (Ps. 53:6).

The prophetic books judge the oppressive actions of the dominating classes and see in their perversities the provoking of divine wrath.

> And I said:
> Listen, you leaders of Jacob, rulers of Israel,
> should you not know what is right?
>   You hate good and love evil,
> you flay men alive and tear the very flesh from their bones;
>   you devour the flesh of my people,
>   strip off their skin,

> splinter their bones;
> you shred them like flesh into a pot. . . .

> Therefore, on your account
> Zion shall become a ploughed field,
> Jerusalem a heap of ruins. (Mic. 3:1-3, 12)

On the other hand, utopian visions of a renewed Israel, free, enjoying abundant life, justice, and peace, come from a spiritual resistance to accepting captivity as a definitive and irreversible fact.

> I will restore the fortunes of my people Israel;
> they shall rebuild deserted cities and live in them,
> they shall plant vineyards and drink their wine,
> make gardens and eat the fruit.
> Once more I will plant them on their own soil,
> and they shall never again be uprooted
>   from the soil I have given them.
> It is the word of the Lord your God. (Amos 9:14-15)

The historical and prophetic books, as well as a sizeable number of the hymns and confessions, grow out of the experience of the exile and not of the Exodus. Latin American theology, in its anxiety to emphasize popular liberation as a central biblical event, has exaggerated the role the Exodus played in the genesis of the Judeo-Christian Scriptures. It has also failed to perceive the significance of the captivity and exile in the formation of the Old Testament canon.

The oppression-liberation dialectic becomes even more urgent from the perspective of the captivity. This new national enslavement gives the Hebrew Scriptures their intense moral character. If the Exodus reveals God as Liberator, the exile shows God to be the eternal demand for justice. When the Exodus is seen in isolation, it degenerates into triumphalism. This happens in Israel and can be seen in the Old Testament in numerous signs of national pride. Thanks to the experience of the captivity, of defeat and national tragedy, we still have the extraordinary ethical-theological reflections of the prophets, where divinity is defined in relation to justice.

> These are the words of the Lord: Deal justly and fairly,
> rescue the victim from his oppressor, . . .

> Shame on the man who builds his house by unjust means
>   and completes its roof-chambers by fraud,
>   making his countrymen work without payment,
>   giving them no wage for their labour!
> Shame on the man who says, "I will build a spacious
>   house with airy roof-chambers . . . panel it with
>   cedar. . . .
>   If your cedar is more splendid,
>   does that prove you a king?
> Think of your father: he ate and drank,
>   dealt justly and fairly; all went well with him.
>   He dispensed justice to the lowly and poor;
>   did not this show he knew me? says the Lord.
> But you have no eyes, no thought for anything but gain,
>   set only on the innocent blood you can shed,
>   on cruel acts of tyranny. (Jer. 22:3, 13-17)

This terrible prophetic diatribe against King Jehoiakim concludes with the threat of national captivity.

> I spoke to you in your days of prosperous ease,
>   but you said, "I will not listen." . . .
> Never have you obeyed me. . . .
> I will hand you over to those who seek your life, to those
> you fear. . . . I will fling you headlong, you and the mother
> who gave you birth, into another land, a land where you
> were not born; and there you both die. (Jer. 22:21, 25-26)

In a historical-critical investigation of the Old Testament, the *exile*, not just the *Exodus*, is seen as a source of canonical formation. This has cardinal importance for our principal interest.

Fourth Critical Note:
The Utopian Biblical Visions of Peace

The depth of the significance of the utopian-prophetic visions of the Old Testament can be seen only from the perspective of the centrality of the captivity in the Israelite national consciousness. They come from the heart of a captive people who long for redemption. "I will bring my people Israel out of captivity . . . and never more will they be pulled up from their land. The Lord your God has spoken" (Amos 9:14-15).

In an analysis of the utopian biblical visions and images, the Latin American hermeneutic has correctly emphasized the aspiration to overcome slavery, oppression, and misery. It has justifiably pointed out the presence in these texts of the hope of an abundant life, a freedom from subjugating work, from an unjust social order.

Silva Gotay, in the book we have already cited, has seen a "new Christian ethic of liberation" grow out of the new Latin American hermeneutic, one which raises "the ethical question of violence in the taking of power."[26] The class struggle of the oppressed against the oppressors, from the biblical perspective of the Exodus, assumes an unprecedented image: God acts with force through revolutionary violence. Love for the poor leads to rebellion against those who exploit.

Nevertheless, another important dimension of such visions has not been adequately perceived: *the aspiration for peace.* This myopia is due to a failure to understand the centrality of the captivity, of desolation caused by war, violence, and military conquest. Its exegetical consequences are, first, the neglect of an essential element of these visions and, second, the extreme difficulty in relating biblical eschatological images to the contemporary problem of the technical possibilities of human extinction through a nuclear Armageddon.

The key biblical passage for the apocalyptic hope for a new heaven and a new earth is found in Isaiah 65:17-25. "For behold, I create new heavens and a new earth. Former things shall no more be remembered" (v. 17). This new condition of historic existence presupposes peace, the absolute absence of aggression and violence of war, as an indispensable requisite of an abundant, free, and just life. Therefore, it says: "I will take delight in Jerusalem and rejoice in my people; weeping and cries for help shall never again be heard in her" (v. 19). The suffering and cares typical of wars will disappear. In the place of the agony produced by the violence of war, the joy of peace will prevail. "For I create Jerusalem to be a delight and her people a joy" (v. 18). The text ends with a utopian image (with cosmic nuances) of the universal reconciliation of adversaries. "The wolf and the lamb shall feed together and the lion shall eat straw like

---

26. Silva Gotay, *El pensamiento cristiano revolucionario,* p. 307.

cattle. They shall not hurt or destroy in all my holy mountain, says the Lord" (v. 25).

Peace as the fundamental content of biblical utopia is expressed emphatically and dramatically in the promise to abolish the arms race and war.

> He will be judge between many peoples
> and arbiter among mighty nations afar.
> They shall beat their swords into mattocks
> and their spears into pruning-knives;
> nation shall not lift sword against nation
> nor ever again be trained for war,
> and each man shall dwell under his own vine,
> under his own fig-tree, undisturbed. (Mic. 4:3-4)

The instruments of war, of the destruction of life, are transformed into instruments of labor, cultivation, and the building up of life. The apparently impossible is achieved eschatologically: the abolition of war and violence—universal peace.

In the midst of the suffering produced by the national desolation, there flowers utopian hope for perpetual peace that was part of the messianic ideology of the Davidic dynasty, shown, for example, in Psalm 72 (a prayer hymn, probably sung in the ceremony of the coronation of a new monarch).

> O God, endow the king with thy own justice,
> and give thy justice to a king's son,
> that he may judge thy people rightly
> and deal out justice to the poor and suffering.
> May hills and mountains afford thy people peace. . . .
> In his days justice shall flourish, and peace
> until the moon is no more. (Ps. 72:1-3, 7)

Isaiah took up again this messianism of justice and peace with the promise of a final kingdom free of oppression and the violence of war.

> For a boy has been born for us, a son given to us
> to bear the symbol of dominion on his shoulder;
> and he shall be called
> in purpose wonderful, in battle God-like,
> Father for all time, Prince of peace.
> Great shall the dominion be,
> and boundless the peace.

> bestowed on David's throne and on his kingdom,
> to establish it and sustain it
>> with justice and righteousness
>> from now and for evermore. (Isa. 9:6-7)

This perennial peace proclaimed by the prophet, which channeled symbolically the deepest aspirations of the afflicted people, does not lead to the preservation of a wicked social order. Peace is a consequence of justice. Social righteousness is its indispensable condition.

> until a spirit from on high is lavished upon us.
>> Then the wilderness will become grassland
>> and grassland will be cheap as scrub;
>> then justice shall make its home in the wilderness,
>> and righteousness dwell in the grassland;
>> when justice shall yield peace
> and its fruit be quietness and confidence for ever.
>> Then my people shall live in a tranquil country.
>> (Isa. 32:15-18)

The intimate relationship typical of biblical utopian-prophetic visions between justice, abundance ("may the desert be converted into a fertile field"), and peace is repeated in this passage. As is proper for religious faith, utopia is established by the irruption of divine power into history (the "spirit from on high"), but its effects are temporal and earthly. The kingdom of God is the regime of perpetual human felicity.

The justice referred to in these biblical texts is not retribution; rather, it is soteriological and restorative. It is seen in the redemption of the poor and oppressed. Only the overcoming of injustice against the humble establishes the authentic bases for peace. Let us look again at the prayer hymn of enthronement:

> O God, endow the king with thy own justice,
>> and give thy righteousness to a king's son,
> that he may judge thy people rightly
>> and deal out justice to the poor and suffering. . . .

> In his days righteousness shall flourish,
> prosperity abound until the moon is no more. . . .

> For he shall rescue the needy from their rich oppressors,
>> the distressed who have no protector.

> May he have pity on the needy and the poor,
> > deliver the poor from death;
> may he redeem them from oppression and violence
> and may their blood be precious in his eyes.
> > > > (Ps. 72:1-2, 7, 12-14)

Isaiah gives utopic expression to this dialectic between justice, abundance, and peace for the Davidic Messiah.

> Then a shoot shall grow from the stock of Jesse,
> and a branch shall spring from his roots.
> The spirit of the Lord shall rest upon him, . . .
> > he shall judge the poor with justice
> > and defend the humble in the land with equity;
> > his mouth shall be a rod to strike down the ruthless,
> > and with a word he shall slay the wicked.
> Round his waist he shall wear the belt of justice,
> > and good faith shall be the girdle round his body.
> > Then the wolf shall live with the sheep,
> > and the leopard lie down with the kid;
> the calf and the young lion shall grow up together,
> and a little child shall lead them;
> > the cow and the bear shall be friends,
> > and their young shall lie down together.
> The lion shall eat straw like cattle. (Isa. 11:1-2, 4-7)

Peace, founded on justice, and the consequence of divine eschatological action, allows for the full and serene satisfaction of vital necessities. It results in tranquility, which comes from freedom from the anguish of war and from the joyful participation in the fruits of nature. Only in peace can human labor be free from slavery and create goods for the benefit of its existence. The utopian-prophetic visions are consistent at this point.

> For behold, I create
> new heavens and a new earth. . . .
> Rejoice and be filled with delight,
> you boundless realms which I create;
> for I create Jerusalem to be a delight
> > and her people a joy; . . .
> > weeping and cries for help
> > shall never again be heard in her. . . .
> > > Men shall build houses and live to inhabit them,
> > plant vineyards and eat their fruit;

> they shall not build for others to inhabit
> nor plant for others to eat.
> My people shall live the long life of a tree,
> and my chosen shall enjoy the fruit of their labour.
> They shall not toil in vain or raise children for misfortune.
> (Isa. 65:17-19, 21-23)

Human labors, according to this utopian vision, will be free of the curse that weighs upon them. They will be dedicated to the building up of life and to truly human and humanizing tasks. The basis of this serene and free creativity is justice. It guarantees this peace.

This utopian vision of perpetual peace arises repeatedly in the midst of a people who have too often experienced violence, aggression, and war. Its history has been that of building and planting "in vain," of seeing its houses destroyed, its crops sacked, its men assassinated or enslaved, its women violated or converted into servants. The aspiration for peace is not an abstract illusion, the product of idle fantasy. It comes from the very entrails of the sufferings of a weak, oppressed, and violated people. It is the experience of the exile, of the military destruction of the nation that occasions the most lyrical biblical passages about the unity between justice and peace. "Justice and peace shall kiss each other" (Ps. 85:10b). Psalm 85 comes from the exile[27] and reflects the conviction that it was caused by the evil of the people. The restoration of the kingdom of peace demands divine pardon, the celestial word of peace. It is God's *shalom* that restores serene and just life to the people.

> Turn back to us, O God our saviour,
> and cancel thy displeasure.
> Wilt thou be angry with us for ever?
> Must thy wrath last for all generations?
> Wilt thou not give us new life . . . ?
>
> . . . Let me hear the words of the Lord:
> are they not words of peace,

---

27. This is an arguable subject among exegetes, but it seems to me the weight of evidence favors understanding the Psalm as exilic. See Moses Buttenwieser, *The Psalms Chronologically Treated with a New Translation*, rev. ed. (New York: KTAV Publishing House, 1969), pp. 271-81.

peace to his people and his loyal servants
and to all who turn and trust in him?

. . . and justice looks down from heaven. (Ps. 85:4-5a, 8, 11b)

The utopia of the *eschaton,* where justice and peace kiss each other, also promises material well-being: "The Lord will add prosperity, and our land shall yield its harvest" (Ps. 85:12).

Ezekiel 34 brings together, perhaps as no other biblical text does, the messianism of justice and peace rooted in the consciousness of Israel, thanks to the sufferings produced by the violence of the captivity. The passage begins with the typical prophetic condemnation of the leaders of the nation.

> You shepherds, these are the words of the Lord God: How I hate the shepherds of Israel who care only for themselves! Should not the shepherd care for the sheep? You consume the milk, wear the wool, and slaughter the fat beasts, but you do not feed the sheep. You have not encouraged the weary, tended the sick, bandaged the hurt, recovered the straggler, or searched for the lost; and even the strong you have driven with ruthless severity. They are scattered, they have no shepherd, they have become the prey of wild beasts. My sheep go straying over the mountains and on every high hill, my flock is dispersed over the whole country. (Ezek. 34:2-6)

The theme is familiar: the captivity of the people and their dispersion are due to the injustice and oppression of the national governors. The theodicy is evident. God is just and God's power is absolute. The destruction of the kingdom is rooted in the evil of its authorities. This becomes a threat and a promise: a threat for the governors and a promise for the people.

> These are the words of the Lord God: I am against the shepherds and will demand my sheep from them. I will dismiss those shepherds: they shall care only for themselves no longer; I will rescue my sheep from their jaws, and they shall feed on them no more. (V. 10)

God proposes to bring down the royal house of Israel because it has not fulfilled its mission to be vigilant for justice and to protect the weak and defenseless. On the contrary, its avarice and corruption have led it to benefit itself socially and economically through its political authority. For this, God, the eternal epitome of justice, will destroy the nation.

The people, on the other hand, will be rescued and redeemed. The text goes on to develop the vision of the future of salvation, of the "covenant of peace" in which the messianic eschatology, justice, abundance, and peace are brought together.

> For these are the words of the Lord God: Now I myself will ask after my sheep and go in search of them. . . . I will bring them out from every land . . . and lead them home to their own soil. . . . I will feed them on good grazing-ground. . . . They will rest. . . . I myself will tend my flock. . . . Then I will set over them one shepherd. . . . He shall care for them and become their shepherd. . . . I will make a covenant with them to ensure prosperity . . . and men shall live in peace of mind on the open pastures and sleep in the woods. . . . They shall know that I am the Lord when I break the bars of their yokes and rescue them from those who have enslaved them. They shall never be ravaged by the nations again nor shall wild beasts devour them; they shall live in peace of mind, with no one to alarm them. (Vv. 11-29)

Let us return to the initial hermeneutic observation: If it is true that the event of the Exodus shows God as the Liberator, exclusive emphasis on it can lead to excessive confidence, to blind triumphalism, to an absolute identification of divinity and the nation. Israel does not always escape this defect. It is rather the tragic and traumatic experience of national desolation of the captivity that gives to biblical faith some of its principal characteristics. These include the following:

1. Its exceptional ethical depth. The exile leads to an inclusion in the canon of prophetic passages highly critical of the nation, such as the following:

> This word came from the Lord to Jeremiah: "Stand at the gate of the Lord's house and there make your proclamation: Listen to the words of the Lord, all you men of Judah who come in through these gates to worship him. These are the words of the Lord of Hosts the God of Israel: Mend your ways and your doings, that I may let you live in this place. You keep saying, 'This place is the temple of the Lord . . . !' This catchword of yours is a lie; put no trust in it. Mend your ways and your doings, deal fairly with one another, do not oppress the alien, the orphan, and the widow, shed no inno-

cent blood in this place, do not run after other gods to your own ruin. Then will I let you live in this place, in the land which I gave long ago to your forefathers for all time." (Jer. 7:1-7)

2. The sensitivity to peace as a fundamental human aspiration, an essential dimension of every authentic eschatological vision of the kingdom of God. "May hills and mountains afford thy people peace and prosperity in righteousness" (Ps. 72:3).

This messianic aspiration of justice, peace, and abundance is taken up by the New Testament and given expression in various ways. First, in the special blessing Jesus gives to peace makers: "Blessed are the peace makers for they shall be called the sons of God" (Matt. 5:9).

For Paul, therefore, it is a revolutionary idea that the universal reconciliation brought about by Jesus Christ eradicates every earthly division and hostility:

> For he is himself our peace. Gentiles and Jews, he has made the two one, and in his own body of flesh and blood has broken down the enmity which stood like a dividing wall between them; . . . so as to create out of the two a single new humanity in himself, thereby making peace. This was his purpose, to reconcile the two in a single body to God through the cross, on which he killed the enmity. So he came and proclaimed the good news: peace. (Eph. 2:14-17a)

Here Paul refers to the church, the body of Christ, in which the former earthly distinctions are eliminated. The church is "the bond of peace" in Christ (Eph. 4:3). Consequently, it is the space where the eschatological reconciliation of all things is anticipated (Eph. 1:10). This is expressed in the practice of ecclesial solidarity, which binds together in a new way the themes of justice and peace.

> True justice is the harvest reaped by peacemakers from seeds sown in a spirit of peace. What causes conflicts and quarrels among you? Do they not spring from the aggressiveness of your bodily desires? You want something which you cannot have, and so you are bent on murder; you are envious, and cannot attain your ambition, and so you quarrel and fight. You do not get what you want. (Jas. 3:18-4:2)

73

Finally, the Old Testament aspiration for peace is recaptured in the apocalyptic vision of a new heaven and a new earth, which leads to a renewal of the suffering people and the elimination of the suffering caused by violence.

> He will wipe every tear from their eyes; there shall be an end to death, and to mourning and crying and pain; for the old order has passed away! . . . "Behold! I am making all things new!" (Rev. 21:4-5)

Peace is seen in the Bible as an ardent human desire, as utopia, and as divine promise. Its importance grows out of the popular character of the Bible. The people are the great victim, in every time and place, of the violence of war. Therefore from their midst come the dramatic visions of perpetual peace.

These exegetical determinations are important for a reflection that leads to an adequate *theology of peace* for our day, the era of the nuclear threat.[28] They help the Christian communities to overcome the spirit of arms and militarism that, under the control of the frightening nuclear arsenal, threaten to unleash a universal Armageddon.

The *theology of liberation* developed by the popular Christian communities and the clamor against oppression should, for the recovery of the context of the biblical dialectic, culminate in a *theology of peace* capable of discovering in the eschatological and apocalyptic utopias of the Judeo-Christian Scriptures a more profound meaning of final human harmony, of joyful participation in the goods of creation.

In this context, we should not forget that the most important document of the Second Conference of the Catholic Bishops of Latin America (in Medellín, Colombia, in 1968 and which some consider the starting point for the theology of liberation) was the document called "Peace," in which it is affirmed that

> Peace is above all a work of justice. It presupposes and requires the establishment of a just order in which men can be fulfilled as men, where their dignity is respected, their legiti-

---

28. With respect to the theme of war and peace in the history of Christian theology, the classic work of Roland Bainton, *Christian Attitudes toward War and Peace,* is still unsurpassed.

mate aspirations satisfied, their access to truth recognized, their personal freedom guaranteed. . . . The integral development of man, the path to more human conditions, becomes the symbol of peace.[29]

29. Second General Conference of Latin American Bishops, *The Church in the Present-Day Transformation of Latin America in the Light of the Council*, vol. 2: *Conclusions*. (Washington: U.S. Catholic Conference, 1975), p. 59. See Jorge Pixley, "La Paz: Aporte biblico a un tema de actualidad," *Revista Biblica* 35 (1973): 297-313.

Hagar and Sarah

MILTON SCHWANTES   *(Lutheran, Brazil)*

"Say That You Are My Sister"

In this discussion we will focus on Genesis 12–25. It is useful to begin with an observation of a general nature. I will enlarge the perspective, then we can turn to a more specific consideration.

"Proclaim liberty to the oppressed" (Luke 4:18). This text is programmatic. It sums up Jesus' project and synthesizes what the evangelist, Luke, wants to witness about Jesus of Nazareth: he proclaimed liberation and liberty to the captives. Passages such as this one serve the purpose of bringing together, in a few words, the meaning of all Scripture. Another central focus is found in the Exodus of the Hebrews oppressed by Pharaoh. They are the axis around which the history of salvation moves.

I want to read Genesis 12–25 in connection with this axis. We shall not be speaking explicitly of Luke 4, but rather illuminating the story of Hagar and Sarah with the "project" of Jesus. "Proclaim liberty to the captives" will serve, then, as our hermeneutic key. The oppression and liberation of the Hebrews will be the entry point and final destination of the reading of Genesis 12–25.

Hagar and Sarah

Two texts consider Hagar and Sarah: chapter 16 and part of chapter 21, where the important verses are 7-21. These texts are highly favorable to Hagar and are not at all sympathetic to Sarah and Abraham. Abraham appears in both, but he is clearly a secondary figure. The role he plays is quite different from that portrayed in the chapters where he is linked with Lot.

I begin with a general introduction of the two texts, and later I will look explicitly at one of them.

Initial Observations

These two texts, of which Hagar and Sarah are the theme, are certainly not eyewitness reports. They went through a long process of oral transmission and multiple rereading. Even so, they clearly come from a semi-nomadic environment. The typical conditions of life for families who survived in the semi-arid region of the Palestinian plateau are mirrored here. In general, we can say that these two chapters about Hagar and Sarah are closer to the semi-nomad period than are the texts that deal with Abraham and Lot.

This semi-nomadic world is characterized by radical confrontation with the cities of the plains. Cities are antilife. We learn in the stories that counterpose Abraham and Lot that the basic conflict is between the city (on the plains) and the nomads (in the mountains).

Beyond this central conflict, there are other tensions within the nomadic world itself. We see the differences between Abraham and Lot, both shepherds. Another tension was that between man and woman. There is also the conflict between free persons and slaves. This is the focus of these two chapters.

Semi-nomadic people are free persons, not a slave-holding society. Since production does not depend on them, there are very few slaves. The few slaves who may exist have household duties and are integrated into the family. This is the context of the narratives of Hagar and Sarah.

Hagar is Sarah's slave, not Abraham's. Consequently, the decisions about her are taken by Sarah; Abraham carries them out. There is no great tension, however, between Sarah and Abraham. With regard to Hagar, they both have the same interests.

Hagar is an Egyptian. This makes her especially interesting in these two chapters. In the Bible, Egypt is the house of slavery, because there the Israelites-Hebrews were themselves enslaved. Here, in the case of Hagar, the place of servitude is the house of Abraham and Sarah. The roles are reversed!

Our two texts apparently had independent origins that represent more or less parallel traditions, which were later correlated. We must attribute them to two distinct groups. In the ancient version of chapter 16, Hagar did not return to the house of her mistress. Verse 9, in which the word comes to Hagar, "Go back to your mistress," was added, in part, to give viability to the narrative of chapter 21, in which Hagar and her son are once again found in Sarah's house.

Who might have preserved these two texts? It would have been hard for men to have done so. Abraham plays a secondary, almost ridiculous, role. Mistresses such as Sarah would not have repeated stories such as these. If they had done so, they probably would have given them other interpretations. As they are, they are truly sympathetic to the slave. Therefore, I believe these two chapters constitute the memories of a slave people, such as Hagar. The pain, suffering, labor, and sweat of slaves is expressed in them. These texts are not just letters and words; they are exploited bodies who create their memory of resistance and succeed in transforming them into Scripture. These memories about Hagar are not just syllables, they are also sweat, struggle, unsubmissive pride. As a matter of fact, Scripture is full of this phenomenon.

In fact, taken as a whole, Scripture is the memory of the poor. This is true not only because it speaks about the poor but because they themselves speak in it. Here, in profound depth, is the inspiration of Holy Scripture! The suffering, resistance, and utopia of impoverished men and women are visible in it.

In these texts, we can also see the hands of editors and scribes. They are not just the memories of enslaved women. They also contain the notations of persons who can read and write, skills slave women would not have possessed. These editors did not, however, falsify the memory of the slaves. They preserved them so well that we are able to identify the addenda and alterations. We have already discovered that Genesis 16:9 is such an addition, almost necessary as a bridge to chapter 21. Other texts which must have been added are 16:15-16 and 21:11-13. Such interpolations tend to give importance to Abraham's role, to defend him (21:11-13). In these cases, the contributions and intentions are easily identified. We can disagree with the interpolations of these editors, but at the same time we must be immensely grateful for the fact of their having transmitted to us so faithfully the memory of the slave women. Thank God, they neither substituted nor suppressed these two marvelous stories of the resistance and emancipation of Hagar.

Hagar Frees Herself! (Chap. 16)

Hagar is presented as a slave woman. She is dependent on her mistress, Sarah, whose decisions control her life. Sarah is childless. This situation of the mistress is determinant in the life of the servant. She is used so that her mistress "may be edified through her" (v. 2)—that is, so that she may "found a family through her."

Thus, besides being a slave, Hagar is also used as a reproducer (a test tube for artificial insemination?) for her mistress. Sarah had taken advantage of the labor of Hagar's arms, now she wants to make use of her uterus. Hagar conceives—she has to conceive. She is a slave, nothing more. A slave is there to satisfy the needs of her masters.

Sarah and Abraham are her masters. While she originally belonged to Sarah alone, she now belongs to Abraham also. They have made a deal about her. Verse 3 puts this in juridical terms: Hagar was "legally" given, by the woman, to Abraham. Certain legal norms of the period are respected; Sarah and Abraham agree, and there is no quarrel between them. Against Hagar their interests come together.

Pregnancy, however, creates a new fact. It shows how much the masters depend on the slave woman. Hagar discovers her importance. She grows in self-respect. She understands what her dignity is. She raises her head, faces the world. She becomes somebody. She becomes the subject of the child she is carrying, not an object of her masters.[1] Thus, rebellion appears. Hagar laughs at her mistress. Verse 4 says she "despises" her. Insubordination follows subjection.

Once again Sarah and Abraham agree on their strategy.

---

1. Editor's note: this is a particular use of "subject" and "object" very important in Latin America. It refers to the oppressed as the active subject producing their revolution, rather than continuing to be the passive object used by the powerful to maintain the status quo.

Hagar had been given into the hand of Abraham, but is returned to Sarah's jurisdiction. The articles of the law, obviously made to benefit the masters, are fulfilled.

Sarah punishes her slave. Some traditions use the word *humiliate*, which in a certain sense is a civilized, elegant term. The truth is, the Hebraic text speaks of "oppressing," "beating," "flogging." Hagar was punished because she would not submit to the orders and whims of her masters. We would say she was taken to the public *pelourinho* (flogging post), except that this well-known Brazilian institution had not yet been created.

From the whipping post, Hagar becomes a fugitive. She heads for Egypt, her native land. She makes her own exodus. She emancipates herself. She takes her life into her own hands. On the road of liberation, Yahweh finds her. God finds her near a well, fatigued, recouping her strength to continue her journey. This Yahweh approves of her decision (some later editors added verse 9, which ordered the return of the slave woman). The divine support was in the promise of the son, Ishmael, and in the description of the future of her child. He would be a rebel! Unsubmissive! A people would be born of Hagar, from this symbol of insubordination.

Finally, Hagar becomes a theologian. She interprets her meeting with Yahweh. She gives a name to the place of the revelation. She describes its meaning. Unfortunately, the original text is somewhat problematic for an understanding of the name of the place. It seems to mean Yahweh is the God who cares for the oppressed people, for the slave woman Hagar.

Hagar continues on her way to liberation, seeking it in her native land, Egypt. Later editors reversed the direction of her movement, making her return to her jailers. This made it possible to tell the story in chapter 21. In this chapter there is full affirmation that the divine purpose is liberation and not slavery. Therefore, the editors who added verses 9 and 15-16 did not discredit the emancipatory dimension of this first story of Hagar. They only transferred it to chapter 21. Let us look at it, then. But first, I must emphasize certain aspects that have not yet been pointed out.

Chapter 16 is a very interesting text theologically. Verses 7-14 have to do with Yahweh. They are not a mere narrative, interested in a description of the actions of the characters. They are concerned about this, as we see in the details narrated in verses 1-6, but their principal focus is theological.

The Yahweh presented especially in verses 8, 10-14 is clearly a liberator. What is seen all through Scripture is seen here: Yahweh is the liberator of the Hebrews. God is the one who redeems the poor from slavery. The Divine is the defender of the oppressed. In this regard chapter 16, once again, reaffirms what is the heart, the central axis, the charismatic nucleus of the history of salvation.

There is, however, a significant difference. Hagar—the oppressed and used slave—is Egyptian. This makes a great difference. After all, in general, the Bible only speaks to us of God's liberating action in relation to the poor of the People of God themselves. Here Yahweh is the liberator of the foreign woman. Her liberation is international!

Yahweh Hears the Disinherited (Chap. 21)

In chapter 21, only verses 8-21 speak of Hagar. When I make general reference to chapter 21, I am thinking specifically of these verses.

This second story of Hagar is also extremely theological, as seen in the number of verses that speak of Yahweh (vv. 11-13, 17-20). Facts are not the center of attention in the stories of Hagar; the theological mystique is central. We shall return to this. First let us look at some other peculiarities of this text.

Hagar is on one side, Sarah and Abraham on the other. There is a repetition of what we had already learned in chapter 16. A confrontation is apparently brought about by a quarrel between the two boys, Ishmael and Isaac. Ishmael, son of the slave woman, made fun of Isaac, son of the wife. I say that the dissension was only apparently created by the children. After all, little spats between children are part of everyday life. If they become a motive to increase the repression against a slave woman, it is because of a deeper fact. They are only used as a pretext.

If chapter 16 portrayed a Sarah without a commitment to justice, chapter 21 goes a step further. Sarah is unjust. She uses an everyday affair as an excuse to free herself of a competitive heir. Even verse 10 expresses this real motive as the basis of the rejection of the slave woman and her son: "The son of the slave woman shall not be an heir with Isaac, my son." The inheritance is at stake. This provoked the expulsion of Hagar. Strictly speaking, the exclusion of Hagar and her son amount to the death penalty. In the world of that time, there was no way to survive alone. In semi-nomadic life, the solitary or wandering person is a condemned one, as can be seen in the story of Cain in Genesis 4. When Abraham sent mother and son into the desert, he doomed them to death. As a matter of fact, Sarah and Abraham are not presented to us here as paradigms of justice. The editors of the stories perceive this, so they added verses 11 and 13, which defend Abraham (the same is not true of Sarah). God allows him to expel the slave woman and her child because he promises to defend them.

Thus, Hagar and her child become wanderers. They are the millions of the disinherited of Latin America, and all the Third World, who are without shelter, land, water, and bread. Hagar and her child live with us daily.

Hagar's desperation is described in minute detail. After her abandonment comes the life of wandering without goal or direction. Then there is the lack of water. Her desperation is complete with weeping and a death wish. The cause for such suffering, laid out in verses 14 and 16, is the inheritance. In order that the son of the slave woman should not inherit from his father, it became "necessary" to eliminate him. The pretext was a little quarrel of children at a picnic. That is the way logic and the cycle of deprivation function, yesterday and today!

Nevertheless, Yahweh hears! When Hagar seemed to be at the end of her rope, when the child was in agony and the slave woman fainting from weakness, God intervened. It is impressive that this awakening of Hagar to continue in the struggle for survival is not primarily tied to the well of water that appeared near to her. It is related to the grand utopia of being the mother of a people who will not submit to slavery and will not bow its head under the lashes of the oppressors: "Arise, take the child, take him by the hand, because I will make of him a great people" (v. 18) This utopia lifts her, takes her to the well. The well is not the cause but the consequence of Yahweh's grace! Hagar is reborn within this new people which "grew and dwelt in the desert" (v. 20), rebellious, unsubmissive, emancipated, free—like their mother!

Yes, God hears the disinherited. This means: God transforms them into a people!

Long Live Hagar!

The two stories of Hagar are marvelously surprising. Their content is fascinating. They celebrate the defense of women, slaves, foreigners, the single mother, and the abandoned child.

They are very theological texts. They possess a mystical radicality. They differ from other passages in two aspects: usually the Bible commemorates the presence of Yahweh with the Chosen People and with poor *men*. Here, a foreign *woman* is enslaved, the mediator and symbol of divine justice. The liberating presence of Yahweh in the midst of weakness is not circumscribed by certain given characteristics. The liberating presence of God is a priori. It is as absolute as God's love and divine justice.

And Hagar is the example. Here neither Abraham nor Sarah is the paradigm. They defend the same interests. They are the masters who live in the big house. They are opposed to Hagar and her son, who live in the slave quarters. Yet Hagar receives God's blessing. Long live Hagar!

Women and Christology

NELLY RITCHIE   *(Methodist, Argentina)*

"Who do you say that I am?" (Mark 8:29) . . . The answer Christians give to this everlastingly historical question is always a historical one, since believers are themselves historical.[1]

Because we accept the historicity of the question as well as of the answer, we consider it necessary to begin with a brief exposition of our own situation as Latin American women. Our particular situation controls the question. Our historic protagonism controls the answers.

The acceptance of this historicity—of the questions and the answers—should alert us to the transitory nature of certain affirmations. We do not question their veracity, because they do not depend on absolutes, but rather on the reality in which they are made.

This means that what is permanent—life, justice, grace, salvation, freedom, pardon—in the midst of historical conflict is changed into a new relevance.

To say "Jesus is the Christ" from this standpoint gains new dimensions. It is not a matter of a doctrine to be applied, but rather of a truth to be discovered. A name translated into words and actions will gain its historical veracity, its liberating force. Therefore, to affirm "The Christ is Jesus" will bring us to new historical commitments with the God revealed in Jesus of Nazareth, and with God's project, revealed in him as the kingdom Jesus inaugurated.

To speak of Christology is to try to delineate that which is relative to:

1. Jon Sobrino, *Jesus in Latin America* (Maryknoll, N.Y.: Orbis, 1987), p. 3.

Messiah ———→ Jesus Christ: God revealed and manifested in the heart of the historical conflict;

Saviour ———→ who incarnates the liberating project of God for all humanity;

Lord ———→ who calls the people to be protagonists of their own liberation, where the answer demanded by the Lord of history—the option presented by the call of Jesus—means to assume the role of active subject in the kingdom of God now present.

This attempt to give answers is made within our reality as Latin American women, a situation that, as mentioned earlier, controls the questions and the answers, and must be analyzed. Only in this way will we begin a fruitful dialogue with the Word of God. A rereading from our specific context will nourish our search with fruitful answers and provoke new questions.

Beginning from Our Reality

As Women

Confronted daily with that which is "expected" of us and that which we really want to be, we search for new models of being the active subject in our lives. We rebel against structures that limit, oppress, and annul our full development. We are women in search of new ways of cooperation, solidarity, and life, who discover the necessity to organize, to unite our strength with others, and to resist together those who are against true freedom and the full dignity of being human. We are discovering the necessity to overcome schemes of individualism and to confront oppressive structures.

As Latin Americans

This is not just a geographical location and a past history we have in common. More than that, it is a reality that wounds and alienates. It is the reality of a continent subjugated, dominated, exploited, bled, fought over—and yet hopeful. It is the reality of people impoverished by enemies, external and internal: a contradictory reality.

Because of this, as Latin American women we speak not of our liberation "by ourselves," but of the liberation of our people, a reality that includes and transcends our personal history. It is a liberation of men and women, within the Latin American liberation, with its regional particularities but also within a continental project.

In this sense we are also able to speak of Latin America as our mother earth, as our sister, who unites and encourages us in the search for an integrated future in which we will see made real this dream of the elimination of barriers others have set up among us.

As Christians

Christian is not a "religious" term. It is a cosmo-vision. It indicates the motive and basis for our struggle, of our strength. Jesus Christ as the incarnated Word of God is a revealing word. Because of this, we fight against all "use" of that word to cover up the reality. We propose a dialogical word that reveals and transforms that reality.[2]

We are already a land of hope, a people of equals. We want to see the realization of this project in our time, in our geography, and we want to be its protagonists.

Because of this, from our reality as women of this Latin American homeland and as members of the Christian body, we throw ourselves into this adventure to offer our humble contribution with the assurance that together we will enrich and accompany each other in supporting the continental project of liberation.

What follows is a dialogue, from our reality, with the reality of the Word of God. It is a search for those lines of action that are enriched by such a transforming dialogue. From the re-

2. Much has been said and written about the role of various Christologies in the process of conquest and subjugation of the Latin American continent, and how the "internalization" of certain christological images made the domination easier. See the chapter "Christology, *Conquista,* Colonization" by Sául Trinidad, in *Faces of Jesus,* ed. José Míguez Bonino (Maryknoll, N.Y.: Orbis, 1985).

ality → to the Word of God; from the light of the Word → to the transforming action and again → to a biblical rereading.

The choice of Luke for this biblical reference is not a casual one. His evident concern for the poor of his time, the sick, the marginalized, the women and children brings him to emphasize certain christological lines that, it seems to me, enrich our reflection in Latin America.

Our intention is not to begin nor end in christological affirmations of a doctrinal character, absolute and closed. Nor does it cause us to want to "apply" known christological titles to our reality. Rather, our intention is to provoke new questions, to open ourselves to the amazing manifestations of the God who in Jesus is always revealed as Liberator, and to discover the God of life in the concrete acts of the Christ of yesterday and always.

> The historical Jesus is being recovered in Latin America lest in Christ's name the coexistence of the misery of reality and the Christian faith be acceptable or even justifiable. Or positively: the purpose of the recovery of the historical Jesus in Latin America is that salvation history be historical salvation.[3]

Jesus: The Christ of Life

"Woman, do not cry ..."

A mother crying over the death of her son: this is not a strange scene in this suffering land of Latin America where hunger, scarcity, lack of possibility, aggression, and repression daily kill the young.

A mother crying over the absence of her son: an image of Argentina, where mothers of the disappeared have come to be symbols of resistance against the terrorism of the state that plunged our nation into the darkest era of its history.

3. Sobrino, *Jesus in Latin America*, p. 59. See José Porfirio Miranda, *Being and the Messiah: The Message of Saint John*, trans. John Eagleson (Maryknoll, N.Y.: Orbis, 1977), p. ix; and Ignacio Ellacuria, *Freedom Made Flesh: The Mission of Christ and His Church*, trans. John Drury (Maryknoll, N.Y.: Orbis, 1976), pp. 23-25, 3-19.

The Mothers of the Plaza de Mayo are symbols of the consistent and valiant women who decided to confront the powers of death. They risk their own lives to defend the life of those to whom they had given life. It is a struggle extended to "other children."

> When we see a mother looking for help we offer it without questions. Defend life above everything. . . . We do not search only for our children. . . . We search for all those disappeared and have taken the larger commitment to defend life, justice, freedom. We are not only looking to the past, but projecting toward the future. . . . When they take away a child, they also take away fear. I have discovered that the most beautiful form of death is for a cause.[4]

In the presence of this organized outcry, many, pretending a Christian posture, tried not to hear, to be quiet, or, even worse, to justify the disappearances and death.

> As Jesus approached the gate of the town he met a funeral. The dead man was the only son of his widowed mother; and many of the townspeople were there with her. When the Lord saw her his heart went out to her, and he said, "Weep, no more." With that he stepped forward and laid his hand on the bier; and the bearers halted. Then he spoke: "Young man, rise up!" The dead man sat up and began to talk; and Jesus gave him back to his mother. (Luke 7:12-16)

Let us look briefly at this scene: a woman who has lost her only companion and support; a God who stops before human pain and is moved. Every time the gospel speaks of this feeling of "compassion," it speaks of a total identification with a situation of the other, of creative, active solidarity. Compassion in Jesus is a sentiment that produces change by searching for the cause of the pain and then transforming the totality of the circumstances which provoke the hurt.

This feeling with the other brings Jesus to relieve hunger, eradicate illness, take away burdens that limit life. Here his compassion not only translates into "don't cry" but also in restoring the lost, so that crying is really transformed into joy.

4. Hebe Bonafini (president of the Mothers of the Plaza de Mayo), reported in "La Voz Semanal," Sunday Supplement, June 16, 1985.

Woman ⟶ don't cry ⟷ Young man ⟶ rise up.

The resurrection, the restitution of life as a miracle, is a "sign" that anticipates the totally new that is begun with him. Jesus the Christ is making known to the "beneficiaries" of his action, and to all those present, the purpose of God to restore life and defeat death. He is calling all who proclaim the Lordship of Jesus Christ to "get up." He is speaking of a God who judges all those who take power over the lives of others, of his solidarity with those who cry and search. His purpose is restitution.

To be witnesses to the resurrection is to give the lie to the triumph of death, struggling against all that limits the fullness of life; to be witnesses of the new life in the midst of hopelessness and the bitter taste of defeat, proclaiming and building ways of hope.

When we read of the life of the early church (in the book of Acts), we discover that the faith was shared with joy because this faith was more than a "message" of the triumph of life over death. It was living family love in advance. Sharing bread and fish opens eyes to the faith. It was new life—experience of the resurrection—a "kerygmatic" life, and the community a "sign."

Jesus: The Christ of Grace

"Woman . . . your faith has saved you, go in peace."

Nothing so separates the human being from God as a piety that is sure of itself. Nothing brings us so close to God as the recognition of the gratitude of pardon, the offer of a new opportunity. "The ultimate language of faith is love. Those who would verify their own truth concerning Christ will in the last resort have to question themselves about their love for Christ."[5]

We look now at Luke 7:36-50:

One of the Pharisees invited him to dinner; he went to the Pharisee's house and took his place at table. A woman who was living an immoral life in the town had learned that Jesus was dining in the Pharisee's house and had brought oil of

5. Sobrino, *Jesus in Latin America,* p. 54.

myrrh in a small flask. She took her place behind him, by his feet, weeping. His feet were wetted with her tears and she wiped them with her hair, kissing them and anointing them with the myrrh.

When his host the Pharisee saw this he said to himself, "If this fellow were a real prophet, he would know who this woman is that touches him, and what sort of woman she is, a sinner."

Then turning to the woman, he said to Simon, "You see this woman? I came to your house: you provided no water for my feet; but this woman has made my feet wet with her tears and wiped them with her hair. You gave me no kiss; but she has been kissing my feet ever since I came in. You did not anoint my head with oil; but she has anointed my feet with myrrh. And so, I tell you, her great love proves that her many sins have been forgiven; where little has been forgiven, little love is shown." Then he said to her, "Your sins are forgiven. . . . Your faith has saved you; go in peace."

Jesus constantly rejects the pretensions of "merit," especially on the part of those who make faith a mere fulfilling of the law, excluding the most important law of all, love. For this reason he often uses the image of the slave, the little one. He calls himself a "servant" (cf. John 13).

Jesus not only proclaims the good news of salvation, that in his person the kingdom has come close, and that the year of the grace of God is the present time, but by his acts of love and pardon he reveals the Christ of grace. He incorporates all of his acts—healing, sharing bread with the marginalized, stopping with the "beggars" on the side of the road—in stories that speak of the new age of grace with its:

- scandalizing of those sure of their piety,
- happiness of the dispossessed and satisfaction of the hungry.

The image is of a woman judged by her society, condemned and marginalized. For Jesus—the Christ—she is a person not afraid to make known her feelings of unconditional love, who offers what she has, who "spills" her life. She is a person who has already entered—perhaps without knowing it—the ambience of grace. "Grace is not something mysterious in the sense of being impalpable. Grace is the personal, living presence of God in life itself, dwelling there to make it more fully life."[6] Only those able to love without strings are able to reach this dimension. "This was Christ's revelation. To be saved is to reach the fullness of love; it is to enter into the circle of charity which unites the three Persons of the Trinity: it is to love as God loves."[7] The word of Jesus explicit in the woman's act of love and gratitude incorporates her in this new community, where pardon is the way of new life, where "the forgiven debt" motivates one to follow the path of the kingdom, in which:

- the weak are restored
- the poor receive Good News
- the blind see, the deaf hear, and the lame walk
- the year of grace appears in the present (Luke 4).

This new time of grace[8] is pregnant with joy and hope. Pardon is restored, gratitude is given, love is the language of solidarity.

Jesus: The Liberator Christ

"Woman . . . I set you free!"

Traveling the roads of Latin America we meet the woman and her "burden":

- the *campesina* woman, stooped over the land from which she may be able to extract food for her children.
- the woman who from early morning carries buckets of water, washes the clothes . . . carries the children.

6. Leonardo Boff, *The Maternal Face of God*, trans. Robert R. Barr and John W. Diercksmeier (San Francisco: Harper & Row, 1987), pp. 131-32.

7. Gustavo Gutiérrez, *A Theology of Liberation* (Maryknoll, N.Y.: Orbis, 1973), p. 198.

8. The word *grace* belongs to Pauline language: "God is grace, the inexhaustible source of the favor he evidenced towards man and which reached its culmination in Jesus Christ. In this way was the rule of grace inaugurated (succeeding that of the Law), one in which man gratuitously received—in contrast with any notion of a retribution that was owed. Such was the Good News" (X. Léon-Dufour, *Dictionary of the New Testament*, trans. Terrence Prendergast [San Francisco: Harper & Row, 1980], p. 215).

91

- the woman bent double in the factory, close to others but not knowing them, selling her work strength.
- the woman in the home, trying to respond to all the requirements in a work not recognized by others.

We meet the peasant woman, the worker, the housewife, and many others who don't know the meaning of rest, who live in a small world that consumes them day by day in hopelessness. These are women who are not able to project the future, but have only enough strength to confront the present. They are women exhausted by double exploitation: that which goes with being an oppressed people and that of being a woman. Many of these search in "religion" for an escape from their situation, but find there only justification for more "burdens."

> One Sabbath he was teaching in a synagogue, and there was a woman there possessed by a spirit that had crippled her for eighteen years. She was bent double and quite unable to stand up straight. When Jesus saw her he called her and said, "You are rid of your trouble." Then he laid his hands on her, and at once she straightened up and began to praise God. But the president of the synagogue, indignant with Jesus for healing on the Sabbath, intervened and said to the congregation, "There are six working-days: come and be cured on one of them, and not on the Sabbath." The Lord gave him his answer: "What hypocrites you are!" he said. "Is there a single one of you who does not loose his ox or his donkey from the manger and take it out to water on the Sabbath? And here is this woman, a daughter of Abraham, who has been kept prisoner by Satan for eighteen long years: was it wrong for her to be freed from her bonds on the Sabbath?" At these words all his opponents were covered with confusion, while the mass of the people were delighted at all the wonderful things he was doing. (Luke 13:10-17)

According to the Gospel of Luke, this is the last occasion on which Jesus entered the synagogue before going to the cross. He confronted institutionalized religion. It must not escape our notice that this was the environment in which he met the burdened woman. There are many occasions on which, speaking to religious leaders, he calls them hypocrites, because they expect of others what they themselves do not do. This is the final episode in the atmosphere of institutionalized religion, on the day of rest (which cannot be that for those under submission). The act of Jesus is thus converted into:

• an act of judgment on the establishment
• an act of liberation for the subjected woman.

And in this judgment of the establishment he shows the falsity of those who pretend to serve and honor God without reference to humanity.

> It is not enough to say that love of God is inseparable from the love of one's neighbor. It must be added that love of God is unavoidably expressed *through* love of one's neighbor. Moreover, God is loved in the neighbor.[9]

This is revealed in the healings that free persons from their burdens. In the light of this, a day of rest has meaning! Liberation makes possible a new pathway:

• where it is possible to envision the future
• where the horizon of action and creation is widened
• where it is possible to share joy with the people
• where it is possible to rest, because it is possible to act.

Jesus, the Christ, reveals the permanence and the relevance of the liberating project of God. In him this liberation is made "act," and the act has its own value and at the same time is part of a larger reality. "Liberation is not only an all-encompassing social process. It is also a form of making concrete and anticipating the absolute liberation to be accomplished in Jesus Christ."[10]

Jesus: The Christ of the Kingdom

The militant woman: . . . "has chosen the best part . . ."

The following is a transcription of some of the testimonies of Argentine women who have committed themselves to the struggle for dignity and human rights.[11]

9. Gutiérrez, *Theology of Liberation*, p. 200.
10. Boff, *Maternal Face of God*, p. 192.
11. These testimonies are by several women who participated in

Referring very specially to the working woman in her condition as a worker, mother, and housewife, we should say that the more than 500,000,000 women who work to create the riches of the world, represent a third of the salaried productive force of the world. . . .

In every union there is a large percentage of women, and during all the years of the dictatorship they have been in the streets carrying the flags for freedom, against repression, for the reincorporation of those on strike, the return of the disappeared, and freedom for those detained. . . .

Having demonstrated that we are capable of leadership, discrimination is obvious. There are only seven women in Parliament, no Ministers of Government . . . to say nothing of the unions. (Delia Boschi de Blanco, telephone worker)

Susana Pérez Gallart, vice president of the executive committee of the Permanent Assembly for Human Rights, says:

Women have to assume their obligation as citizens, en masse, each one in her own role, because being political is not only being active in a political party. Doing politics is working in a neighborhood center, a cooperative, a professional, cultural, or union association, or whatever, because they must contribute, because the base of democracy is to be dynamic. Democracy cannot be static. . . .

Women are going to win their place and really make a difference in national liberation, in the day when they actively and massively take up this fight for liberation.

Referring to the theme, "Women Victims of Repression," Graciela Fernández Meijide (of the same executive committee) pointed out:

Women were not repressed as women, but for having dared to come out of their role and take up the fight along with the men for the rights which belonged to them in their new role. Therefore, it is certain that torture of women is aimed at the parts which are specifically female, with a sadism and vengence, for having dared to do so. Also it was directed toward her offspring as in the case of a mother who is detained with

---

a round table discussion on the theme "Women and Human Rights," Buenos Aires, May 16, 1984. They are recorded in a Spanish publication of the Permanent Assembly for Human Rights.

her children, as a pregnant mother who is hit until she loses her child.

The hard experience of the woman who "dares"; the one who confronts and rebels against a reality that subdues, marginalizes, denigrates her; the one who does not accept "the given" as an absolute, or as something unchangeable, but who dares to act, participate, to claim a dignified life which makes hope possible—is not this choice, this militant option, what the gospel calls "the better part," which, according to the very words of Jesus, "nobody can take away"?

Felicidad Abadia Crespo and her sister Dominga were workers in the Lozadur factory.

One of them was a representative of the factory. There was a conflict between the owner and the workers over the question of wages. The factory was audited by the military. The union was also. There was a meeting at which the auditor threatened those present and all the Board of the factory. They were ordered to tell their companions to abandon their demands or be fired, their homes broken into or taken. We never heard any more about them.

Felicidad and Dominga disappeared because they were defending their rights as workers. (Graciela Meijide)

Jesus came to a village where a woman named Martha made him welcome in her home.

She had a sister, Mary, who seated herself at the Lord's feet and stayed there listening to his words.

Now Martha was distracted by her many tasks, and said, "Lord, do you not care that my sister has left me to get on with the work by myself? Tell her to come and lend a hand."

But the Lord answered, "Martha, Martha, you are fretting and fussing about so many things; but one thing is necessary.

The part that Mary has chosen is best; and it shall not be taken away from her." (Luke 10:38-42)

The choice of the way of commitment with the struggle of the people, the search for life for everyone, is from our faith perspective the way to proclaim the Lordship of Jesus over all other power.

Putting ourselves "at his feet"—as in the text—in the attitude of disciple and beginning truly to follow him, getting ourselves involved in the cause of his kingdom, brings us to discover him, to meet God in the middle of pain, struggle, work, and the hope of those who are victims of injustice, who have consecrated themselves to the cause of justice. It is to choose the better part which cannot be taken away from us. It cannot be taken away because it is the cause of God's own self.

The "activism" that is known and accepted—the attitude of Martha—is put in opposition to the defiant attitude of Mary, "who is the one who dares" by her actions to announce, to proclaim, the totally new Jesus. Her decision and her actions are christological proclamations.

> After the announcement of the Kingdom, that is to say, of the new social and political reality which is constructed on the land of Israel, after the certainty that history is brought about by the invisible Lord, who created the people and called his prophets, there is the construction of this society of new persons which will live according to revolutionary criteria, which will give women the same dignity and responsibility as to men. . . .
>
> These are the germs of a cultural and human revolution which began in that time (and which was promptly blocked) and from time to time breaks out again.[12]

New Questions

If we accept our reality as our point of departure, if the dialogue with the Word of God and especially with the Incarnate Word, Jesus Christ, illuminates our analysis and gives strength to our commitment, then this presupposes a return to our reality with some questions and with eyes open and ears attentive to read the signs of the times and to hear new questions, new demands.

Because of this, rather than end with a "conclusion," I prefer to end by paraphrasing the Apostle Paul, who in his ancient christological hymn reveals "who it is" who gives breath and nourishment to our journey.

> Among us, let us adopt the style of Jesus: He, being God, did not take on the benefits of his condition, on the contrary, he accepted service to humanity and was one of us. His giving of love was total. He did not avoid pain nor fear the cross.

12. Giorgio Girardet, *A los Cautivos Libertad*.

He followed his cause to the end. Because of this, he did not die but received from the Father a new life. By his resurrection from the dead a totally different world is being born. Because of this we, his sisters, do not fold our banners, nor are we fearful of the struggle. From liberation comes true life. (Paraphrase of Phil. 2:5-11)

The Priesthood of All Believers

JERJES RUIZ   (*Baptist, Nicaragua*)

The Baptist Convention of Nicaragua has assumed the principle of the priesthood of all believers as part of the theological legacy it should disseminate. It is worthwhile to cite the entire Article 2 of its by-laws, approved by the General Assembly of the convention in Managua in January 1982, and also approved by the Council of State of the Republic of Nicaragua:

Article 2—The purpose of this Convention is the proclamation and realization of the Gospel of Christ. Toward this end it will use the following means:

a. The spoken and written word and other legitimate and honest audio-visual means permitted by the law.

b. The service of pastors, preachers, missionaries, evangelists, Bible distributors, professional and other lay workers.

c. The churches, mission fields, high schools, other schools, institutes, hospitals, seminaries, homes, cooperatives and other institutions of social welfare.

d. The organization of assemblies of children, youth and adults. Permanent campaign for the unification of the Baptist community.

e. Dissemination of the following Baptist principles which are held by our denomination:

1. The Bible is the only and supreme rule and practice.

2. The Church is formed of believers who have been converted and baptized by immersion.

3. The priesthood of all believers.

4. The autonomy of the local church.

5. Freedom of conscience.

6. The separation of church and state.

The fact that we have assumed such a principle has led us to think of it as "Baptist," but we are aware that it does not identify us; it is not a principle unique and exclusive for Baptists. All Protestant denominations assume it. In the polemic with Catholicism, the focal point of the discussion has been the distinction between the general priesthood and the special priesthood, not the denial of the priesthood of all believers as such.

I wish to make a hermeneutic of the third principle, taking into account the practice of faith of the Baptist Convention of Nicaragua in the context of the Sandinista Popular Revolution, and the biblical-theological base on which this principle has traditionally been defended.

We, the Nicaraguan Baptists . . .

We were born in Nicaragua, the navel of America, a country that offers (1) the embrace of nature: the living together of the flora and fauna of North and South America, and (2) the embrace of history: the mutual cultural influences of the Toltecs and the Nehuas from the north and the Chibchas and pre-Incas from the south.[1]

Nicaragua's geography both charms and frightens us. It charms with its beauty—and we are not the only ones who say so.[2] At the same time this geography frightens us: earthquakes, droughts, floods, volcanic eruptions, the greed of demagogues, pirates, and traitors, as well as foreign powers who occupy our national territory.[3]

1. Pablo A. Cuadra, *El Nicaragüense*, 8th ed. (San José: EDUCA, 1978), pp. 20, 21.

2. Another is George E. Squier, historian and North American diplomat, who was in Nicaragua in 1848. His delight in Nindiri from New York is an example, and is cited by J. Guerrero and L. S. de Guerrero in *Masaya* (Managua, 1965), pp. 128-29.

3. Harold N. Denny, *New York Times* correspondent, wrote in 1928: "It has been Nicaragua's fate, often an evil fate like that of a woman too lovely, to be desired by many nations. Geological forces laid out the area which was to be Nicaragua at a point destined to be of enormous strategic importance to the great powers of the world." Quoted by Miguel D'Escoto in his introduction to Richard Millet's *Guardians of the Dynasty* (Maryknoll, N.Y.: Orbis, 1977), p. 4.

Nicaragua's history is filled with vigor and glory—as Dario has said—but at a very high social cost. Few people have received from life so high a share of pain as ours: savage, brutal colonization; a postindependence era saturated with civil wars; neocolonialism culminating in the military dictatorship of Somoza, of whom it has been said he left a balance of several hundred thousand truncated lives, not only by the slow death of oppression but by the cruel death of repression; the third earthquake of Managua (1972), which left ten thousand dead and some one hundred thousand wounded; the war of liberation that cost fifty thousand lives; and the current war, which has already cost more than twelve thousand deaths. Pablo Antonio Cuadra gives expression to our historic drama in his poem "Prayer to the River":

> Flower of night pinned
> to the florid forehead:
> We beg you
>
> on behalf of the land of which we sing.
>
> Shoot of the rose of silence!
> And water lily:
>
> Aroma of the sadness of Nicaragua!

Our ecclesiastical history within the national history is brief, but has a very significant quality. We are a result of the twentieth-century missionary movement. We bear two marks typical of Latin American Protestantism: (1) We have arisen from a denominational division, and (2) we have been organized by missionary agreements.

The first missionary was sent in 1916. The First Baptist Church of Managua was founded in 1917 by a group of brothers and sisters who had come out of the Central American Mission because of a disagreement with the missionary of that mission.[4]

About April of 1937, the National Convention of the Baptist Churches of Nicaragua was formed, with seven churches.[5] Since then its history has been that of one denomination among

---

4. Arturo Parajón, *Veinticinco años de labor bautista en Nicaragua 1917–1942* (Managua: CBN, 1942), pp. 17-19.

5. Augustín Ruiz, *Hacia las bodas de oro 1942–1967* (Managua: CBN, 1984), p. 24.

many in Central America. The sacrificial labor of the pioneer Baptist pastors in the work of evangelism is worthy of our admiration. It has been especially difficult due to the strong opposition of Catholicism. In San Gregorio, Department of New Segovia, a cross inside the sanctuary marks where one of the elders was hacked to death by aroused Catholics.

From 1916 to 1978 our history went along with the history of our country. We had no understanding of the meaning of this history. We were not critical of the economic and sociopolitical system within which we were living, nor were we self-critical of the mission of our church in its context.

Nevertheless, we believe that by means of pastoral work, evangelization, and service, God has worked in genuine conversions, giving health and education within the limitations of a work carried out in a dependent capitalist society. We have a sincere debt of Christian love for the missionaries and pastors who laid the foundations of Baptist work in Nicaragua. Children of their times, they gave and continue to give their best for the sake of the kingdom of God in our country, through the formation of churches and missionary fields, and the founding of such institutions as a high school, a university, a seminary, a school of nursing, other schools, a hospital, and clinics.

Since 1978, the Baptist Convention of Nicaragua has begun to achieve a new Christian conscience. This is because of new leadership, the majority of which was trained in the Baptist Seminary, with a very contextualized theological education embodied in the national reality, and with an ecumenical mentality that would lead the convention to involve itself in CLAI (the Latin American Council of Churches) and the World Council of Churches.

Today, Nicaraguan Baptists—with the interecclesiastical difficulties and ideological tensions that the Sandinista revolution implies—as children of God and children of the country that gave us birth, identify ourselves with the historic project of the liberation of our people. This option is an act of Christian priesthood and is also a profoundly human and patriotic act.

What Is Our Priesthood?

The Traditional Interpretation

We cannot deny the fact that Catholicism came to Latin America along with Spanish colonialism and Protestantism came along with North American neocolonialism. Although those of the Catholic community were unaware of its ideological implications, evangelical Protestant preaching represented an interpretation and a style of life nearer to the Holy Scriptures. The Protestants of the first generation in Nicaragua understood it that way, even though we cannot deny that there was anti-Catholic fanaticism.

The presence of evangelical Protestantism in Nicaragua, a country eminently Catholic, was characterized by polemic. For the Protestant, to be Catholic meant to be "impious," "lost," "an unbeliever," "unconverted," and so forth. The Catholic considered the Protestant as a "heretic," "lutheran," "apostate." In the midst of all this, we ask, How are we to interpret the priesthood of all believers?

Baptists, like all Protestants, made this principle an axis in the polemic against Catholicism, basically attacking at two points: first, the exaltation of the priest, and second, oral confession.

In the first case, the attack was on the three-pronged concept of a special priesthood, which excessively exalted the priest, putting him very high above the laity. In this case the Protestant principle pointed to the democratization of the priesthood. Every believer is a priest at the altar of Christ, offering daily the sacrifice of life to God in the name of Jesus Christ, who is the only Eternal Priest.

In the second case, the criticism pointed to the fact that when the Catholic priest heard the confession of sin and gave absolution, he took the place of Christ. So the priesthood of all believers meant the ability to enter into relationship with God without the need for a *padre*. It meant the freedom God gives to the believer to confess sin directly to God without the necessity for a Catholic priest.

Even today, this interpretation is found in the mentality of Baptists and Protestants in general, even though it is no longer held with the emotion of yesterday. The polemic has been practically overcome, or even better, no longer occurs.

We need to call attention to the fact that there is a reality which is lost to view in the polemic: Catholic theology does not deny the priesthood of all believers, but rather distinguishes between a general (common) priesthood of all baptized Christians, and a special (ministerial) priesthood of the ordained.

Especially beginning with Vatican II, there has been a reevaluation of the common priesthood. The distinction continues in practice and the solution still does not satisfy all Catholic theologians, as can be seen in the writings of Hans Küng and Leonardo Boff.

On the other hand, Protestant interpretation of the priesthood of all believers falls into an individualism that strips it of any communitarian value. We must recognize that there is not a well-developed doctrine in the Baptist theology of Conner and Mullins, who translated into Spanish the texts used by the first generation of pastors. The more recent work of James Giles[6] also lacks a development of this principle. The interesting thing is that, despite the poor development of the doctrine, Nicaraguan Baptists have always affirmed the priesthood of all believers. It is usually one of the lessons in classes for candidates for baptism.

Purified of all anti-Catholicism and individualism, the principle is of vital importance for the life and mission of the church, and therefore should be reaffirmed and made fruitful from a new hermeneutic horizon.

Returning to the Bible

In the beginning his disciples did not understand these things; but when Jesus was glorified, then they remembered that these things had been written about him and about what he had done.

(John 12:16)

It appears to us that this biblical text was written to remind Christians that God's word always has a hidden meaning whose mystery will be revealed only by salvific historic events. We

---

6. *Esto Creemos los Bautistas (This Is What Baptists Believe)* (El Paso: CBP, 1977).

therefore return to the Bible aware that we must have a militant reading of it that can answer the questions growing out of our daily reality. The question we shall have in mind is: What does the living priesthood mean to us Nicaraguan Baptists in the context of the Sandinista revolution?

Priesthood in the Old Testament

The institution of the priesthood has a long history that goes back to the earliest worship of Yahweh and stretches to the destruction of Herod's temple by the army of Titus. In the ancient history of Israel there was no professional priesthood. The head of the family or tribe functioned as the priest. An organized, official priesthood is found only after the conquest, especially when David conquers Jerusalem and this city becomes, under Solomon, a sanctuary for all Israelites.[7]

There were priestly families: that of Moses in Dan (Judges 18:30), and that of Ely in Silo, in Not, and in Jerusalem. Nothing more is known of Moses, but the priesthood of the family of Ely enters into the genealogy of Aaron, of whom all priests are descendants.

During the reign of David a third priestly family appears: that of Sadok, who supplanted that of Ely (1 Kings 2:27-36) to become the dominant priestly family. After the exile, when true priests are mentioned, the reference is to the Zadokites. Other priests, descendants of Levi, but not of Aaron, are eclipsed and can officiate only in secondary functions of the temple.[8]

The head of the priesthood was the High Priest. The priests were distributed by classes in twenty-four priestly lines; their order and service were determined by lot (Luke 1:8) or heredity.

The text of Exodus 19:6 is important because it speaks of election of the people of Israel as a "priestly kingdom"[9] even

7. Haag, van der Born, and de Ausejo, *Diccionario de la Biblia,* 8th ed. (Barcelone: Herder, 1981), col. 1750.

8. Ibid., cols. 1750-51.

9. The term does not refer to the internal structures of the people of Israel, but to a relation with God. For a scientific analysis of the term see G. Schrenk, "hieráteuma," *Theological Dictionary of the New Testament,* ed. Gerhard Kittel, vol. 3 (Grand Rapids: Eerdmans, 1976), pp. 249-50.

though not all Israelites were in reality priests with the ministry of worship. This leads us to think that Israel as a people was the priest of all other peoples, the intermediary between God and all humanity. She was to stand before the people on behalf of God and stand before God on behalf of the people. She should stand as a blessing, which would be a fulfillment of the promise to Abraham (Gen. 18:18; 22:18) that in his seed all nations of the earth would be blessed.

Philo expressed the priestly vocation of Israel in these words:

> The Jewish nation is to the inhabited world, as the individual priest is to the city. . . . She offers prayers, feasts, first-fruits for the totality of all humanity and offers worship to the only true God. This worship is offered in her own name and also for all the others who have abandoned the adoration which God deserves.[10]

When Israel mistakenly understood her election as a nationalist privilege, which would be in this case a divine favoritism, she lost her efficacy as a priestly people and failed in her mission.

The importance of all this is the purpose of the priesthood. Why the priesthood? According to von Rad, "the priestly priesthood in its totality was a service of mediator taking the place of others, above all, if they ate the flesh of the sin offering."[11] Even more, the prophetic ministry itself had a priestly as well as an intercessory role. "The prophetic service of mediator takes on theological significance when the received ministry enters the sphere of personal life and places in danger the human existence of the mediator himself."[12]

The priesthood was an all-embracing ministry that had to do with all relationships of the people with their God. It was the only competent mediator of all divine decisions. It had teaching functions (Deut. 33:10), but above all it was the ministry of

10. Quoted by E. Cothenet, "La primera epístola de Pedro," in *El Ministerio, y los ministerios según el Nuevo Testamento* (Madrid: Cristianda, 1975), p. 136.
11. *Teología del Antiguo Testamento*, vol. 2 (Salamanca: Sígueme, 1976), p. 520.
12. Ibid., p. 521.

the cult and of the expiatory rites. That is, the priest was the decisive key to mediate between God and human beings (a need that is basically soteriological), which in the Old Testament has a ritual and cultic solution. The reason for this solution is the insufficiency of moral perfection. People must come to God and find salvation in God.[13]

Priesthood in the New Testament

In the New Testament, priesthood *(hiereus)* is never mentioned except in relation to Christ (Heb. 7:15) and to the Jewish and Christian priests. No importance was given to the Jewish priesthood, although Jesus had recognized its authority (Matt. 8:4). The reason for this is twofold: the Christian conviction that Jesus was greater than the temple (Matt. 12:6; John 2:19), and the gradual rupture with Jewish worship.[14]

In the New Testament, Jesus is called the High Priest (especially in Hebrews, the primary literary witness to the subject) who had reconciled humanity with God by his death on the cross (Rom. 5:10). He was the mediator par excellence before God on behalf of humanity and before humanity on behalf of God. Jesus' sanctification (John 17) did not consist in his purifying his life by distancing himself from the sinful world, but in the greater dedication to the salvation of the human being.

With regard to believers as priests, it must be said that the letters of Paul do not speak of this, but they come close (Rom. 12:1; Phil. 2:17). The letter to the Hebrews is silent regarding it, but is chiefly concerned with the priestly office of Jesus Christ. This is clearly expressed in 1 Peter 2:4-10 (following Exod. 19:6) and Revelation 1:6.[15]

We can say in general that in the New Testament the early church appears to have been a church without priests. The ex-

---

13. J. Sobrino, "Hacia una determinación de la realidad sacerdotal. El servicio al acercamiento salvífico de Dios a los hombres," *Revista Latinoamericana de Teología* 1/1 (March-April 1984): 47-81; J. M. Castillo, "Sacerdocio," in *Conceptos Fundamentales de Pastoral* (Madrid: Cristiandad, 1983), p. 888.

14. Haag, van de Born, and de Ausejo, *Diccionario*, col. 1751.

15. Otto Kuss, *Carta a los Hebreos. Comentario de Ratisbona al Nuevo Testamento*, vol. 3 (Barcelona: Herder, 1977), pp. 478-79.

istence of a priesthood as specialized personnel within the church is completely unknown.[16] Moreover, priestly vocabulary is avoided in referring to the ministers of the new covenant.[17]

All of this indicates there was a new and radical way of understanding the relationship with God and the practice of faith.[18] This indicates that a radical change in the priesthood comes about when salvation is understood in the same radical way.[19]

At this point I want to look briefly at 1 Peter 2:4-10, since it is the passage most preached about in our Baptist churches in Nicaragua when we speak of the priesthood of believers. For reasons of space we shall leave aside the discussion about the authorship and other introductory matters of the letter, except to point out the hortatory character of it in the face of the difficult situation through which the Christian communities of Asia Minor were passing: "persecuted, lied about, offended by the pagans and the Jews."[20]

In this perspective it is of interest to us to analyze exegetically the terms *holy priesthood (hieráteuma hágion)* and *royal priesthood (basíleion hieráteuma)* in the context of the letter.

The passage is found in the first part of the epistle where the writer is emphasizing the greatness of the Christian vocation (1:3–2:10). After giving thanks (1:3-12) to the Father, to Christ, and to the Holy Spirit, the author points to the life of Christians as the true exodus of Israel with all of the implications carried by such a privilege. He makes six recommendations and a recapitulation.[21] The term *holy priesthood* is found in the sixth recommendation:[22] to come to Christ as the living stone (2:4-6).

As the church, the Christian community is built through

16. Castillo, "Sacerdocio," p. 893.
17. See B. Sesboüe, "Ministerio y sacerdocio" in *El Ministerio,* p. 439.
18. Castillo, "Sacerdocio," p. 888.
19. Sobrino, "Hacia una determinación," p. 80 n. 1.
20. José Salguero, *Biblia Comentada,* vol. 3 (Madrid: BAC, 1965), p. 92.
21. Following the outline of B. Schwank, *Primera Carta de San Pedro* (Barcelona: Herder, 1979), p. 11.
22. The first five are: arm yourself with hope, be holy, obedient, loving, feed on the Word of God. Ibid.

the unity of believers on the cornerstone, which is Christ. This analogy has an Old Testament base (Ps. 118:22; Isa. 28:16). The metaphor of the stone rejected by the builders is found in the synoptic teachings (Mark 12:10), in the Acts of the Apostles (4:11), and in the letters of Paul (Rom. 9:33; Eph. 2:20). Christ is the living stone: an image in which two things are contrasted, the hardness of a rock (something inanimate) and the life that gives life. That is, Christ is the stone who is life and gives life to others. The building God raises with living stones (Christ and believers) is a spiritual edifice because of the divine Spirit that fills the house (1 Cor. 3:16).

While Christians should be living stones, they should also be a holy priesthood. The idea is that of a priestly community consecrated to the service of God, to offer spiritual sacrifices to God through a life acceptable to God.[23] Such sacrifices can be prayer (Rom. 12:1), praise (Heb. 13:15), holiness of life (James 1:21), ministry (Rom. 15:16); the ultimate consequence can be martyrdom. This spiritualization of sacrifice is based in the Old Testament (Ps. 51:19; Hos. 6:6; Mic. 6:6-8) but is developed in early Christianity.[24]

Royal priesthood appears in the recapitulation (2:7-10), where it seems almost to be a hymn. It is worth mentioning that the author applies the titles of honor of Old Testament Israel to the believers in Christ: "chosen line," "royal priesthood," "holy nation." Of the three, we are interested in the second. The expression had been applied to Israel (Exod. 19:6) in the sense that the Israelites were the kingdom of God, in a theocratic sense since Yahweh was their king. They were destined to offer to God a worship other people could not offer. Metaphorically, they were a people whose members were all priests because they belonged to a holy nation dedicated to the worship of the true God.[25] By analogy, the author applies the title of royal priesthood to Christians.

The term *royal (basíleion)* means belonging to the king; the priesthood serves the king. *Priesthood (hieráteuma)* carries a corporate sense according to the Septuagint: it is a community

---

23. Kuss, *Carta a los Hebreos*, pp. 473ff.
24. Salguero, *Biblia Comentada*, p. 114.
25. Ibid., p. 116.

of believers that as the priestly body has immediate access to God. Thus, they could truly fulfil the ideal established for Israel, since the one who comes definitively to God through his paschal sacrifice and has presented the believers as a holy offering (1:19; 3:18) is united to Christ.[26]

From the hermeneutic point of view, what the sacred writer has done is what we would call today a rereading of the priesthood from his own hermeneutic horizon. He has tried to answer for his time and context the question, What does the priesthood mean? In response, he has reached two conclusions: all believers are priests, and the sacrifices we offer today are spiritual. There is, then, a spiritualization of the priesthood even when there is neither temple nor institutional priesthood.

On the other hand, remembering that in the New Testament priesthood does not appear as a special ministry, we are led to think it is at the base of all other ministries (apostle, prophet, etc.). In other words, the priesthood is an existential attitude implicit in all ministries. Everything in the life of Christians has a priestly character by the work and grace of Jesus Christ, High Priest of our faith.

Let us compare this New Testament concept of the priesthood with that of the Old Testament. While in the Old Testament the problem of human salvation is given a *ritual* solution, in the New Testament the solution is *existential*, which is possible thanks to the priesthood of Christ. The radical change is due to a new way of understanding salvation experienced in the encounter with and following of Jesus of Nazareth.[27]

A Hermeneutic Proposal Based on Our Reality

We are going to leave aside for the moment the Reformers' interpretation of the universal priesthood of believers, as well as the interpretations of contemporary Catholic and Protestant theologians,[28] even though we recognize they are implied in our work.

---

26. Schrenk, "hieráteuma," p. 250; Cothenet, "La primera epístola de Pedro," p. 136.

27. Castillo, "Sacerdocio," p. 893.

28. We must honestly recognize that a broader work on this theme should take seriously the contributions of Luther and other Reformers, although pointing out their interpretative and practical limitations.

There are two fundamental assumptions in our proposal. First, as already pointed out, priesthood is essentially related to human salvation, the saving approach of God to humanity. The understanding of the priesthood grows out of our understanding of salvation. Second, our understanding of salvation today is holistic and radical. Salvation is the liberation of the oppressed in the concrete history of their times.[29]

From our hermeneutic horizon, the universal priesthood of believers should be expressed today as Christian solidarity. The spiritual sacrifices in our continent in general, and in our country in particular, are the acts of solidarity with the processes of liberation, with the struggle for peace with justice and dignity. Solidarity today is "living sacrifice holy and acceptable to God." It is authentic worship, the liturgy of sacrificial service, with no other lamb than the flesh of our bodies, no other blood than that of our heroes and martyrs, no other incense than our sweat, no other water for absolution than the tears of our mothers and war orphans. All of this takes on meaning in the redemption once for all realized in the death of the Lamb of God who takes away the sin of the world. It is in the humanity of the crucified one that the flesh and blood of those who die to take away the structural sin of the world are redeemed, so they become the new "living stones" of the new spiritual edifice: the humanity of the future. The life of Jesus of Nazareth offered in his death-resurrection gives meaning, worth, and effectiveness to lives that, united to him, seek life in abundance for our impoverished and bleeding peoples.

It is in Christ that those who were no-people are today *the* people of God; it is in Christ that the disinherited of the world, the condemned, the anonymous ones have come to be the historic subjects, "the architects of their liberation."

Today our solidarity has different ways of expression; we can summarize it this way:

1. Christian solidarity is pastoral priesthood and priestly

29. This truth comes to us from the Latin American theology of liberation with its extensive bibliography on the theme of salvation. I am indebted to two works: I. Ellacuría, "Historicidad de la Salvación Cristiana," in *Revista Latinoamericana de Teología* 1/1 (March-April 1984): 5-45; and J. Sobrino and J. Hernández Pico, *Theology of Christian Solidarity* (Maryknoll, N.Y.: Orbis, 1985).

pastoral: it is the celebration of the daily struggle, it is intercessory prayer for the pain of a people before the throne of the Father through Jesus Christ.

2. Solidarity is prophetic priesthood and priestly prophecy: it demands from the governors of this world a conversion to justice, peace, and love for the least of the kingdom; whether it was Somoza or is Reagan, the sin is concrete: oppression, repression, aggression. The demand is the same: "let my people go."

3. Solidarity is missionary priesthood and priestly mission: the truth of our people and our insertion in their cause seeks for solidarity with those who first brought us the Good News; with those who taught us that the only way to come to God is through Jesus Christ.

Today we turn back to say to them with all Christian love, the way of coming to Jesus Christ today is through our impoverished and wounded people. This is an important work because the Lord is forming cells of the kingdom in the United States that can have a positive influence to avoid a direct invasion of Nicaragua.

4. Solidarity is a teaching priesthood and a priestly teaching: of those in the faith who do not understand or do not agree with us or the process of Nicaraguan liberation, whether from traditional religious scruples or from the marks of imperfection and sin of the human process.

In the past decade the Baptists of Nicaragua have taken six steps we consider profoundly priestly:

1. *The prophetic fast of the community of students of the Baptist Theological Seminary.*[30] Beginning April 10, 1978, in reaction to the assassination of Pedro J. Chamorro, the students were fasting and praying in the Ebenezer Baptist Church, Managua. In a communique to the Nicaraguan people through press and television they said:

> Motivated and guided by the spirit of God, we have decided to break and humiliate our bodies in living sacrifice, holy and acceptable to God, in fasting, reflection, and intercession for our people, to the end that God may show divine justice and

---

30. The Baptist Seminary is an institution with ecumenical work. In the past the majority of the students have been Baptists, but there have also been some from other Protestant denominations.

liberating power on behalf of those who suffer.

We confess with shame before God that the critical situation of the country is the result of structural, institutional, and individual sin of each and every one of us.

This priestly prophetic fast had a marked effect on the conscience of these future pastors.

2. *Baptist support of the Declaration of the 500 Pastors, October 5, 1979, from the Second Interdenominational Retreat of Evangelical Pastors.* Two paragraphs will suffice:

> We, 500 pastors and evangelical leaders of Nicaragua . . . in the name of our Lord Jesus Christ give thanks for the victory of the Nicaraguan people and their instrument of liberation, the Sandinista Front of National Liberation. We share the joy of all our people and we celebrate the freedom which strengthens our hope and consolidates our faith in the God of history. . . .
>
> We call on our churches in this hour of deep significance to live the Christian commitment to the gospel, which is to be salt and light to the world. To offer intercessory prayer for those in our government; to stimulate in our congregations confidence in the government (1 Tim. 2:1-4) and to exercise the ministry of reconciliation in all the life of our Nicaraguan people.

3. *Manifesto of the Baptist Seminary in response to the Sandinista document on religion (1980).* Confronted by confusion created by reactionaries who accused the Sandinista government of using religion for the moment in order later to suppress it, the National Directory of the FSLN issued an official communique on religion that broke with all the dogmatic molds of revolutions. The compatibility of Christianity with the revolution was made clear, the important role of faith as motivation for militant revolutionaries. The revolutionary state was declared to be secular. The deepest respect was shown for the beliefs and traditions of our people. The government declared its openness to the participation of Christians (regardless of their religion confessions) and incorporation in the revolutionary process.[31]

31. Christians in the Sandinista Popular Revolution, *Comunicado Oficial de la Dirección Nacional del FSLN sobre la Religion,* Managua, 7 October 1980.

Faced with such a document, the Catholic hierarchy took a backward step. By contrast, as though it were a fulfillment of the gospel statement that the last would be first, the community of students and professors of the Baptist Seminary issued a public manifesto to the Nicaraguan people and the evangelical churches on October 29, 1980. The following words reflect clearly its profoundly priestly and pastoral sense:

> If the FSLN opens all doors for the participation of Christians in revolutionary militancy, we believe there is no biblical nor doctrinal impediment to such action; quite to the contrary we are called to be agents of change, carriers of the liberating message of Jesus Christ, which commits us to work in everything which dignifies the human being. . . .
>
> The section of the document refering to the secular character of the separation of church and state has deserved our special attention. . . . It is clear power corrupts. The Gospel is upheld only by the Gospel, needing neither the support nor recognition from the state. We believe that Christian objectives lead us to see ourselves as servants of the people and not as those served by the people.

4. *Solidarity with the priests in the government.* We have always felt sympathy and even pride that there are Catholic priests in the government (Miguel D'Escoto, Edgard Parrales, Ernesto and Fernando Cardenal), without denying that we are Baptists. In the face of the attacks by the hierarchy and the harassment by the newspaper *La Prensa*, our sympathy has not been obscured, because we consider the work they are doing on behalf of the people through the revolutionary government as an authentic priesthood. A letter of solidarity from the Community of the Baptist Theological Seminary to Father Edgard Parrales, at that time Minister of Social Welfare, received the following telegram reply: "Thank you for your gesture of solidarity and fraternity" (June 30, 1981).

5. *Pastoral letters of the Nicaraguan Baptist Convention.* From 1982 to 1985 the Baptist Convention has denounced to the secular and religious world the North American war of aggression against the Nicaraguan people. It has made its own the pain of numbers of assassinated and orphaned children, and the destruction of schools and other centers of social service by the counterrevolution. This is a priestly sorrow. It is not only ex-

pressed in offering the sacrifice of service, but in being part of the sacrificial lamb as Jesus was. We know that our priesthood has already been costly. Baptist clinics have been broken into and destroyed by the contras. Churches have been closed by the aggression. Lay leaders and other believers have been killed, threatened, or falsely accused ("Baptist Leninists").

The pastoral letter of May 10, 1985, directed to the whole world on the occasion of the economic blockade decreed by the government of the United States against Nicaragua, deserves our attention:

> On the basis of our Christian faith in the Holy Scriptures we denounce and condemn the blockade put into effect by the government of the United States. We consider it anti-christian, anti-biblical, inhuman, unjust, illegal and arbitrary. . . .
>
> The government of Nicaragua has been the first to recognize the mistakes it has made. We, as part of the royal priesthood of God, intercede for the sins committed by all. As believers we recognize we need the grace and divine pardon given through Jesus Christ our Redeemer. We give thanks to God for the laudable achievements already effected and for the efforts of our people and governors and, along with them, we continue to pray, "Thy Kingdom come."

6. *Our brother and sister missionaries to and from the North Atlantic.* The pastoral letters would not have sufficient force if it were not for our sisters and brothers who go to the United States and Europe to explain to the churches what is happening in Nicaragua, to defend our faith in solidarity with the historic process of liberation, and to call them to unite with the acts of God in Nicaragua.

We feel strengthened and supported when these churches send their delegates in response, to see and hear the reality in our nation and church; and even more when the churches support projects of salvation such as the National Literacy Crusade, health and educational projects., etc. We say sincerely that the support of the Christian, and especially of the Protestant, world to the Nicaraguan process has no parallel in the history of revolutions. Protestantism is writing beautiful pages of history by its constant and decisive support of the liberation of the Nicaraguan people. With honesty we confess that the building of the new society in Nicaragua is a historic-salvation experiment in which Christians of the whole world are collaborating.

Conclusion

With honesty and modesty we believe as Baptists of Nicaragua that as we strengthen and consolidate Christian solidarity already expressed in our process of liberation, we are giving life to the priesthood of all believers. However, along with our daily labor, we pronounce the prayer-poem of Dario, the father of Nicaragua:

> Come, Lord, for your own glory
> come with the shaking of stars and the horror of
> cataclysms
> come to bring love and peace over the abyss.
>
> And your white horse, which the visionary saw,
> may it pass. May the divine trumpet sound.
> My heart will be the coals of your incense.

The Trinity from the Perspective of the Woman

MARIA CLARA BINGEMER   *(Catholic, Brazil)*

The central objective of this chapter is to reveal the feminine aspect of God. A number of valuable works have been written on this theme.[1] There is more to say, however, especially in Latin America, where the problematic of the woman is integrated into the wider global context of the struggle for the liberation of the poor and marginalized.

Any theological word spoken within the context of struggle will not be complete if it is not solidly based on the one who is the central mystery of Christian faith and all theology: God.

The divine mystery that creates, saves, and sanctifies us is not identified in a privileged way with only one of the two sexes that form humanity. It integrates and harmonizes the two without suppressing their enriching differences, and at the same time it transcends them. We believe there is a feminine principle in our creation as God's image, in our salvation made possible by the incarnation, passion, and resurrection of Jesus Christ, and in our new being formed by the Spirit of God, just as there exists (as has been expressed ad nauseam) a masculine principle.

Why is it that the language and images that the Chris-

1. This chapter is an edited version of an article originally published in *Revista Eclesiastica Brasileira* (May 1986). Cf., e.g., L. Boff, *The Maternal Face of God*, trans. Robert R. Barr and John W. Diercksmeier (San Francisco: Harper & Row, 1987); R. Haughton, "Deus é masculino?" *Concilium* 154 (1980): 63-71: C. Halkes, "Por que se protesta contra Deus 'Pai' no Teologia Feminista?" *Concilium* 163 (1981): 122-31; R. R. Ruether, "A natureza feminina de Deus—Um problema na vida religiosa contemporanea," *Concilium* 163 (1981): 72-79; M. Hunt and R. Gibellini, *La sfida del demminismo alla teologia* (Brescie: Editorial Queriniana, 1980).

tian faith found to express the central mystery that energizes it are so markedly masculine: Father; Lord; All Powerful; Strong Warrior; Son? What are the cultural, anthropological, and theological problems found in the origins of this language and typology?

The Origins of the Problem: A Triple Dualism

Theological anthropology, in its affirmation that the human being is the image of God, is basic. Observing the concept we have of image (human being), we are able to perceive, analogically, the characteristics of the model (God). This concept, in the Judeo-Christian world and in the so-called Western and Christian civilization, is markedly *androcentric*.

The creation is interpreted as a hierarchical relationship between the two sexes. Woman is created *after, from,* and *for* the man. The result is the ontological, biological, and sociological dependence of the woman. Even more serious is the concept that only the human being of masculine sex is *theomorphic* (has the image of God). This typology, which has been projected in all later theology, establishes what may be called "a theological sexology."[2]

In later doctrine, especially as developed by St. Augustine, the woman is the image of God in her rational soul, but not in her feminine sexual body, where she is subordinated to the male. The masculine sex, therefore, symbolizes in itself the excellence of the divine image, and beginning with the *body-soul dualism*, is theomorphic in the primary sense. God, the universal God, the God of all peoples and all times, becomes *andromorphic*. This is how we understand the meaning of the masculine images of God almost always presented as king, judge, patriarch, husband, lord, and father. The woman rises to equality with man to the degree to which she is defeminized; that is, to the degree she renounces the functions of her sex, transcending her auxiliary function of procreation.[3]

---

2. Cf. K. E. Borresen, "L'anthropologie théologique d'Augustin et de Thomas d'Aquin," *Recherches de Science Religieuse* 69/3 (1981): 394.
3. Ibid. p. 397.

The *soul-body dualism* that determines this anthropology reaches its apex and releases its consequences even within the very person of God. A disassociation between humanity and femininity in the order of creation and salvation leads to the conclusion that woman is not created in the image of God, as long as she is woman.

The *second dualism*, the origin of the concept of a preponderantly masculine God, is based on a cosmic vision that makes a static separation between *heaven and earth:* that which is from on high, invisible, transcendent, and that which is from below, palpable, imminent. The divine being, which humanity has worshiped in all times and in all cultures, always is mediated by the archetypal symbolism, *paternal and maternal.*

In this way Christianity and Judaism are and have been eminently masculine religions. Judaism and Christianity were established on this cosmic vision that concedes privilege to the heavens over the earth; to the vertical over the horizontal. Between this God and the *Abba* of Jesus there is little relation. "On the contrary, this God of patriarchy arises from the first division of the world into heaven and earth: heavenly father—mother earth."[4]

A *third dualism* characterizes our modern society: the dualism between *efficiency and gratitude,* between *pragmatism and experience,* between *action and contemplation.* Our society is eminently active and gives almost exclusive value to power, productivity, and command: in other words, attributes identified as masculine. Those identified with the feminine (receptivity, shelter, protection of life, intuitive perception, and gratuitous praise) are normally minimized as "lesser" or "useless" because they are not "efficient" or "productive." These attributes, in a world almost exclusively masculine, find their correspondence in the attributes of the divinity. So God is strong, powerful, absolutely transcendent, the Lord, the Dominator, the one who with the power of his arm brought the Hebrews out of Egypt and led them to occupy other lands, the Lord whose service demands carefully elaborated plans, feverish activity, efficiency, and urgency. This emphasis on power and dominion arouses associations of con-

4. Elizabeth and Jürgen Moltmann, *Humanity in God* (New York: Pilgrim Press, 1983), p. 114.

trary character, of debility, subjection, and inferiority in those dominated,[5] and consequently, of all the dimension represented by passivity, receptivity, and gratitude. The almost exclusively patriarchal image of God that strongly marked Judaism and Christianity, especially in certain periods of their histories, presents a strict interaction with the masculine positions of power in society; an interaction that appears also in the emphasis on transcendence at the expense of concrete life on earth and of the authentic living of our love and familial relationships.

Our objective will be to try to show that these dualisms and their consequences do not have their base in the Christian revelation. We intend, then, to make use of language and images that allow us to see in Scripture traces of the feminine in God, in a way that permits us to call on him as strong Father, but also as Mother who supports, consoles, shelters, and protects; as Spirit of creativity, balance, and beauty.

The God of Christianity is not a solitary and dominating patriarch, definitively and perennially installed in his distant heaven. God is the community of love between persons (Father, Son, and Holy Spirit) where the differences and plurality are integrated without being suppressed, where the strength of the masculine is enriched and complemented by the delicacy and tenderness of the feminine, where life is a complete and laborious process of conception and childbirth. The human community finds its image in this divine community. The poor and marginalized, of every kind, feel themselves included as responsible subjects of history. Among them the woman rediscovers herself, companion of the man, in action and in the dignity of being, as he is, on an equal footing, the image of God.

Open Possibilities for a Theology of the Trinity from the Feminine Perspective

What are the indications that the inclusion of the feminine in the intimate mystery of God, along with the masculine, is not a product of our imagination, but has authentic roots in the Christian revelation?

5. Halkes, "Por que se protesta," p. 123.

The Feminine Characteristics
of the God of the Bible

Among the Old Testament terms that refer directly to God, the term *rahamim* is used constantly to describe mercy, attribute par excellence of Yahweh, the God of Israel. In its root (*rehem*—maternal bosom, entrails)[6] the term refers to a markedly feminine part of the feminine body. The uterus is the place where life itself is conceived from the seed, enfolded and nourished so it may later grow and come to light. *Rahamim* is used, then, to indicate the love of God in direct parallel with the love of a mother who experiences compassion for the child from her entrails.

The Old Testament attributes these characteristics to God. Isaiah 49:15 makes the comparison with the mother:

> Can a woman forget the child she suckled, without compassion for the child of her entrails? Because even if these forget, I will not forget you.

Jeremiah 31:20 refers directly to the divine entrails:

> Is Ephraim still my dear son,
> a child in whom I delight?
>   As often as I turn my back on him
> I still remember him;
> and so my entrails yearn for him
>   I am filled with tenderness towards him.
>   This is the very word of the Lord.

Again, Isaiah 42:14 refers to the maternal sorrow that affects the bowels of Yahweh, afflicted by the child conceived in God's maternal love.

> Long have I lain still,
> I kept silence and held myself in check;
> now I will cry like a woman in labour, . . .

This faithful and invincible love, thanks to the mysterious and intimate strength of motherhood, is expressed in the Old Testament in diverse ways: as protection and salvation from dangers and enemies, as forgiveness of the sins of the people,

6. Ernst Jenni and Claus Westermann, "*rhm* pi: sich erbarmen," *Theologisches Handwörterbuch zum Alten Testament*, vol. 2 (1976), pp. 761-68.

and even as faithfulness in fulfilling promises and nourishing human hopes despite infidelity (cf. Hos. 14:5; Isa. 45:8-10; 55:7; Mic. 7:19; Dan. 9:9). The *hesed* of God, whose profound attitude of goodwill cannot be unfaithful to the divine nature, gives permanence to God's love, despite infidelity and sin. The disposition to perennial mercy is evident in God's maternal entrails, *rahamim*, predisposed to the compassion of infinite tenderness (cf. Isa. 14:1).

The faith of the Israelite was directed toward God as toward the fertile womb of a mother, calling for protection with ardent and filial love:

> Where is your zeal and strength,
> the stirring of your bowels?
> Are your entrails closed to me? (Isa. 63:15)

> Has God forgotten to be gracious,
> in anger shut up his entrails? (Ps. 77:10)[7]

To this God experienced and worshiped by the chosen people, would it not then be possible to attribute as basic, alongside the liberating force of a strong warrior and powerful lord, the loving and tender feminine features of a woman in the sacrificial exercise of her motherhood?

Another helpful term is *ruach*. Its basic Old Testament meaning is "wind," "spirit," "breath of life," and is almost always in the feminine. With some exceptions throughout the Old Testament, everything from soft breeze to violent wind (cf. 1 Kings 19:11; Isa. 57:13; and others), from the epiphany to the frighteningly luminous theophany (Ezek. 1:4; Dan. 7:2), even to the breath of God, life itself, is said in this way to be "materialized" (2 Sam. 22:16; Ps. 18:16; Isa. 11:15; etc.). The *ruach* is the presence of God, carrier and cause of life in motion.

Our special attention is called to one of the manifestations of this divine *ruach*, the moment of the creation of the world (Gen. 1:2), when the *ruach* moved and fluttered above the waters of the primeval chaos, as the breath of creative childbirth.[8]

---

7. Cf. also Pss. 25:6; 40:12; 51:3; 69:17; 79:8; 103:4; 106:46; 119:77; 156; 145:9; Lam. 3:22; Dan. 9:9, 18; and others.

8. Cf. G. Philips, "Le Saint Esprit et Marie—Le Vatican II cet prospective du probleme," *Bulletin de la Soc. Fr. d'Etudes Mariales* 1 (1968): 30.

In this line, Paul Evdokimov, the great Russian Orthodox theologian, refers to the woman in this way: "She is under the sign of the Spirit who in the creation narratives, 'covers' the egg of the world."[9] The *ruach*—Spirit of God—appears as the *Great Mother* who, from her loving and fertile entrails, gives birth and makes the universe appear.

The same *ruach*, mother and mistress of life, who brings things out of nothing into being, is transformed by the prophets to speak of the life Yahweh inspires (cf. Ezek. 36–37; 1 Sam. 10:6-10; 2 Kings 3:15ff.). In the later texts it will be identified with God's self (Isa. 63:10-11; Ps. 51:13), giving basis for what will appear later in the New Testament as the Third Person of the Trinity, the Holy Spirit, who comes down like a dove on the Messiah in the River Jordan (cf. Mark 1:9-11 and parallels), and is called by the Syriac texts not only Comfortor, but Comfortress.[10]

Other terms in the Old Testament could throw light on our subject. For instance, Wisdom (the *Hochmah*, the *Sophia*) is described as the daughter of God through whom God mediates the work of creation and who Solomon, paradigm of the king, invokes as "the wife of his soul" (Wisd. of Sol. 7-10). This image of the *Sophia* disappears in rabbinic thought after the coming of the Christian era, possibly because of its use in Gnosticism. It reappears, however, in the form of *Shekinah*, a new image of the mediating presence of God as feminine. The *Shekinah* brings about the reconciliation of Israel with their God. In the mystic speculations of the rabbis about the exile, the *Shekinah* is imagined as going into exile with Israel when Yahweh, the Lord, turned aside his face in anger.

> Each Sabbath celebration is considered as a mystical matrimonial embrace by God with his *Shekinah* anticipating the final reunion of God with his creation in the messianic era. The Exile of Israel, far from their land, is considered an exile within God's own self, separating God's "masculine" aspect from his "feminine" aspect.[11]

9. P. Evdokimov, "La maternité théandrique—figure de la paternité divine" and "Panagion et Panagia," *Bulletin de la Soc. Fr. d'Etudes Mariales* 3 (1970): 65.

10. Philips, "Le Saint Esprit et Marie," p. 30.

11. Cf. Ruether, "A natureza feminina de Deus," p. 74.

In the New Testament, we do not find a semantic nucleus so clearly feminine applied to God as in the Old Testament. Jesus, the *Son* of God, is clearly, and without doubt, a man; the God on whom he calls and whom he worships is *Abba-Father*, clearly masculine; and the Holy Spirit, the third divine person, is called in Greek *Pneuma*, a neutral term that gives no room for partiality on either the masculine or feminine side.

In the Johannine writings, however, there is a notable term that has roots in the Christian tradition as definition of the mystery of God: *Agape*, translated as "love." *"God is love"* (1 John 4:8-16). We believe this term helps to clarify our thought, not so much because it is in the feminine gender in Greek, but because of the deeper reality it expresses. Johannine *agape* is the love of God that comes down from on high and is poured out on the world, evoking family and community, which allows for the return of humanity to the very bosom of the Love which is God.

> In brotherly love the circle of the Father, the Son and the people of the Son constitutes a fellowship which is not of this world. The love of God is the final reality for the life of this fellowship, and abiding in His love is the law of its life. . . . This love is a vital movement, a form of existence, an actualization of God in this world.[12]

The love God produces in the midst of humanity, in its trinitarian form, is an image of the deepest reality. This mysterious reality is a love of communion, inclusive and global, where the poor and the little ones occupy the chief places, where the masculine and the feminine are united in radiant and fertile harmony. This is the semantic nucleus that defines God as *agape*—love—projected in the Christian world in a very excellent way by the eucharistic banquet,[13] which will permit us, we hope, to continue to seek for the feminine traces revealed within the three divine persons.[14]

12. *Agape*, in *Theological Dictionary of the New Testament*, vol. 1, ed. Gerhard Kittel, trans. Geoffrey W. Bromiley (Grand Rapids: Eerdmans, 1964), p. 53.

13. Ibid.

14. We are aware of the danger of falling into unilaterality or seeking tendentially for an interchange of terms that could lead to a new, inverted "theological sexology."

The first image that comes to mind goes back to the *priestly narrative of creation*. There, in the first chapter of Genesis, the human being, man and woman, appears as the radical image of God: "Let us[15] make man in our image and likeness" (Gen. 1:26). The plural God uses there to realize the highest work of creation, where some holy fathers insinuated the "vestige" of the Trinity, is followed by the term that designates the object of creation: humanity ("man") as a collective being. The plural, then, follows naturally: "Let them have dominion over the birds of the heavens and the fish of the sea" (v. 26a). And further along: "Then God created the human being in the Divine image, in the image of God he created, male and female God created" (v. 27).

To be male (man) and to be woman appear in this context then, not of a separation made up of hierarchy and subordinations, but as a *reciprocity*, one being for the other, which reflects *the eternal face-to-face relationships of the divine persons*. Just as the Father is only Father in relation to the Son, and vice versa, in the intimate living together *(perichóresis)* of the Spirit, so also man is only man in relationship to woman, and she in relation to him, by analogy, as in the Trinity.

The other image we find is of God *engaged in activities appropriate to the woman, and more concretely to the mother*. Besides the passages already cited we can also mention the beautiful second chapter of Hosea, where Yahweh teaches Ephraim to walk, takes him in his arms and, as one who raises a child against his cheeks, leans toward him and feeds him (Hos. 11:3-4). In Isaiah, God is presented as a mother who consoles Israel (Isa. 66:13), who is incapable of forgetting her own child (Isa. 49). Also in the Wisdom literature, in correlation with the woman, Wisdom identified with God is hypostatized (Prov. 8:22-26; Ecclus. 24:9; Wisd. of Sol. 3:12; 7:28; Prov. 19:14; 31:10; 26:30).

In the New Testament, Jesus refers to God and God's merciful love for the sinner as *a woman who lost one of her ten coins*, lighted the lamp, closed the door, and searched for it until she found it. Having found it she called her neighbors and friends to celebrate the event (Luke 15:8-10). In another passage, Jesus himself, casting his look of sorrow over Jerusalem, compared himself to a protective mother as *the hen who gathers her chicks*

15. See footnote h in the Jerusalem Bible.

beneath her wings (Luke 13:34). In the final book of the New Testament, the Apocalypse, God appears in a classic and traditional maternal gesture:

> And he shall wipe every tear from their eyes,
> and there shall be neither death nor weeping,
> neither crying nor weakness,
> because the old earth has passed away. (Rev. 21:4)

Why is it not possible here to establish an analogy of a mother with her child, who in the midst of nightly terrors dries the eyes, puts an end to the sobbing, restores harmony to the senses, and assures the child it does not need to fear?

Such images allow us—even in the face of the unutterable mystery of God as Love—to dare to affirm that there is a feminine principle in the divinity that allows us to believe in, praise, and love God, not only as a Strong Father who creates us and frees us with powerful arms and from whom life proceeds, but also as Mother responsible for tenderness, grace, beauty, receptivity, who as Mother receives the seed of life and shelters it in her womb, to give it back converted into a being in the full light of day.

Some Witnesses from the Tradition and History of the Church

We can affirm that the revelation of God shows feminine features not only on the basis of the Holy Scriptures, but also from the history and tradition of the church. We want to point out, much too briefly, some of the historic witnesses who can be of help. These are only illustrative, worthy of more complete study.

The first text is from the apocryphal *Gospel to the Hebrews*. A reference to the Holy Spirit as feminine is placed in the mouth of Jesus, more concretely referring to her as his mother: "In the same moment my mother, the Holy Spirit, took me by the hair of the head and led me up the great Mount Tabor."[16] The author expresses here a characteristic in the concept of God that certainly comes from his or the community's experience of faith.

16. Cf. P. Benoit and M. E. Boismard, *Synopse des quatre évangiles en français*, 1 (1981): 153.

The identification of the Divine Spirit as maternal is found in the oldest Christian tradition.

The second witness is from a respected church father, *Clement of Alexandria*. Writing in Egypt about the year 180, in a beautiful text, Clement characterizes God in terms as much feminine as masculine.

> The Word is everything for the child, father and mother at the same time, teacher and governess. The food is the milk of the Father . . . and the Word alone supplies us, the children, the milk of love and only those who nurse from this breast are truly happy. Therefore, to seek is a synonym of to nurse; the loving breasts of the Father give milk to the children who seek the Word.

The third witness is from a much later time, *Juliana of Norwich*, English mystic of the fourteenth century. Her vision of God integrates the masculine and feminine in the divinity: "And so I saw that God rejoices that he is our Father, and God rejoices that he is our Mother, and God rejoices that he is our true spouse, and that our soul is his beloved wife."[17] The most characteristic note of Juliana's mysticism is this divine maternity. When Christ was willing to do the will of the Father, he became the mother of our souls: "Our Saviour is our true Mother, in whom we are endlessly born and from whom we shall never depart."[18] She adds:

> All the lovely works and all the sweet loving offices of beloved motherhood are appropriated to the second person, for in him we have this godly will, . . . from his own goodness proper to him.[19]

We have seen that the revelation of the feminine in God, through Holy Scripture and throughout history, occurs in trinitarian rhythms and dimensions.

The Feminine and the Divine Persons

We now turn our attention to each of the divine persons to perceive the feminine traces in them.

17. Juliana of Norwich, *Showings* (New York: Paulist, 1978), p. 279.
18. Ibid., p. 292.
19. Ibid., p. 296.

The Son: The Founder of a Community of Men and Women

What we can learn about the *historic Jesus*, through the gospel narratives, shows him as the originator of a charismatic itinerant movement, where men and women are admitted in relationships of familial friendship. Unlike the movement of John the Baptist with its emphasis on asceticism and penitence, unlike the community of Qumran where only men are admitted, the movement Jesus inaugurates is characterized—beyond its central concern for preaching the kingdom—by joyfulness, by participation without prejudice in feasts and banquets to which sinners and the marginalized are admitted, and by the breaking of a series of taboos that characterize the society of his time.

One of the most evident of these broken taboos is the one that had to do with the woman. In the Judaism of Jesus' time, women

> suffered discrimination at the hands of both society and religion. First, they were not circumcised, and hence could not be a part of God's covenant. Next, they were subject to a series of rigid laws of "purification," by reason of their female biological condition. Finally, they had been personified in Eve, with all of the inferiority that that implied.[20]

Every day the Jewish man was to give thanks to God for the triple honor bestowed on him: having been born not a Gentile, nor ignorant of the Law, nor a woman. In this context, Jesus's practice is not only innovative, but shocking. His attitude toward women is so unprecedented it surprises even the disciples (John 4:27).

A common element in the four Gospels is that women form a part of the assembly of the kingdom, convoked by Jesus. They are not merely accidental components, but are integrated actively as participants (Luke 10:38-42), even privileged beneficiaries of his miracles (cf. Luke 8:2; Mark 1:29-31; 5:25-34; 7:24-30; and others).

Jesus' promotion of women has a double theological significance for us today:

20. Boff, *Maternal Face of God*, p. 65.

1. It deals with the special and most essential aspect of the gospel: *the Good News preached to the poor*—the disinherited, the rejected, the pagans, the sinners, and the marginalized of every kind—liberated by Jesus as a priority. And among these are women and children, not given consideration by Jewish society. Jesus gives all of them a privileged place in his kingdom, integrating them fully into the community of the children of God because, with his divine vision, he can see among all these poor people—women included—values that are being ignored.

2. With his liberating practice toward women, Jesus overthrows one of the three dualisms we pointed to earlier: the *body-soul dualism*. Accepting women with the body their culture considered weak and impure, he proclaims an integrated anthropology that gives value to the human being made up of body and spirit. It is important to remember here some episodes in the Gospels where Jesus appears in contact with the feminine body.

- Curing with a touch the woman who suffered a flow of blood (impure for the Jews), exposing himself to the risk of becoming impure himself (Matt. 9:20-22).
- Reviving Jairo's daughter, taking her by the hand (Matt. 9:18-29).
- Allowing a publicly-known sinner woman to touch, kiss, and anoint his feet, so that the Pharisee who was his host came to doubt whether Jesus was a prophet (Luke 7:36-50).

Unfortunately, this dualism was implanted into Christianity because we lost contact with the gospel practiced by Jesus.

Having analyzed Jesus' attitude toward the female, we should now look at *the feminine in Jesus*. The understanding we have from modern psychology that every human being is simultaneously and in different proportions *animus and anima,* masculine and feminine, gives us an opening in this regard.[21] Jesus, a man in whom the masculine mode of being predominated, also integrated the feminine dimension.

Overcoming the androcentrism of his time, "he had himself personally integrated so many male and female behavior

21. Cf. Boff, *Maternal Face of God,* pp. 87-90.

characteristics that one could consider him the first maturely integrated person."[22]

The Gospels portray Jesus as a man who did not show the celebrated masculine "shame" for his own sentiments. Just as he is capable of speaking harshly, reprimanding the Pharisees and the disciples, his lips can also sing with joy and thanksgiving to the Father in confirmation of the revelation given to the little ones and hidden from the wise (Matt. 11:25-27); he does not hold back the overflowing tenderness when he sees the defenseless and fragile children so little thought of by the society of his time (Mark 9:36 and parallels).

We even dare to say that Jesus experienced in his own most intimate inward parts the emotions and sorrows that afflict the *rahamim* of Yahweh in the Old Testament. This can be seen when he weeps at the death of his friend Lazarus (John 11:35), when he pours out his pity over the city that would be responsible for his martyrdom (Luke 19:41), when he mourns for the fate of the cities that would not accept his salvation (Matt. 11:21), and in his cry of a frustrated maternal desire to bring together the dispersed and rebellious "chicks" of Jerusalem (Luke 13:34).

All of this femininity in Jesus, expressed as tenderness, compassion, and infinite mercy, which reaches its highest point in the painful childbirth of the cross,[23] was taken up eternally, definitively, and hypostatically by the Word, the second person of the Trinity. So we can say that in Jesus, his life, his words, his praxis, his person—in the most intimate part of his being—the feminine is made divine and belongs to the deepest nucleus of the mystery of God's love.[24]

The Spirit: Uncreated Maternal Love

Looking further at the Triune God among us, in order to perceive the feminine features of the Revelation, our attention is

22. Moltmann, *Humanity in God,* p. 38.
23. Cf. this with what was said before about the experience of Juliana of Norwich.
24. Some reflection on the mystery of Mary may also be relevant here. However, we purposely do not take up this theme because it would need to be a chapter in itself.

now focused on the Holy Spirit. Faith and the Scriptures say to us that the Spirit took the place of Jesus in the midst of the community of faith, as "another Paraclete," at the side of the baptized as defense and counsel, in the absence of the Son. Jesus himself referred to the Spirit with maternal accents. It is he who does not leave us orphans (John 14:18), who consoles, exhorts, and comforts us as a loving mother (John 14:26). Paul also attributes functions to the Spirit that normally are fulfilled by the mother: she teaches us as children to learn and stammer the name *Abba-Father* (Rom. 8:15) and the name of the Lord Jesus (1 Cor. 12:3), and she teaches us to seek and pray to God as is pleasing to him (Rom. 8:26).[25] Further, the Hebrew word *ruach*,[26] legitimate predecessor of the New Testament *pneuma*, not only is of the feminine gender but is constantly related to the creation, to the sources and protection of life, to the elements that identify motherhood.

One of the earliest Syriac fathers wrote:

> The Spirit is our Mother, because the Paraclete, the Comforter will comfort us as a mother her child (Isa. 66:13) and because the believers are "reborn" out of the Spirit and are thus the children of the mysterious mother, the Spirit (John 3:3-5).[27]

Can theology seriously affirm this motherhood of the Holy Spirit? Some leading theologians today are inclined to do so.[28] We choose to be more prudent and affirm the tradition of the church that the mother of Jesus is Mary, the *Theotokos*, as proclaimed by the Council of Ephesus (A.D. 431). Thus, beginning with the church's belief in the fertilization of Mary by the Holy Spirit, we can say the Spirit is Uncreated Love that possesses Mary and makes her pregnant. It is delicate and difficult to separate the Father and the Holy Spirit respectively as Father and Mother of the Incarnate Son, since there is only one God in three persons. It is still possible to say that the Holy Spirit is a person distinct from the Father. If it is possible to say the conception of

25. Cf. Boff, *Maternal Face of God*, pp. 63-103.
26. Cf. what we have already said about this word from the Old Testament.
27. Moltmann, *Humanity in God*, p. 103.
28. Cf. ibid.; and Boff, *Maternal Face of God*.

the Word in Mary is the work of the Father, it can, on the other hand, be said this work of the Father is carried out through the Holy Spirit. Maternal Love, "Conceiving Love," divine receptivity, fertilizing and being fertilized, conceives so that the seed of the Word may appear in Mary and glory be given to the Father, who engenders the Son in this virginal womb.

If it is delicate to affirm the Holy Spirit as the "Divine Mother" of the man Jesus of Nazareth, we can still say without doubt that the Holy Spirit, the *ruach* of the Old Testament and the *pneuma* of the New Testament,

> is the divine-maternal Love in the Father in relationship to the divinely conceived Christ; he is the same divine-maternal Love in the Virgin in relationship to the humanly conceived Christ.[29]

This divine-maternal Love formed in Mary allows Christians to see in her the Maternal Face of God.[30] Thus the Holy Spirit allows us today a social understanding of the image of God that would not otherwise be possible for us. The discovery of the feminine and maternal dimension of the Holy Spirit opens a possibility (breaking the body-soul, heaven-earth dualisms we earlier stated as the origin of the predominate "masculinity" of God) to appreciate the human being in its totality.

This frees us from the false images of a monotheistic God and helps us experience the fullness of God with our entire being, with our community of men and women, where the abandoned and exploited of this world, the orphan, the widow, the poor, and the stranger have an ultimate and definitive place of shelter, tenderness, and protection.

The Maternal Father and the Paternal Mother

The Son and the Spirit lead us to the invisible Father, the Abba of eternal love, Origin without origin, endless Mystery of life

---

29. H. M. Manteau and O. P. Bonamy, "L'Esprit Saint, divine Mere du Christ?" and "Et la Vierge conçut du Saint Esprit," *Bulletin de la Soc. Fr. d'Etudes Mariales* (1970): 22.

30. Cf. the final document of the Conference of Roman Catholic Bishops of Latin America in *Puebla and Beyond*, ed. John Eagleson and Philip Scharper (Maryknoll, N.Y.: Orbis, 1979), p. 162, para. 291.

and the world. This Mystery is all paternity, called by Jesus *Abba-Father!* at times with an explosion of joy (Matt. 11:25-27), at others with serene and solemn unction (John 17:1ff.), at still others with inward sorrow and struggle (Mark 14:32-42 and parallels). Is it possible, then, for theology to find in this Father some trace of femininity drawn from some maternity capable of coexisting with divine paternity?

God the Father is, therefore and above all, the Father of his Son Jesus. Only the relationship of Jesus with the God he lovingly calls *Abba-Father* can be the key to the interpretation of the true significance of this paternity. Entry into this love of the Father and the Son can be possible to us only by the Spirit. Any understanding we may have regarding the mystery of the maternity of the Father must have a trinitarian foundation.

The trinitarian Christian doctrine, with its affirmations about the mystery of the Abba of Jesus as Maternal Father and as Paternal Mother, definitively opens the door to the formation of a community of men and women that "in the communion of the Holy Spirit" (2 Cor. 13:13) is able to overcome privileges and dominations of every kind.

The Maternal Father of Jesus also makes it possible to overcome, with the eternal begetting of the Son and with his *rahamim* of loving divine childbirth, the body-soul dualism. The monotheistic God, understood in patriarchal terms, is a distant and sovereign God, invulnerable to the sorrows and sufferings through which the poor of humanity go, silent before the cross of the Son that continues in history. The Abba of Jesus, the Mystery of life that engenders and gives birth, participates passionately in the sufferings of the people of Israel. He dwells among the little ones and the humble through his *Shekinah*, which is exiled along with the deported ones of Jacob.[31] He feels in his merciful *rahamim* the entire range of the shame of Ephraim to the most concrete level possible (Deut. 8:3; Gen. 12:7; and others).

In delivering the beloved Son into human hands to be crucified, the Abba also delivers himself and suffers, in his

---

31. See the rabbinic writings on this special point of the theology of the *Shekinah*; F. Rosensweig, "L'étoile de la redemption" (Paris: Ed. du Seull, 1982).

divine entrails of maternal Father, the infinite sorrow, the anguishing impotence, the death of his maternal fatherhood. In the same movement of trinitarian love, the passion of the God who is maternal Father, Son, and Spirit of love throws wide the doors of definitive salvation to all the abandoned of this world.

In the passion of the Son, the maternal Father participates through the Spirit of Love in the filiation of those men and women who have learned, lived, and suffered to be family in an *agape* more communitarian and profound. In the passion of trinitarian love there is the ultimate possibility of integration and redemption of the human being in all its dimensions.

Conclusion: The Trinity as the Ultimate Possibility of the Integration of the Masculine and the Feminine

The progressive emergence of the feminine in all the areas of our lives today marks a true revolution in theology.

> The androcentric scriptural prism and its classical interpretation is being fragmented into a thousand pieces. The disappearance of patriarchal structures implies a true "revolution" which affects all human language about God. It has to do with the change of paradigms, deeper than anything which has been known in the history of Christian doctrine.[32]

In this profound transformation, it seems to us that trinitarian theology will play a decisive role. As mystery that integrates pluralism into divine unity, it is capable of integrating in the same way the masculine and the feminine in a happy synthesis, understanding them in the light of their basic oneness: God. Such an understanding of trinitarian theology affects not only human verbalization about the divine but also the symbolic system.

With relationship to anthropology and the concept of God: if the divine image is found as much in the woman as in the man, if the God in whom we believe has both masculine and feminine characteristics and ways of acting, it is necessary from now on to describe God by using masculine and feminine words, meta-

---

32. Borresen, *L'anthropologie théologique*, p. 403.

phors, and images. If the woman as well as the man is *theomor-phic*, the image of God, this image must not be simply andro-morphic, but *anthropomorphic*.[33] We know we have only the poverty of our human language, which is limited in ability to express the majesty and the ineffability of the Divine. Neverthe-less, the combination of the two symbols, the two metaphors—masculine and feminine—is more apt to the totality of the Divine, since they are modeled on the totality of the human.

With respect to the structure of society and social relation-ships: the trinitarian mystery of God is, fundamentally, a mys-tery of social, communitarian dimensions. Therefore, one in-dividual alone cannot be this image of God.

This has direct consequences for us in Latin America today. A society where the poor and needy are excluded and marginalized carries within itself neither the seed of the king-dom preached by Jesus nor the possibility of achieving it, nor even faintly the image of the Triune God. In the same way, a society in which women are kept in subjection, where they do not occupy their place as companion, shoulder to shoulder with men in the struggle for justice, is very far from the trinitarian mystery of God.

The Patristics saw the analogy and image of God in the three persons of the original nuclear family: Adam, Eve, and Seth.[34] Despite the problems and limitations in such an analogy, it can throw some light leading to a better understanding of human relationships. The human family as the image of God in-dicates that God is the mystery of love and of fruitful love. The trinitarian being is not shut up within the being of God, but is realized by surrender and the pouring out of self.

On the other hand, if the woman, man, and child are the image of God on earth, then the eternal fatherhood, the eternal motherhood, and the eternal infancy are revealed to us in the Triune God.[35] Femininity and infancy have their place restored in the bosom of the divine mystery.

This permits, above all, the visibility of true masculinity

---

33. Borresen, *L'anthropologie,* p. 404.

34. Cf. esp. Gregory of Nazianzus in Moltmann, *Humanity in God,* p. 100.

35. Moltmann, op. cit., p. 101.

in its original dignity, without being deformed by patriarchal domination. It makes it possible, also, to overcome the spirit-body dualism, because the body and everything related to it is reintegrated in the glory of the image of God. The total human person, man, woman, and child, in corporate nature and spirit are the image of God on earth. The body can be the temple of the Holy Spirit because it is the intelligible image of God in the world.

Even more, this implies that human and social relationships are not shaped nor do they take their guidelines exclusively in terms of their efficiency, which can easily degenerate into a desire for power and obsessive pragmatism. Rather, they are harmoniously balanced by the more "feminine" characteristics of gratuity and receptivity, the more "infantile" ones of purity and of trust. The social doctrine of the Trinity, which brings together the divine differences in an agapic unity of love, without suppressing them, allows us to find a theological basis for the building of a "social personalism" and of a "personal socialism"[36] as an alternative to the society in which we live.

Trinitarian theology and the rediscovery of its feminine aspects have foundations in the sacred Scriptures and the traditions of the church. Therefore, it should be written on the signposts of the people for whom the covenant and the company of God are a constant reality, that they desire *liberation from every form of oppression.*

In the church in Latin America today, which has made a fundamental option for the oppressed, the announcement of the God of life, who is a protective and strong Father, and at the same time a loving and eternal Mother, finds its human image in the community of liberated men and women who, shoulder to shoulder, join in the building of the kingdom of God. Together they hope and pray for messianic times in which, beyond all patriarchal or matriarchal domination, lords or slave, there may exist a future without either domination or subjection. This messianic humanity, in which there is "neither Jew nor Greek, neither slave nor free, neither man nor woman" (Gal. 3:28) is to be constructed in Latin America today *beginning from and moving*

---

36. The term is Jürgen Moltmann's in the book he wrote in cooperation with his wife, *Humanity in God,* p. 106.

toward the greater mystery of *love* which we call *Father, Son, and Holy Spirit,* and which in infinite mercy is revealed not only as begetting and creative strength, but also as entrails that give birth and feel compassion.

Reinterpreting the Doctrine of Two Kingdoms

WALTER ALTMANN *(Lutheran, Brazil)*

The Meaning of the Question of "Church and Politics"

I am interested in the question of "Church and Politics," with the urgency and priority due it, because it focuses on the well-being of persons, of oppressed people and, finally, of all humanity. It is certainly a theme that raises much anguish in our Latin American historical moment and context, where we are living with situations of centuries of dependence, domination, and oppression, but are, at the same time, looking for and rehearsing ways of liberation. The church can, by no means, leave this question behind and practice neutrality. Neutrality has never existed; it cannot.

Throughout the whole of Latin American history the churches have been, for the most part, an instrument of domination. Could they become now, in this historic hour, an instrument of liberation? No doubt the question will remain open. Only the historical process as such will be able to answer it. In any case, it is possible to observe that where the church puts into practice its prophetic mission and transforming action, it gets into the center of the conflicts that, after all, characterize our societies.

The belief is widespread, however, that the church cannot, by any means, get involved in politics. This is not an exclusive problem for Lutherans, since this concept can be found in all churches, including the Catholic, which traditionally has not been against direct political participation. Nevertheless, it was in the sphere of Lutheranism that the so-called doctrine of the two kingdoms, which has been used as an ideological legitimation of such belief and posture, was developed.

There are, however, remarkable variants of this doctrine, as the studies done by the Lutheran World Federation between 1970 and 1977 have shown. In the United States the doctrine has served to corroborate the traditional liberal-bourgeois concept of the separation of church and state. In a very unique configuration, the doctrine also served to conform the majority of German Christendom to the despotism and atrocities of the Nazi regime during the Third Reich. More recently, this same doctrine was used as legitimation in Chilean Lutheranism, when a few groups began to give support to Chileans and foreign refugees under the military government headed by Pinochet.

Nevertheless, it is important to point out that this problem does not rely only on the explicit formulation of a doctrine named "the two kingdoms." For example, during the twenty-one years of the military dictatorship in Brazil (1964–1985) an increasing number of voices identified with the government denounced the undue intervention of the church in issues of the competence of the state in the economic, political, and social arena. The rationalizing character of this "pseudo-theological" reasoning becomes even clearer when we realize that the coup d'etat of 1964 took place precisely "in the name of God" and with the public support of Catholic and Protestant churches.

In other words, the reasoning regarding the division of competencies between church and state only took place when the church (or meaningful and representative sectors of it) started to take a critical posture toward the state and the politics of the military regime. Thus, the objectives of the rationalization become evident: to silence the voice of the church that was then on the side of the weak and marginalized and to hinder the action of the church in solidarity with these outcast people. The purpose was to limit the church—its voice and, even more, its concrete performance—to a very circumscribed sphere. Obviously the economic, political, and social questions would be excluded. So the legitimizing dimension of this pseudo-theological reasoning is perfectly clear.

During the first years of the military regime (approximately until 1968), the dominant powers in Brazil did not look for the silence of the church, but rather for its public support in mobilizing people to maintain the secular system of social domination. As soon as the posture of the churches changed, a dichotomous concept of the church and state arose.

Let us take a very brief look at what has happened inside the churches. In 1964, the CNBB (the National Conference of Brazilian Catholic Bishops) supported the military takeover, not coming to a more critical posture until after 1968. In 1970, the IECLB (the Evangelical Church of Lutheran Confession in Brazil), reacted very negatively to and repudiated the decision of the Lutheran World Federation to transfer its Fifth General Assembly planned for Porto Alegre, Brazil, to Evian, France. The Lutheran World Federation did this as part of an international movement of awareness of the tortures systematically practiced in Brazil. The IECLB understood this as an affront to itself and to the country, and denied the reality of torture in Brazil. It also decided not to participate in the assembly in France.

In the same year, at its general convention in Curitiba, the IECLB issued the "Curitiba Document," which critically analyzes the relationship between church and state in regard to the violations of human rights and to the ideological interests in the introduction of civics and moral education in the Brazilian educational system. Here we have the principle of the church watching over the state. So the "Curitiba Document" became the starting point for a change in the official statements of the IECLB in regard to economic, political, and social matters.

Inside the Catholic church this new attitude also became evident. The imprisonment, murder, and expulsion of priests and religious workers were representative of the suffering of the Brazilian people at large.

Why did these changes take place? In my opinion, we have to list factors in the internal, as well as external, life of the church. The end of the fifties saw a growing number of new pastoral initiatives with workers, peasants, and university students. There was a reawakening of Christian lay action. A model of industrial ministry was being developed in the churches at the precise moment transnational corporations were entering Latin America.

A widespread renewal took place in the Catholic church in the sixties. Though not as deep, courageous, or significant, a similar renewal can be observed among some Protestant denominations. From a Latin American standpoint, these early efforts show signs of a developmental philosophy not based on structural change. I do not need to emphasize the tremendous relevance for Latin America of the Conference of Catholic Bishops in Medellín, Colombia (1968), and of the emergence of liberation theology.

If we look at the global context in which the churches live, we observe in the sixties the rise of popular organizations. Among students there were large demonstrations, not only in Brazil, but worldwide from the United States to China, crossing France and Czechoslovakia. Parallel to this, in Brazil something new and fundamental was happening: the military takeover. While people talked and dreamed of an imminent revolution and liberation, Brazil was thrown into captivity. Military regimes followed in other Latin American countries, always with the support of the United States.

My very simple thesis is that while the churches were opening themselves, the regimes were closing. While the churches were declaring themselves more and more on the side of the workers, the governments were cutting the workers' means of survival. While the churches were providing space for peoples' meetings, the political participation of the people was being repressed by force.

It is ironic that today the opposite is happening: while the political space is enlarging, at the same time the churches are closing. This is seen most clearly in the Catholic case, coming from Rome. The situation is, however, very ambiguous. Almost all Latin American countries have rid themselves of military regimes (except for the terrible Chilean case) and established a liberal-bourgeois democratic regime. (Central America and the Caribbean deserve a special analysis.)

The end of authoritarian, repressive regimes is, in fact, a concrete answer to the strong commitment of the people and must be seen as their achievement. On the other hand, social and economic change has not yet followed. Only a few reform measures of very limited scope have taken place. The structures of social discrimination and economic spoilage are still present. International dependence remains intact. That means the national and international systems of social and economic injustice work with the same cruelty. With a few concessions, mainly at the political level, the privileged classes have been able to stay in power and to preserve the social and economic structures that benefit them.

From another perspective, since the political space has been enlarged and direct repression diminished, the groups looking for real structural change are facing the question of how to use this new political space given to them to achieve the goals of social and economic change. There are many difficulties facing the churches in this situation. They do not know what to do with political freedom and fear social and economic transformations. They could well become again a legitimizing force of the status quo, which is exactly the position in which the owners of power would like to see them.

This tendency is obviously reinforced by the closing process going on inside the Catholic church. The same role is played by a large number of neoconservative U.S. missions working in Latin America at the service of the hegemonic interests of the United States.

It is in this context that we will examine the so-called doctrine of the two kingdoms. Can a dichotomous interpretation really be ascribed to Luther? Can we learn anything from Luther on this precise question?

Church and Politics under the Kingship of God

The Two Realms of God's Action

I wish to state very clearly at the beginning that we cannot legitimately ascribe to Luther the dichotomous dualism between church and state.

It is true that he drew a distinction of competencies between the two, but he never separated them as autonomous identities. This distinction seemed for him indispensable. His purpose was clear: to stand against the corruption of the church, which was becoming a temporal and political power. This comes through in the Ninety-five Theses, where he condemns the traffic in indulgences. The church must offer the free forgiveness of God in Christ and not take advantage of it as a source of enrichment. This distinction can be found, very clearly stated, in the writing "To the Christian Nobility of the German Nation concerning the Reform of the Christian Estate" (1520), where he turns radically against the political power of popes and bishops (who were often political authorities), against the system of feudal ecclesiastical properties, against the civil jurisprudence of the church, against its complicated and diversified fiscal system, and so forth. All this created, in the name of the gospel, a concrete system of spoilage.

At the same time, there is in Luther a dignifying of the social and political office in the widest sense, even and particularly for Christians. Luther addresses himself to the Christian nobility, making them aware that their political office did not originate from their own autonomous and arbitrary competence, but from their universal priesthood as baptized Christians. Therefore, as Christians in a political office, they have to put into practice the necessary economic, political, and social reforms of the German nation. In an analogous way, Luther answered positively the question about the legitimacy and necessity of Christians taking public jobs in the areas of law (e.g., as judges), education, and even the military.

So Luther never meant to make the church and the state autonomous entities. It was the responsibility of political authorities to achieve economic, political, and social reforms that would also affect the church; and it was the task of the church to confront the political authorities with God's will. Thus, the "two kingdoms" can be distinguished with regard to their duties and means, but overlap each other in terms of space. God is the Lord of both, and of the human being, their final goal. Church and state are, therefore, instrumentalized, limiting and binding themselves reciprocally. The state limits and regulates the church as a social institution (e.g., in matters of property). The church proclaims God's will to the state (e.g., criticizing its arbitrariness or calling it to work for social, political, and economic transformations). Thus, Luther was always compelled to address the political authorities, princes, nobles, or city councilors with advice and economic, political, and social claims. These claims were often wise but sometimes regrettable and tragic. But he never looked for neutrality.

Thus, Luther never thought of the "secularization" of the

political sphere, in the sense of modern liberal separation between church and state. When he talked of "secular authorities," he had in mind a determination of functions, not the autonomous nature of the political office.

At this point I would like to insert an observation about the Latin American theology of liberation, many times—by both Catholics and Lutherans—mistakenly considered antagonistic to Luther's vision. It is true they have taken contrary paths, since their starting point is different. On the other hand, the point of arrival is perfectly analogous, taking into account the historical differences.

One elementary and well-known aspect of the theology of liberation is the overcoming of the distinction of two planes: the natural and the supernatural. Consequently, the affirmation of only one historical process, within which Christians play a part through their experience and faith, is essential. In some places this is used in a reformist (and thus not revolutionary) renewal of the church. It requires the political participation of the Christian but does not consider the deep conflicts in the historical process. Such a praxis employs the term *liberation* but does not convincingly explain "from what" people are to be liberated. This praxis does not do justice to the central intention of the theology of liberation, which acknowledges "one history only" but also reflects dialectically upon this history as a process marked by antagonism, conflict, and transformation.

The theology of liberation has had to clarify this aspect better than it did in its beginning. However, the dialectic perception was not missing in Gustavo Gutiérrez's book *The Theology of Liberation*. He emphasizes that there is only one history, yet because it is marked by conflicts, distinctions within it are necessary. It is just such a dialectic we find in Luther's writings.

Models of Relationship between Church and State

My reinterpretation of Luther's position will be clarified by giving some examples of the relationship between church and state in various models. Permit me to do so in a schematic way:

Model of Separation between Church and State

State	Church
Secular	Spiritual
Social order	Ecclesiastical order
Public order	Private order
Body	Soul
The power of the sword	The power of the word
Law	Gospel
Repression	Love
Punishment	Forgiveness

In this first model, the state and church are seen as separate powers, as if in tight compartments. Each has its own field of duties, completely separated from the other. Generally it is maintained that the state is responsible for the secular order and the church for the spiritual order. Or, the church is supposed to deal with its internal organization while the state regulates society as a whole. On one side, we have the public order under the state's responsibility; on the other, the private and intimate order is for the church to sustain. In a simpler way it is said that the state takes care of the body, whereas the church nourishes the soul. The church uses the word, the state the sword. The church preaches the gospel, the state enforces the law. The state has to watch over the order and punish the delinquents; the church is the instrument of love and forgiveness.

Admittedly, this model of separation has often been defended by Protestant churches and by liberal secular movements. Further, it can take two forms, one apparently excluding the other, but based on the same premise of separation. The first variant we could call the demonization of politics. It makes the following claim: everything belonging to the political sphere is characteristic of the fallen world, an expression of human sin or even the work of the devil. Politics is something dirty, and renewed Christians should not take any part in it. They already live in a regenerated world in the midst of the old and fallen one. Consequently they have the new life, which they might endanger by taking part in politics. So they confine themselves to their private sphere or to the company of the redeemed. We can find persons or groups with this line of thinking in all churches, including the Roman Catholic, but it is doubtless more frequent in Protestant churches or sectarian groups of an apocalyptic character. Such groups demonize the political order of the world and consequently of the state, taking their refuge in the spiritual order. They tolerate the world, since to live in it is inevitable, but they do so in expectation of heaven.

The second variant is the autonomy of politics. This variant shares the basic vision that the competencies of state and church are clearly separated, but it does not demonize politics. On the contrary, it expresses a clearly optimistic view of the state. As part of God's creation, it is therefore good. The same is true of the social and economic spheres. Even so, the church should never interfere with the specific realm of the state, because politics, economics, and society are governed by their own laws. They have an inherent rationality whose rules should be known and applied. The church would pervert these definitions if it raised questions from its own spiritual order.

Thus, the church may talk about God, Jesus Christ, and the gospel in the private realm; it may awaken and strengthen personal morality; it may promote the unity of the family; but it should not tackle political, social, or economic questions. These should be taken care of by those with technical understanding. These realms are considered autonomous and the church is not allowed to invade them.

This variant is especially tempting to Protestantism. Lutheranism experienced the tragedy of that vision intensely in Germany. It is also found widely in the United States, a country where the principle of separation of church and state has been firmly established, permitting capitalism to develop with its own rationality, justified by the ideology of such a theological concept. This, however, does not impede the North American missionary expansion, hand in hand with the international implantation of technocratic capitalism.

Thus we observe that the two variants share the premise of separation between church and state. As a result, both serve to legitimate the status quo. Whether one divinizes or demonizes politics is unimportant; both leave it untouched.

Model of Alliance *between Church and State*

Visualization of this model is very simple:

> STATE + CHURCH

At first glance, this model seems contrary to the first. This is, however, a mistake, because here, too, there is a division of spheres of competency. The difference lies only in the fact that the separation is changed into cooperation—active, conscious, and deliberate. The fields of action are divided, but each side works with the other toward a common project. One task falls to the church, another to the state.

We can distinguish two variants in this model, also. When two bodies cooperate, the question of the division of tasks inevitably arises. Who shall have the power? Who shall decide over whom? In the last analysis, will the church dominate the state or the state the church? The best example of this model today has to be taken from outside Christianity: the control by Shi'ite Islam of the state and politics in Iran. It would be difficult, if not impossible, to find similar examples in present-day Christianity. This shows that the modern evolution of the state and the process of secularization either leads to the separation of church and state or is likely to make the church dependent on the state.

I shall give two examples of this second variant, where the state dominates the church. The first refers to Lutheran churches. Luther found it necessary in his time to protest the authority of the church over the state. Historical development brought the division of Christianity into two ecclesiastic bodies—against Luther's desire for evangelical restoration within the one church of Christ. The task of Reformation was carried out in Germany by the nobility, the princes, who could count on Luther's support. Measures Luther had meant to be only temporary were made permanent, such as the establishment of territorial churches. There the religious affiliation of the citizen was determined by the option of the ruler (the principle of "cuius regio, eius religio"). Even if the relationship between church and state in modern times is mostly defined in terms of division, there are still Lutheran state churches, as in Scandinavia.

The second example comes from Latin American history. Colonization is marked by the alliance between state and church. There was certainly much tension and resistance between them, but in the establishment of Christendom the state and church were allies. The sword and the word formed an alliance in order to conquer the continent and its indigenous population, and even to import black slaves. This alliance is also marked by the state's power over this church. The model was that of Christendom which linked the economic and political system of the colonizers with the implantation of Spanish culture and the Christian faith. Through the patronage system, the state was in charge of sending out missionaries and, consequently, it could also call them home in case of conflict.

This discussion raises an important question: Who are the absent ones in the schemes so far presented? The people and God. These models deal with institutions—the state and the church—but make no mention of the concrete necessities of the people nor the actual will of God. The next model will seek to rectify this lack.

Model of the Relationship between Church and State in the Context of the Struggle for Justice

Here I shall try to schematize Luther's position (see the chart on page 148).[1] The relationships become more complex because both the church and the state have to find their proper places in God's struggle against the idols (in traditional language, the devil), in favor of the implantation of the kingdom of God.

The situation of creation and humanity is in no way characterized by neutrality. On the contrary, creation is a disputed territory, humanity lives in a situation of conflict. The ongoing dispute is between God and the idols (devil). It is not a matter of a dualistic Manichaeism, because the result of the dispute is already known. God is superior to the idols. The victory belongs to God. The final result will be the kingdom of God, the new heaven and the new earth. Nevertheless, creation and humanity still continue to be objects of struggle.

A lot of terms could characterize what is at stake here.

1. I shall simplify and actualize a scheme elaborated by Ulrich Duchrow in "Lutheran Churches—Salt or Mirror of Society" (Geneva, 1977), p. 65.

GOD	CREATION/HUMANITY	DEVIL/IDOLS
justice truth hope faith conscience love liberty fraternity equality resurrection etc.	new reality | old reality (Christus victor) 1. the human being faith | disbelief hope | despair love | egoism 2. the church (word and sacrament) communion | instrument and | of liberation | domination 3. the state (coercive power, "sword" and rationality) defense of | instrument of the oppressed | the oppressors social | dominating well-being | interests participative | divided and and equalitarian | discriminating society | society	injustice lie despair sin alienation exploitation oppression domination egoism discrimination death etc.

THE KINGDOM OF GOD ——————————→A NEW HEAVEN
AND NEW EARTH

Some of them appear in the side columns. God defends justice against injustice, truth against lie, liberation against domination, and so on. The final outcome is no longer uncertain, since it became reality in the death and resurrection of Christ, to whom the idols are subject.[2]

This battle does *not* take place in a nonhistorical manner without human participation. Rather, history is the battlefield of this struggle in which humanity and creation are not specta-

2. This terminology in Luther is a heritage of an apocalyptic-Augustinian tradition. On the other hand, the distinction between "secular" and "spiritual" emanates from the medieval question of the "two worlds" and is significant in Luther's writings only in the context of the major duality between God and the devil.

tors but protagonists. Persons may be instruments of oppression or of liberation. Faith centered in Jesus Christ, dead but risen, gives a certainty of victory even if at the moment it seems to be "against appearance" (Luther). Against the apparent victory of injustice, despair, oppression, and death, faith clings to reality and to the divine promises, trusting the supremacy of justice, hope, liberation, and life. I have tried to show this conflictive situation in the central columns of the above chart.

History, not just the individual, turns out to be the scene of the conflict between justice and injustice, in the chart called "new" and "old" reality. The whole present reality is penetrated by the new and the old. When we evaluate the human being, the church, and the state, we should always ask this question: Which are they serving, the old or the new reality? Of course, *old* and *new* here are terms of quality, not of chronology. *Old* is everything that in the light of God's victory is doomed to disappear, even if it is very active and apparently prevailing. *New* is everything that in the light of the kingdom of God is predestined to triumph, even if at present it seems weak.

Frequently the division between the old and the new is a line that passes through the whole reality, the human being, the church, and the state. This is shown above through the broken line. As long as we still expect the kingdom to come in its fullness, nobody, no institution—including the church—can claim to be totally characterized by the new. On the other hand, nobody needs to resign in the face of the old because, since Christ, the kingdom is already present even if it is contested by that which is overcome. At each step we suffer the anguish of the old reality but also see signs of the new.

Everywhere the old and new realities are manifest, coincident, and antagonistic. The relationship between church and state, which we have been considering, is too narrow if it is not set into the greater sphere of God's will and the antagonistic reality. Thus, what interests us is not the relation of church-state in itself, but in the cause of justice. When considering persons and institutions, we always have to ask if they represent the new or the old reality, that is, whether they favor justice or protect injustice.

Within this outline we can imagine many different variations. First, it may be we have such an oppressive and disturbed situation that both the church and the state are on the side of the old reality. They form a "holy" alliance as instruments of domination.

Second, we could imagine an inverse situation in which the church is fundamentally an instrument of communion and liberation, at the same time that the state defends the oppressed and promotes a participatory, egalitarian society. Since we are still on the way to the full consummation of the kingdom of God, we will not find this possibility in a "pure" stage, but always only approximate, requiring the permanent, critical vigilance of both institutions.

Third, we can imagine a perverted state, an instrument of domination, and a church really serving Christ—and thus in critical resistance to the state. We can also imagine the opposite, in which the church continues to defend the old reality, desires its institutional preservation, built on privileges, while the state is the instrument of the popular wish for transformation and the construction of a just society.

Pure cases, however, are difficult to find. Mostly there will be a complex situation involving the people, the church, the state, and the institutions. Ultimately it is always a question of discovering one's place in the midst of God's fight against the idols, and in favor of the kingdom.

Criticism of the Secular Power

Even though the image of a Luther subservient to the political authorities, especially the princes, is very widespread, one can find much harsh criticism against them in his writings. I would like to illustrate this with Luther's interpretation of Psalm 82 (1530). Significantly, this text is not found in any of the popular editions at my disposal (Spanish, English, or German).[3]

According to Luther, this is a political psalm. The first verse describes God "standing up," that is, as judge, in the middle of the congregation to judge the "gods"—the political authorities, the princes. Their judgment takes place in the congregation, so the church transmits the judgment of God's words

---

3. I am using the edition by Erwin Mühlhaupt, *D. Martin Luther's Psalmen-Auslegung*, vol. 2 (Göttingen, 1962), pp. 466-85.

to the political authorities. In his introduction, Luther shows how the princes, after having been liberated from the pope's tutelage through the Reformation's proclamation of the gospel, now want to be liberated from the gospel itself in order to be the dominators—putting themselves above even God. They want to shut the mouths of the preachers who criticize them, accusing them of being "revolutionaries" and "agitators." But the gospel is revolutionary, and it is part of the preacher's task to denounce evil.

Luther understands verses 2 to 4 as a description of political office. Each ruler should have the duties of office written "in his room, over his bed, at his desk and also in his clothes." Luther distinguished three tasks: (1) to guarantee the free preaching of the gospel—critical, prophetic preaching; (2) to defend justice and the rights of the weak and abandoned; (3) to guarantee the order, peace, and protection of the poor. The sequence of the tasks is not coincidental. Free preaching comes first, so that through its criticism political power is permanently limited, contested in its claim to be absolute and reminded of its duties. In the second place is the establishment of right and justice as a premise to the execution of the task of maintaining order, peace, and protection. All these tasks, according to the psalm, are not at the service of the rulers but always turned to the weak, the abandoned, the poor, the wronged, the oppressed.

According to Luther, the princes were unfaithful to their political office by disregarding the gospel, putting themselves above God, governing in their own favor, and oppressing the people. Therefore it is necessary that preachers serve as the voice of God's judgment. Luther then criticizes the various kinds of preachers who try to avoid this mission. Among them he distinguishes three kinds: (1) the unfaithful and lazy ones, who prefer to keep silent because of fear of retaliation; (2) the flatterers, who support the political arbitration out of self-interest and connivance; (3) the slanderers, the ones who prefer to criticize behind one's back, who do not have the courage to criticize publicly.

Against all these Luther puts the true preacher, who does not avoid the task of criticizing injustice and oppression, who does not have his own interests to defend.

> Observe the consequence of this first verse: it is not subversive to criticize authorities, when it is done in the way here described, i.e. free, public and honestly, in the ordained ministry and through God's words. On the contrary, it is a rare, noble and praiseworthy virtue—yes, an especially great service to God, as the Psalm here testifies.

Really, with Luther it is impossible to legitimate the total autonomy of politics or restrict the political mission of the church to the so-called spiritual realm.

Conclusion: The Liberating Kingship of God in the Church and Politics of Latin America

The dualist vision of the so-called doctrine of the two kingdoms that separates the gospel and politics, church and state, cannot rightfully be ascribed to Luther. True, he makes a distinction in the competencies of the two, which is of undeniable importance. Without doubt, Luther's historical liberating contribution was that he broke the tutelage of the ecclesiastical authorities over the political ones. It is equally necessary to resist every intention or system of absolute autonomy of politics. In fact, the situation of the modern state is not at all similar to the ecclesiastical tutelage over politics.

The current importance of this distinction of competencies can be illustrated by the political praxis of the Christian base communities. Clodovis Boff[4] explains how base communities played an important political role during the years of dictatorship. As communities of faith, they were also the only space for organization of the people. They now relate to other practices of liberation in a historic period when different possibilities of popular organization develop, such as local concerns groups, labor unions among rural and factory workers, and even political parties. The difficulties experienced by a base community in this changed context range from the fear of strange ideological and political infiltration to the fear of losing command of the popular claims and struggles. The more mature communities,

---

4. *CEBS e Prática de Liberação*, REB, vol. 40, fasc. 160, Dec. 1980, pp. 595-625.

however, are discovering they are a place of faith in which their participants are strengthened to action within the popular organizations themselves, outside the walls of the ecclesial community. Many times there is a close personal and group connection between them, with a division of competencies.

Which tasks belong intrinsically to the base communities and are not transferrable? C. Boff mentions the celebration of faith and education in the faith. Protestant terminology would speak of worship and Christian education. I would add further the propagation of the faith, that is, the proclamation and mission Boff omitted, probably on the false supposition that the entire Latin American population is already Christian. If that were true, it would mean a remarkable success of the colonial project of creating Christendom.

Worship, Christian education, mission—celebration of faith, education in faith, proclamation of faith—make up the Christian community that finds its fountain of life in the gospel of Jesus Christ and its historical concretion in the praxis of the liberation of the poor.

Let us look at the relevance of political action related to the struggle for justice and against oppression. First, oppressive Latin American governments are confronted more and more by the critical voice of the churches (if they are true to their prophetic calling) as well as by the direct force of popular organizations. Even if they manage to win a small part of society for themselves, a part becoming more and more a minority, at the same time they have to take account of a growing movement of claims for justice among workers, rural laborers, civil servants, and others.

Second, in the period of transition from military to civil governments, the church has an opportunity to rediscover its proximity to the people and its historical task together with the people. It need no longer be the voice of the voiceless, as during the years of harsh repression and captivity. The question the churches now face is: Are they going to be satisfied being an auxiliary voice of a people who are learning to speak for themselves? While they need not be the voice of the voiceless, they can rejoice at the words of the people themselves. Consequently, Latin American churches have completely ceased to be the space for popular organization they used to be in the dark years of repression. Are they going to be content in being "only" a support for these forms of organization the people are trying out in popular movements, labor unions, political parties, and so forth? Or are they going to be victims of the fear of giving up the control of the organizations of the people?

The question of making the churches instruments of other groups may be a real problem, and they have the right, like every other organized group, to be critical and watchful. However, the mark of the real church is not prudence but courage. It is not withdrawal behind its own walls, but its missionary outreach. It is not in settling with the mighty rulers, but in solidarity with the oppressed. Therefore it will be reason for gratitude and joy if Christians and the churches become simply an auxiliary voice instead of a voice speaking in the name of others, a supporting channel for the organization of the people instead of an organism substituting for the people.

Third, the churches would have even less right to aim at commanding the people and, consequently, dominating the state at some favorable moment in the future. That is why we have to reject those ideas that reappear in official Catholicism that the churches should patronize a model of their own, a political, social, and economic model of Christian inspiration and perhaps exclusive authority of the churches. This is like longing for the return of Christendom.

The fundamental option, as we have seen, is not between church and state, but between justice and injustice, truth and falsehood, liberty and oppression, life and death. With this option the gospel confronts both the church and the state. Thus it is not a question of defending the state from the interference of the church or protecting the church from the control of the state. It is rather a matter of participating concretely in the fight for justice and rights, for democracy and popular participation, be it in the order of the state or in that of the churches themselves.

We have come to our final conclusion. For the concrete action of Christians, forms of adaptation to current political-social-economic structures are discarded from the outset, be they the dualist variants of separation or the models of coordination and alliance. Our faith permits only a dialectic posture of distinction and critical participation. The concrete action, even in this understanding, will still be submitted to variations according to the actual historical situation and commanded by political praxis. For many Christians only a critical-constructive participation would be permissible in any situation. This is a nonhistorical vision. The critical-constructive participation is legitimate in situations such as the current one in Nicaragua. It is not advisable when the ruling system is irremediably corrupted by injustice and oppression.

As a second alternative, we can consider the critical-passive resistance adequate when the fight for active transformation is hindered by repressive violence. To maintain the critical conscience throughout captivity is a task of extraordinary importance.

Finally, at this time when spaces for a direct, transforming participation are opened or achieved, the option imposed on the Christian conscience is that of critical-active transformation.[5] This type of action is required on two conditions: (1) the recognition of a fundamentally unjust system characterized by social oppression, and (2) concrete possibilities of action given by the historical process and the circumstantial moment. Both of these conditions are present in most Latin American countries today. The need still remains to call attention to the concrete means of action at the present moment—the organizations of the people such as local concerns movements, labor unions, rural laborers' associations, and populist political parties.

Thus I conclude that supporting the organizations of the people, participating in them, and aiming at the transformation of the established oppressive system is the political praxis (action) which the gospel demands from Christians and the churches in most Latin American countries today.

---

5. I have taken this typology from Duchrow, "Lutheran Churches," pp. 300-307.

Theology of Sin and Structures of Oppression

ALDO ETCHEGOYEN *(Methodist, Argentina)*

Sin Defined from Latin America

We begin our analysis from a Latin American perspective. For this purpose the first question must be: What is happening in our continent because of the structures of oppression?

To get a reading of life in our region, we must speak of the aboriginal (indigenous, Indian) communities, the clearest example of oppression. Originally these communities had their own land and their own culture. Today their story is one of marginalization, of pain, and of suffering. The sword was the instrument of pillage and death. The cross was the symbol of massive, often despotic conversion.

We were taught to call this the "civilizing" advance. For these aboriginal communities, however, it was indiscriminate slaughter. What happened in the past in my country, Argentina, is still the reality in other regions of Latin America, where a war of domination and conquest for the possession of land by the white world is being waged. Carlos Benedetto, a member of the team from the United Mission Board who works in the Toba communities in Argentina, says, "It is an unequal struggle based in the lack of love, on injustice and lies." Following his analysis, I want to compare what land means for the indigenous peoples with what it means within the mentality of oppression.

For the aboriginal communities, land is property on which to live a full and abundant life. For the mentality of oppression, on the contrary, land is private, commercial, capitalist property, the object of profit. From this we can identify some of the characteristics of a structure of oppression: dominating and capitalist possession of the land, and an extermination of the community as a hindrance to control of the land. In two words, possession and reification (people treated as things). When we speak of the aboriginal communities of Latin America we should recognize our own sin, because we are participants in the structures that oppress them.

Our Latin American continent is not only dependent but is caught in a growing dependency. A clear example of this is the voluminous growth of our foreign debt, truly a trap expertly laid and from which it is very difficult to escape. The oppression of Latin American peoples creates a growing dependency. We must call attention to the violence against life that this scheme generates.

The Assembly of the Latin American Council of Churches (CLAI) at Huampani, Peru, emphasized it this way:

> The structures of power are, in the final instance, the causes of the great problems which our continent faces today. These problems include: serious levels of malnutrition, infant mortality, unemployment, lack of housing, limited access to health, educational and social security services, etc. It is not minorities, but large majorities of our Latin American compatriots who suffer these disgraces in their own flesh. With regard to this, the socioeconomic organization dominant among our people, rather than contributing to the improvement of the situation, causes it to become increasingly worse, turning it into a determining factor in the violation of the rights of the working class and of those who defend democratic liberties. . . . The economic system predominant in Latin America means the strengthening of the so-called developed countries and the growing deterioration of the countries of the Third World. International capitalism subordinates these latter countries to their interests for profit and accumulation of capital, leading to the weakening of the conditions of interchange, to technological dependence, to political-military control, to the strengthening of internal domination and the increase of the external debt which reaches astronomical figures.

The doctrine of National Security becomes the justification for power, exercised both by the centers of world capitalism, and by the dominating classes (oligarchies) in the countries of the Third World.

The empire of capital makes oppression a tool for the deepening of dependence. Its reasons are not human but economic. In this kind of scheme, life is turned into an object to be used: human rights have no intrinsic worth, and justice, liberty, truth, and peace are secondary values.

The Doctrine of National Security is a very important element in this structure. In a continent that needs to be unified for its liberation, this doctrine uses division and creates ideological enemies. It goes beyond the concept of enmity created by frontiers or nationality. National Security makes my neighbor an internal enemy, simply because he seeks a political-economic-social change.

In the last decade, when the impact of the Doctrine of National Security hit us most strongly, there was at the same time a marked advance in our dependency, accompanied by massive violation of life by hunger, malnutrition, physical and psychological torture, disappearances, and death. Beyond this is the injustice in the commerce of our raw materials, the poor utilization of our land, the privileges of the dominating classes, the special benefits for members of the armed forces, as well as frustrations and limitations on our human possibilities.

Recently there are signs of an increasingly acute situation. Structures of oppression, for their own security, need spaces carved out in strategically located territories, such as Central America, the Caribbean, and the islands of the south Atlantic. In the face of this demand for security, territorial rights as well as human rights lose their value. Structures of oppression demand their own defenses and prevail through armed power.

We have learned from our experience in Latin America that the structures of oppression are impersonal. Laws can be manipulated to the benefit of the dominating power. The will of the people is given no weight. Education can be, and in fact is, a domesticating exercise. The means of mass communication serve as channels for brainwashing and lies.

As far as the church is concerned, in the face of these structures of oppression its fidelity to the liberating gospel of Jesus Christ is at risk. We find in the church, on the one hand, martyrs of the faith and prophets of the truth. On the other hand are those who hide reality through silence or use the Word of God to support the dominating power.

John Wesley and His Time

Recognizing the differences and distances, it should be pointed out that John Wesley and the Methodist movement took shape in the midst of structures of oppression and domination.

Eighteenth-century England was the center of world economy, laying the foundations of the industrial process. The power of entrepreneurial-banking-commercial capital advanced with giant steps. Great masses of working people, even children, were placed at the service of iron, coal, and the textile industry. This structure certainly does not benefit the poor who work and produce. The large firms benefit through the discovery of a new financial world. A whole gamut of problems and social injustices affect and even destroy life. Thus begins a great tension: the valuation of capital leads to the devaluation of life. John Wesley directly perceived all this human problematic.

The Methodist movement's origin is among working people, miners, marginalized people, such as those around Bristol. Evidently this produced in Wesley a profound change that demanded of him new pastoral decisions, attitudes, and practices. I believe one of these key moments was when he had to choose between his pastoral action in conformity with the ecclesial structure of his church (which would limit his preaching to inside the sanctuary) and the demand of these marginalized and poor people who challenged him to begin pastoral action outside the walls of the churches. His famous affirmation, "the world is my parish," meant for Wesley a liberation from structural domination—in this case, ecclesial—for a pastoral action directly related to life seriously prejudiced by the nascent economic structures of oppression.

Let us analyze, in this context, the Wesleyan theology of sin. It begins with a literalist Bible position that afterward was very much discussed. From Genesis it takes the idea of the primitive state of man, of Adam in paradise. He begins his message about justification by faith by presenting the human state before sin entered human life.

> Man was created in the image and likeness of God, holy as the one who created him is holy. Merciful as the Creator of all things is merciful; perfect as his Father in heaven is perfect. Just as God is love so also man existing in love, existed in God and God in him. . . . He did not know sin in any degree or manner. . . . He loved the Lord his God with all his heart, soul and mind. . . . He should have continued forever in this life of love if he had obeyed God in all things and always.

This starting point, which we also find in many of his other sermons, can be called the Wesleyan theology of the primitive state of man.

This state is affected totally by the fall. A large part of what Wesley wrote about the fall from the primitive state was written in reaction to the ideas of John Taylor, a Presbyterian minister, and published in 1740. In his arguments against Taylor, Wesley emphasized the tragic fact of sin in human life and the effect of evil among the people. The fall produced the corruption expressed before and after the flood. Later it affected the chosen people and culminated in the crucifixion of the only Just One.

To explain the origin of this human corruption, Wesley appeals to the oracles of God.

> They teach us that all die in Adam . . . that by the first man natural and spiritual death entered the world, that by one man alone sin entered the world, and death as a consequence of sin, and beginning with him death passed to all men since all have sinned. . . .
>
> It is an inescapable truth that the death of all men in Adam is the reason why the whole world lies in evil. . . . It is evident 1) that humanity is in a state of sin and suffering; 2) that this was a necessary situation from the moment in which Adam fell. Very well, if it was not his fall which put men into this state, I would like to know what it was. (Letters of Wesley)

If we ask Wesley what the consequences of sin are, he would answer: "Error, guilt, pain, fear, suffering, sickness and death."

When we consider the historic situation within which Wesley carried out his ministry, we discover that his theology of sin is entirely embodied in the very heart of the reality that shook him, and we may be surprised by some prophetic statements still valid today. In his sermon on the reform of customs he affirms:

> Therefore we need, even in this Christian nation—as, out of courtesy, we speak of England—and in this same Christian church—if we are able to give this name to the majority of our compatriots—we need, I said, some persons who will rise up against the evil ones and be united against those who practice iniquity. Never was there felt as in our days the necessity for those who fear the Lord to deliberate frequently together about these things, to raise the flag against the iniquity which floods the entire country. There are more than enough reasons for all those who serve God to unite against the works of the Devil; so that, uniting their hearts and efforts, they may place themselves on God's side and destroy, as far as possible, these floods of iniquity.

The reality that surrounds him is in no way a motive for entering a celestial world, but on the contrary is a call to unity, to assume together a commitment to struggle in the search for changes that destroy and do away with "these floods of iniquity." In response to this call to participation, we see many Methodists, lay and clergy, in labor unions, workers' organizations, and other groups in defense of life and against the forces of death.

In his sermon on the use of money, after strong words against the making and selling of the "fiery liquid which is called spirituous drinks, or liquor," he affirms:

> Is there not equal guilt, even though in lesser degree, of the surgeons, druggists and doctors, who play with the health and life of men to increase their profits; those who prolong the illness they could cure immediately, to rob them of money, charging more than they should? Can it be that God will hold innocent that man who does not shorten any disorder in the quickest manner and cure the illness as soon as possible? God will not hold him innocent, because it is clear that he does not love his neighbor as himself and does not do to others as he would want others to do to him.

So we discover in Wesley a theology of sin that awakens the conscience in the face of a society wounded by the concrete consequences of evil. It is a call to participation on behalf of change and to a courageous prophetic attitude. In an unjust situation, the fight for change demands courage.

He also says in the same sermon:

> Anyone who has faith and confidence in God should naturally be a courageous man. It is extremely important that the members of this society be courageous persons, because when this work is undertaken terrible things happen, so tremendous that beings of flesh and bone fear them. In this undertaking, then, there is need for a high degree of courage. Only faith can supply it. It is in faith that the believer can say: I am not afraid of sacrifice nor sufferings nor temptations because Jesus is near.

It is not possible to speak of Wesley's doctrine of sin and the fall without at the same time speaking of his theology of redemption. This demands reference to justification and sanctification, and also to Jesus Christ, the Just and the Holy. His work is the supreme manifestation of justice and holiness. Only he makes possible redemption and reconciliation with God.

Above all, God helps the individual to have faith in the merits of Jesus Christ. Wesley's personal experience of conversion on May 24, 1738, represents an existential deepening of this doctrine. His words, "He took away my sins, yes all of my sins, and saved me from the law of sin and death," are more than just a testimony. They were converted into a profound experience of the work of Jesus Christ, the Just and Holy One.

Wesley's theology of sin allows him to see and denounce the social evils of his time. His personal theology of redemption is transformed into a dynamic impulse for participation through word and action in the midst of a reality he desires to change.

A Theology of Sin for Today

The structures of oppression deepen, strengthen, and coordinate their action. Julio de Santa Ana affirms: "The present situation of the poor of the world is linked to the process which the modern world has been following since the thirteenth century." He then quotes Simonde de Sismondi, who wrote at the beginning of the nineteenth century:

> A gulf separates the salaried peon from any industrial, commercial or agricultural firm, and the lowest class has lost the hope which it still had in a previous period of civilization. . . . It can hardly maintain a sense of human dignity, love or freedom.

Indigenous America and later Latin America suffered the devastating impact of the structures of oppression. This is the reality in which we live today as believers in Jesus Christ.

As Methodists, we have a rich heritage, and as we go deeper into it, we discover an indispensable facet of our identity. It makes it impossible for us to accept the separation—so tragic—between the temporal and the spiritual, between the individual and the community, between the sacred and the secular. On the other hand, the incarnation of Jesus Christ—the revelation of God to humanity—forces us to see his work as integral and full.

The Bolivian Thesis of the Methodist church in that country affirms it this way:

> True evangelization is integral: the whole gospel for the whole person and for all persons. . . . We reject, therefore, all dichotomies, ancient and modern, which attempt to reduce the gospel to one dimension only or to fragment the human being created in the image and likeness of God. We do not accept it because it is insufficient, the notion that to evangelize is only "to save souls" . . . "to change the eternal status of the individual."

The document entitled "The Strategy of the Methodist Church of Argentina" expresses it in the following form:

> When we consider our goals and priorities we must keep visible the total reach of the term *liberation*. This expression embraces two inseparable concepts, indissoluble and interdependent: personal salvation and the redemption of society. A strategy which does not include in it, in integral form and with solidarity, both dimensions will be incorrect and vacillating. An adequate and relevant strategy must do away with the disjunction between the material and the spiritual, the individual and the social, the present life and the after life. Such

disjunctions are unfaithful to the gospel just as the individual cannot be separated from the community of which he/she is a part, or the spiritual life from the material or the Kingdom from its present significance.

The East Annual Conference of South America, of what was then the Methodist Episcopal Church, said the following in 1935:

The East Annual Conference of South America . . . reaffirms its faith in the democratic system of government, protests against every government which limits human rights, such as the freedom of speech, assembly, press and conscience, and energetically repudiates the trampling by any government on liberty and democracy. . . . It manifests its repudiation in the face of the errors and injustices which exist in the present economic system which permits misery in the presence of abundance and the exploitation of human by human, and expresses its firm purpose to struggle with each and every worthy means at its disposition to obtain a new state of affairs penetrated by the spirit of justice, cooperation and comradeship sustained by the Gospel of Christ . . . having as a base Christian principles which establish dignity, love and human cooperation. We declare:

1. The capitalist system is anti-christian and therefore should be replaced by a cooperative system which guarantees life in great abundance to all people.

2. To achieve this objective, it is necessary to arrive at the socialization of all sources of wealth, the means of production and of the means of transformation.

If we wish to find support in even earlier sources, it would be interesting to note, in the documents of what was then called "The Annual Conference of South America," the nineteenth-century interventions in favor of the abolition of slavery and its rejoicing when it occurred.

As a backdrop for these kinds of declarations in all of Latin American Methodism, we have the words of John Wesley: "Christianity is essentially a social religion, and to change it into a solitary religion is to destroy it."

It is not only interesting but indispensable to remember all of this, because it helps us deepen our roots in the context of structures of oppression and dependence, such as those affecting Latin America today. This deepening is indispensable to overcome the danger of the great contradiction that threatens us: our tradition comes to us from England through the United States; it was also from these same nations that colonialism and dependence came to us. Our Methodist tradition, and with it the knowledge of the liberating and redeeming gospel of Jesus Christ, came to us from those same countries from which also came the forces of money, military instruction, control of news, domination of the laws of commerce, exaltation of violence through the imposition of television, and cultural guidelines completely foreign to the gospel. All of this converted our societies into structures of oppression and domination.

In this historic tension, we should not have the slightest doubt about where our loyalty belongs. To honor it calls for responsibility to our brothers and sisters in those dominating countries. They also live in the midst of structures of oppression that oppose the liberating gospel of Jesus Christ. Our responsibility consists in making our contribution toward the common assumption of a commitment against such political and economic structures that in our countries produce dependence and domination. What is sought in England and the United States is the maintenance of the privileges of a totally unjust "order."

We must grow in our dialogue and reflection with our brothers and sisters of the North without forgetting those in other regions of the world—especially Africa and Asia—since the structures of oppression are not imposed on Latin America alone. The entire world is threatened by them.

Our Connectionalism

On this journey, we must redeem with seriousness the meaning and value of our "connectionalism"—a definitive principle especially of Methodist structural relations. Certainly connectionalism is not exhausted in its institutional meaning, but must be seen in the service of the liberation that Jesus Christ is bringing in every place. It is a connectionalism that speaks to us of our comradeship for service and for the good of the whole people and of all peoples. The rediscovery of the value of this connectionalism will permit us to become aware that in the midst of the many divisions that shake our continent, many of them programmed in detail by the forces of oppression, this comradeship is one method of struggling on behalf of the redemption of Latin America.

Let us not forget, on the other hand, that the power of money, the military, the control of the means of communication, and so forth, also work in a "connectional" form, that is, they mutually assist and complement each other.

In the face of this, our connectionalism should also be a "training" for a mature and broad ecumenism; for united work not only with others in the faith, but also with all those who profess no faith, but who are committed to the struggle for the dignity of life in all persons.

Our connectionalism has both a religious and a secular significance. It is not socially neutral. It is a struggle of life against death. Most important of all is the witness of the Scripture, which declares with total clarity that God also chose this path.

The biblical "signs of the times" as given in our continent are to be seen in the struggle of our peoples for their liberation from the sinful structures of domination and oppression. If our ministry as a Christian church, firmly founded in the gospel, does not place us with increasing solidarity on this path, we shall be negating not only our historic tradition, but also the Lordship of the One Who conquered sin and death.

Idols That Kill: In the "World" and the Church

JORGE PIXLEY   *(Baptist, Nicaragua)*

Biblical Idolatry

To define the theme of what in our Christian language is called "idolatry," we begin with a selection of biblical texts:

> Then God spoke all these words. He said, "I am Yahweh your God who brought you out of the land of Egypt, out of the house of slavery.
>
> "You shall have no gods except me.
>
> "You shall not make yourself a carved image or any likeness of anything in heaven or on earth beneath or in the waters under the earth; you shall not bow down to them or serve them. For I, Yahweh your God, am a jealous God and I punish the father's fault in the sons, the grandsons, and the great-grandsons of those who hate me; but I show kindness to thousands of those who love me and keep my commandments." (Exod. 20:1-6)[1]

> Do not turn to idols, and cast no gods of metal. I am Yahweh your God. (Lev. 19:4)

> If a prophet or a dreamer of dreams arises among you and offers to do a sign or a wonder for you, and the sign or wonder comes about; and if he then says to you, "Come, then, let us follow other gods (whom you have not known) and serve them," you are not to listen to the words of that prophet or to the dreams of that dreamer. Yahweh your God you shall follow, him shall you serve, to him shall you cling.

---

1. Scripture quotations in this chapter are from the Jerusalem Bible.

That prophet or that dreamer of dreams must be put to death, for he has preached apostasy from Yahweh your God who brought you out of the land of Egypt and redeemed you from the house of slavery, and he would have made you turn aside from the way that Yahweh your God marked out for you. You must banish this evil from among you." (Deut. 13:2-6)

Yahweh Sabaoth, the God of Israel says this: "Amend your behaviour and your actions and I will stay with you here in this place. Put no trust in delusive words like these: 'This is the sanctuary of Yahweh, the sanctuary of Yahweh, the sanctuary of Yahweh!' But if you do amend your behaviour and your actions, if you treat each other fairly, if you do not exploit the stranger, the orphan and the widow (if you do not shed innocent blood in this place), and if you do not follow alien gods, to your own ruin, then here in this place I will stay with you, in the land that long ago I gave to your fathers for ever. Yet here you are, trusting in delusive words, to no purpose! Steal, would you, murder, commit adultery, perjure yourselves, burn incense to Baal, follow alien gods that you do not know?—and then come presenting yourselves in this Temple that bears my name, saying: 'Now we are safe'—safe to go on committing all these abominations! Do you take this Temple that bears my name for a robbers' den? I, at any rate, am not blind—it is Yahweh who speaks. (Jer. 7:3-11)

The wood carver takes his measurements, outlines the image with chalk, carves it with chisels, following the outline with dividers. He shapes it to human proportions, and gives it a human face, for it to live in a temple. He cut down a cedar, or else took a cypress or an oak which he selected from the trees in the forest, or maybe he planted a cedar and the rain made it grow. For the common man it is so much fuel; he uses it to warm himself, he also burns it to bake his bread. But this fellow makes a god of it and worships it; he makes an idol of it and bows down before it. Half of it he burns in the fire, on the live embers he roasts meat, eats it and is replete. He warms himself too. "Ah!" says he "I am warm; I have a fire here!" With the rest he makes his god, his idol; he bows down before it and worships it and prays to it. "Save me," he says "because you are my god." (Isa. 44:13-17)

Assemble, come, gather together,
survivors of the nations.

They are ignorant, those who carry about
their idol of wood,
those who pray to a god
that cannot save.
Speak up, present your case,
consult with each other.
Who foretold this
and revealed it in the past?
Am I not Yahweh?
There is no other god besides me,
a God of integrity and a saviour;
there is none apart from me. (Isa. 45:20-21)

You cannot be the slave both of God and of money. (Luke 16:13)

We see, then, a number of similar phenomena included in the term *idolatry*. There are at least the following:

1. The worship of "other gods" rather than Yahweh who brought Israel out of slavery in Egypt.
2. The making of images as objects of worship, whether images of Yahweh (such as the golden calf in Exod. 32) or images of "other gods" whose worship is forbidden (such as that of Asherah, the queen mother, which Asa ordered burned in 1 Kings 15:13).
3. The worship, with the name of Yahweh, of another god who cannot save and who covers up the crimes of the governing powers.
4. The attribution, outside the religious sphere, of the power of life and death over human beings to a thing (such as money) that is not Yahweh and cannot save.

In the biblical text, idolatry is considered a serious offense, deserving of death. This is true even of making images, which would seem the most innocent of the four listed above. In this way the making of the golden calf at Sinai, which was nothing other than an image of Yahweh, caused the death of three thousand persons (Exod. 32:28). According to Jesus, to cling to money is sufficient cause for eternal death (Mark 10:17-27).

In Israel, the problem of idolatry was centered primarily in the struggle between Yahweh and Baal. In the time of Manasseh, a king of Judah, the worship of the stars was introduced in

Jerusalem. But his grandson, Josiah, succeeded without great difficulty in wiping out this worship, which the people perceived to be foreign. But Baal was something else. Baal was an autochthonous god tied to work in the field; so the god became attractive to the country people of Israel, as can be seen in the oracles of Hosea 2. Joash the Abiezrite of the tribe of Manasseh, a line that recognized Yahweh as their god, had a sanctuary of Baal on his property, apparently without seeing in this any contradiction. When Yahweh called Joash's son Gideon to free Israel, the first thing he did was to destroy his father's sanctuary to Baal (Judges 6:25-32).

To understand the hostility of biblical texts to these "other gods," we must examine the origins of the nation. Israel was founded as a peasant movement that rejected the king of Egypt as well as the autochthonous kings of Canaan. Yahweh was their king and they could not have human kings (Judges 8:22-23; 9; 1 Sam. 8:12).

The struggle between Yahweh and Baal was the ideological side of a class struggle. This explains the deep hostility between Yahweh and Baal. In play were the liberty and well-being of the country people. The story of Naboth's vineyard (1 Kings 21), stolen by the king and queen with the legality Baal conferred on them, is a good illustration of this struggle.

But the real danger of Baal was that his attraction was not limited to the royal house and state functionaries. For the country people, Baal represented the certainty of rain, so much so that the prophets, such as Elijah and Hosea, had to assure the people that Yahweh, the Liberator, was also capable of sending them rain.

The struggle between Yahweh and Baal was serious and cost many lives. But it appears that the worship of Baal did not survive beyond the Babylonian exile. The problem against which Isaiah, Jeremiah, and Jesus struggled was deeper and more permanent, that is, the false worship of Yahweh that gave legitimacy to domination in the name of Yahweh.

Solomon is the best representative of this kind of idolatry. By the luxury and splendor of his religiosity, he succeeded in persuading many that his worship of Yahweh was authentic. Even some of the biblical authors (such as the Chronicler) came to believe it.

In a monotheistic culture such as ours, this last kind of idolatry is the most notorious. Nobody believes in a multiplicity of gods anymore, so the question about God is reduced to what or who is the only true God. A President Reagan in the U.S., or a General Rios Montt in Guatemala, practices, in the name of "God," the assassination of those who try to create a just society. In using the generic name, "God," they believe and try to make others believe that they are referring to the God of biblical tradition, who is accepted in our culture as the only existent god.

Our effort as Protestants within this context has to be to demonstrate that the god of Mr. Reagan and General Montt is not the God who brought Israel out of Egypt nor the God who was incarnated as the Son of Mary, born in a stable, with no place to lay his head, who died on a cross as a subversive. That should not be so difficult.

Equally important in our time, even more so than in biblical times, is the idolatry that is not religious but confers on an object that is nothing more than the work of human hands and minds the power of life and death over men and women of flesh and blood. This is what Jesus denounced when he said that it is impossible to serve God, the Yahweh who took Israel out of slavery, and money, today's secular version of Baal. The secularization of our culture is even deeper than that of the culture Jesus knew. The idols of the oppressors only occasionally take on a religious appearance.

Idols That Kill in the "World"

This general introduction to the broad field of idolatry brings us to the theme to be developed here: the idols that kill. First we will deal with idols which are neither created nor disseminated in the religious sphere. Then we will examine the nature of all idols to kill their worshippers. Finally, we must analyze the kind of spirituality that gives the idol an aura of sanctity by tying it to the religious tradition of the culture.

I believe that the gods of the oppressors in our time are only two: capital and military might. They are strongly interrelated. Ours is a theological analysis of these idols, although there are many other aspects that will not come within the focus of our intention here.

From the theological point of view, what is important is that these idols kill by intrinsic necessity, while their capacity to give life is limited and capricious. For theological analysis it is also important to point out that these gods enjoy a relative autonomy, even in relation to persons who benefit from their existence. In other words, not even the oppressors themselves are capable of freely manipulating these gods, which impose their own demands and do not respond to a logic of human needs.

Karl Marx made a masterful theological analysis of capital when he called it a fetish. He apparently did not take the term from the Bible, but from anthropology. I will cite two brief quotations from *Das Kapital:*

> Just as in religion man is dominated by the product of his mind, in capitalist production he is dominated by the product of his hands.

> Through the conversion of the worker into an automaton, the instrument of labor appears during the process of labor itself as capital, that is, as dead labor which dominates and sucks life out of live labor.[2]

We are unable to analyze completely the process by which this god is formed by human labor. Marx did this by pointing out the progressive steps from the fetishism of the merchandise to the fetishism of money to the fetishism of capital. Rather, we will examine the finished form in which it exercises the power of life and death over its creators. Capital is accumulated labor, materialized in a combination of money, raw materials, labor force, merchandise, deposits, trucks, and so forth, which have an imperious need to be in constant movement and to return periodically to the form of money in order to ratify their continuous increase in value.

Live labor is indispensable to the circulation of capital in its various forms, for without it the circulation of capital would cease. There would be no accumulation of surplus value,

2. Karl Marx, *Das Kapital* (Berlin: Gustav Kiepenhauer Verlag, 1932), pp. 571-72, 404.

and thus capital would collapse and disappear. In other words, capital is dead labor that lives from live labor and dies in the moment it no longer has its quota of live labor. This is its secret. This idol cannot live without squeezing the life out of human beings.

The deadly nature of capital is seen with greater clarity in its periods of crisis, which repeat themselves with a certain regularity. There are moments of deceleration of the circulation of capital due to its necessity for repositioning, so that once again it can accelerate its accumulation. In these periods factories are closed, constructions are paralyzed, creditors demand payment from debtors, workers are laid off as production goes down, taxes go up, and services of social assistance diminish.

In these moments of threatened collapse, capital demands human suffering for its own revitalization. When the new cycle begins, some of the workers are declared superfluous, condemned to die of starvation unless they are able to find support among parents or friends who have succeeded in keeping their jobs. Others die from illness because high prices deprive them of health services. Children and the aged suffer the most from the sacrifices the idol demands in order to revive itself. It is an idol precisely because, being a creation of human hands, it survives by demanding human sacrifices.

The spiritual halo that surrounds this idol is freedom. In periods of crisis, capital needs the freedom of prices for the benefit of those in commerce; the freedom of the work force (break the unions) so management can reduce benefits to the workers and lay off superfluous workers; freedom from regulation so the less efficient industries will go broke and leave their clients to the more efficient industries. These liberties have corresponding freedoms at the level of ordinary people: the freedom to look for the most enjoyable employment and to buy the merchandise of their preference.

This idol is presented as one who offers freedom. It is not capable of guaranteeing the satisfaction of basic necessities. It will satisfy the needs, even the whims, only of those who have money. For those who do not have purchasing power, the life of this idol demands sacrifice and in many cases death.

Through more than two centuries, the capacity of the defenders of the idol to link it to the Christian tradition has been perfected. The churches and their pastors are not immune to this fascination with money and capital, and with frightening ease serve as ideologues of the idol, forgetting the preference of the gospel for the poor.

The Protestant system of churches, made up exclusively of believers, has at this point the advantage of being able to exclude, without great difficulty and without its being apparent, the failures of society. The congregation, made up of those who have employment and enjoy the advantages of solvent consumption, have no problem giving themselves over to this god who kills, since those he kills are the others, who in any case are seen as unbelievers.

The other idol of the oppressors is military might. From time immemorial the armed forces have existed to protect against external enemies and internal antisocial elements. Just as human beings create mercantile interchange to satisfy vital necessities, the army is created to defend them from aggressions that are always expected. It happens that in this case, as in the previous one, the instrument acquires autonomy and demands sacrifices of its creator. Let us listen to Isaiah and Habakkuk:

> Woe to Assyria, the rod of my anger,
> the club brandished by me in my fury!
> I sent him against a godless nation;
> I gave him commission against a people that provokes me,
> to pillage and to plunder freely
> and to stamp down like the mud in the streets.
> But he did not intend this,
> his heart did not plan it so.
> No, in his heart was to destroy,
> to go on cutting nations to pieces without limit. . . .
> "By the strength of my own arm I have done this
> and by my own intelligence, for understanding is mine;
> I have pushed back the frontiers of people
> and plundered their treasures.
> I have brought their inhabitants down to the dust.
> As if they were a bird's nest, my hand has seized
> the riches of the peoples.
> As people pick up deserted eggs
> I have picked up the whole earth,
> with not a wing fluttering,

not a beak opening, not a chirp.
Does the axe claim more credit than the man who wields it,
or the saw more strength than the man who handles it?
It would be like the cudgel controlling the man who
    raises it,
or the club moving what is not made of wood!"
                                        (Isa. 10:5-7, 13-15)

You treat mankind like fishes in the sea,
like creeping, masterless things.

A people, these, who catch all on their hook,
who draw them with their net,
in their dragnet gather them,
and so, triumphantly, rejoice.

At this, they offer a sacrifice to their net,
and burn incense to their dragnet,
for providing them with luxury
and lavish food.

Are they then to empty their net unceasingly,
slaughtering nations without pity?
                                        (Hab. 1:14-17)

As far as I know, there is no theological analysis of the
armed forces such as Marx made of capital. The question does
not, however, seem to be so difficult. Continuity between the
modern army and its antecedents is greater than in the case of
economics. All armies—ancient and modern—are created to
kill, even when they do it for the best of reasons. The guardians
of Plato's Republic were to be trained like dogs, to be docile with
those of the household and ferocious with strangers. However,
as Plato's armies acquired a certain autonomy, their interests
began to demand of "those of the household" enormous quotas
of work for increasingly sophisticated and numerous armaments. They came to demand of "strangers" quotas of blood so
they might learn to use their new arms well.

When any military force is not given the equipment it
thinks it needs and the guarantees it considers necessary for its
monopoly on violence, it seizes power and submits the population to an excessive use of force as, for example, in Guatemala

and Chile. The armed forces always want wars, big enough to prove their capabilities but not so big as to threaten their existence and honor. For this reason the army of the United States provokes wars, which it thinks it can win, in Central America and the Caribbean. In countries such as the United States and Chile, the economic demands of the armed forces call for an enormous exploitation of the work force. Wherever there are armed forces of such magnitude, the diplomacy of the society finds itself under obligation to respond to its needs through the manipulation of the economy and other aspects of public administration.

The armed forces also have their spiritual halo, more necessary even than it is for capital, since the benefits they offer are not as evident. In our times, the ideological strength of armies rests principally on the so-called defense of democracy. The United States invaded Granada "to defend" the Antilles democracies against the Cuban-Soviet threat that would spread from that island. In Central America the spiritual defense of the army became a little more complicated: artificial democracies have to be fabricated in order to have allies. The ideology of the armed forces is supported by the spirituality of liberty.

The autonomy of this idol can be clearly seen in Chile, where the armed forces, perceiving that their monopoly of violence was threatened, crushed the legal democracy. They said that although the government of Popular Unity had not violated the letter of the constitution, it had violated its spirit. With this they were doubtless referring to the possibility of a democratic transition to a noncapitalist society.

It is necessary to look more closely at the pernicious character of these worldly idols that kill. Tens of thousands of persons, the majority of whom are children, die every day from hunger and exhaustion, fundamentally because there is no place for them in the cycle of capital as solvent consumers. This fact alone is sufficient to convince us that it is not enough to unmask the idol of capital. We must combat it. The logic of the arms race, seen in its maximum expression in the nuclear competition between the United States and the Soviet Union, has in it the potential to destroy all life on the globe (not to mention the hundreds of lives lost every week in the limited wars it provokes).

Of course, there are a number of ways to combat these

death-dealing forces of the idols. The Cuban Communist Party combats capitalism in the name of the "new man," with a planned economy toward the satisfaction of the basic needs of everyone. The Sandinista revolution does it by taking up again the Christian tradition that celebrates the God of life, and, through a mixed economy, plans to satisfy the basic necessities of the majority without eliminating free competition. The struggle against the arms race takes place through complex international understandings such as the efforts of the Contadora Group in Central America and in the liberal democracy of Raúl Afonsin in Argentina.

It seems to me that we should not reject any of these efforts to destroy or limit the death-dealing forces of these powerful idols. Nevertheless, while cooperating with all these efforts, we Christians naturally will be guided by the God of the Bible who desires the life of the sinner and not his death. This God shows us in Jesus Christ the way of salvation, which consists in solidarity with the poorest: "Remember how generous the Lord Jesus was: he was rich, but he became poor for your sake, to make you rich out of his poverty" (2 Cor. 8:9).

The Ten Commandments and many other biblical texts forbid us to accept idols, because sooner or later the idol demands its quota of blood to continue its own life. The God of the Bible, on the other hand, gives God's own life that all may live.

Idols That Kill in the Churches

The most dangerous idols are not religious idols but those of the world, which we have just examined. It is not unusual for the churches to lend themselves to the legitimization of these worldly idols. We can see this very openly in the case of General Rios Montt in Guatemala. The phenomenon is also notorious in the churches of the United States and Chile. These cases are nothing more than religious manifestations of idols that were neither created by the churches nor have their vitality from within the churches.

But there are also religious idols, that is, those whose natural environment is within the churches. Since the French Revolution, however, political liberalism has achieved such broad success that the churches no longer have the power they had in traditional societies. They have been pushed out of public life and into the private sector. With the churches' loss of power they also lost some of their ability to create and destroy idols.

It was not always this way. For Jeremiah and for Jesus, the most dangerous and deadly idolatry was that practiced in the temple in Jerusalem. The situation in Jesus' day is especially enlightening. He lived in Palestine in a time of open domination by an army that lived from the destruction of people. There was a religious sect called the Zealots, which fought against the idolatry of these Roman legions. Significantly, Jesus did not condemn them; they did a good work. But in his view the idolatry practiced in the temple was more deadly than that of the Roman army. There the people worshiped a legislator God who demanded obedience, tithes, and control of the lives of Palestinians. Let us look at a typical confrontation of Jesus with this idol:

> He went again into the synagogue, and there was a man there who had a withered hand. And they were watching him to see if he would cure him on the sabbath day, hoping for something to use against him. He said to the man with the withered hand, "Stand up out in the middle!" Then he said to them, "Is it against the law on the sabbath day to do good, or to do evil; to save life, or to kill?" But they said nothing. Then, grieved to find them so obstinate, he looked angrily round at them, and said to the man, "Stretch out your hand." He stretched it out and his hand was better. The Pharisees went out and at once began to plot with the Herodians against him, discussing how to destroy him. (Mark 3:1-6)

Jesus' attacks on the temple followed the line of Jeremiah. Quoting the prophet's statement about the transformation of the temple into a den of thieves, he condemned the temple for serving as the religious legitimization of thieves, assassins, and adulterers. But Jesus added another target to his attacks in addition to those of Jeremiah. He particularly accuses the Pharisees of laying unbearable burdens on the people and of taking advantage of their piety to grab privileges and offerings from innocent people. With this they hid the more important things that the God of Israel wished, those that contributed to the life of his people. The idol which religion created had lived off the sacrifices it imposed, taking advantage of the guilt feelings of the people.

In a society such as that of Palestine, in which religion gave national identity to the people, substitution of an idol for the biblical God of salvation was a very serious thing. The presence of the Roman army, and the temptation to serve in it, a temptation to which many young men succumbed, was doubtless serious also. At this stage it is not possible for us to form an objective judgment as to whether the Zealots or Jesus were right in their respective assessments of the danger these two idols represented. Jesus did not see them as mutually exclusive. His attack on the Pharisees and the temple was in contrast to his passivity toward the struggle of the Zealots against the military forces.

It is my impression that the most deadly of idols worshiped in our churches is that same god who was created by forces outside the churches: money or capital, although the principal ambit of this god is not the religious milieu. In addition, the idol of the armed forces also has a certain place within our churches.

If we look for idols that are very specially our own, I believe foremost is the same one against which Jesus struggled: the god of law. If the Sabbath was the touchstone for the idolaters Jesus faced, for us it is other laws.

The legislator idol focuses its commandments on the plane of personal morality with the prohibition of drinking, smoking, and dancing. It lives by the repression of the vitality of the faithful. Or, at times, it expresses itself through the orthodoxies of each church. In the case of the Baptist church, the law has to do with the strict observance of closed communion and baptism by immersion. Pastors can lose their pulpits if they raise questions about these doctrines, even when they do it with the Bible in their hands. With Lutherans, it is individual guilt before God, to be assuaged only by the grace of God received through faith, which is made the principal problem for all Christians. For certain Pentecostals, charismatics, and similar churches, it has to do with the obligatory nature of the gift of tongues as the demonstration of the Holy Spirit in the life of the believer. All of these laws are manifestations of the idol that lives through the imposition of repressive standards on the life of human beings.

Even though this idol may not have the deadly power of

capital or of the armed forces, within the circle of faithful Protestants it is the cause of enormous anguish for many. It causes serious problems of conscience for those who rebel against it in the name of the God of the Bible, or simply in the name of human liberty. For many, this has come to mean painful separation from their brothers and sisters, and for those of us who are pastors, at times it means living with a heavy conscience when privately we do not obey the standards our churches profess. At other times it means losing the job for which we have prepared ourselves through many years of our youth. The ordination examinations in some denominations, including my own, are usually acts of forced submission to this idol.

The principal remedy for the idolatry that gives tribute to the idols in the church is Bible study. In the Bible we discover the prophets and Jesus struggling against the same idols that dominate many of our churches. I have been a Bible teacher for more than twenty years and I am convinced of this. I passed the first twelve years of my teaching career in fighting within the church against the idol that gives ecclesial power to the most hypocritical and least human persons. It is an important struggle.

I have spent recent years fighting against secular idols that kill. This is an even more important struggle. The theological formation we receive in the church is an important weapon for this struggle. But it must be joined by the instruments of social science by means of which the deadly dynamics of idolatry are revealed. Only theological analysis can explain the global pretension of idols. The biblical prophets, including Jesus, are our guides.

The Power of Nudity

ELSA TAMEZ   (Methodist, Costa Rica)

I am going to tell you the story of the birth of Ce Acatl Topiltzin, the famous priest of Quetzalcóatl, god of life, who was later known by the name of this same god: Quetzalcóatl.[1]

According to the Toltec legend, there was a man called Mixcóatl, great chief of the Toltecs. He was a warrior, a man of extraordinary strength. When he settled in Culhuacán and established his capital there, he decided to conquer neighboring peoples. He conquered Morelos, Toluca, Teotlalpan, and others.

The legend says that once during the conquest of Morelos a beautiful woman named Chimalman, who was not a Toltec, appeared to him. When the young woman saw him, she "put her shield on the ground, laid aside her bow and arrow, and stood before him without petticoat and dress." Mixcóatl, confused by the appearance of the woman and her unexpected nakedness, shot his arrows at her: "the first passed over her as she simply leaned over; the second went behind her, bending its shaft; the third, she caught in her hand; and the fourth, she caught between her legs." The great warrior chief, surprised, did not know what to do. He retreated to fortify himself with more arrows.

In the meanwhile, Chimalman fled and hid herself "in the cave of a great cliff." Mixcóatl wanted to see her again. He went to look for her, but did not find her. Then he became angry and began to mistreat the women of Cuernavaca. When these women could no longer bear his mistreatment they said, "Let us go look for her." They found Chimalman and told her, "Mixcóatl is searching for you, and because of you he is mistreating your little sisters."

1. We have taken this story out of the book of Ignacio Bernal entitled *Tenochtitlán en una isla* (Mexico: Fondo de Cultura Económica, SEP, 1984), pp. 84-86.

When she heard this, Chimalman went to meet Mixcóatl. When she saw him, she stripped her clothes off again and placed her clothing and arrows on the ground. Again Mixcóatl attacked her with his arrows, with no result. After this there was nothing left except to couple with her. There they conceived Quetzalcóatl, who is considered the founder of one of the most esteemed cultures of the New World: the Toltec.

This beautiful story, raised to the level of extended metaphor and reread, theologically, from the present situation of the Latin American woman, offers us a plan to recapitulate the present experiences of women actively engaged in theology.

We strip ourselves, then confront and stop various "arrows" shot at woman in our macho society. We look for ways to contribute to the birth of the baby Jesus among us Latin Americans: the Son, whose Father, the God of life, is consecrated to the salvation of the world, the liberation of men and women, and the building of a new way to live in justice, love, peace, and freedom.

Quetzalcóatl and Jesus Christ join hands in an alliance against the gods of war and of the money that produces injustice, and against the gods who demand human sacrifice: against Molok, Mammon, and Huitzilopostli.

Mixcóatl and Nudity

The figure of Mixcóatl, the warrior, can embody a number of negative attitudes toward woman. This can be said of the macho society of Latin America at the socioeconomic, political, ideological, and cultural levels; also included is the male domination of the church and theology—theological education, bibliographical resources, and the topics of theological discourse.

Mixcóatl would embody these instances since the figure of the warrior is woven with peculiarly masculine *stereotypes*. We emphasize the word *stereotype*, because it does not necessarily represent what is and ought to be the male being. Rather, it is popular opinion that characterizes the figure of the man. So Mixcóatl is the powerful warrior, dominator, chief, to whom beautiful women must be brought for his sexual satisfaction.

Female theologians in Latin America are making remarkable advances in their awareness and articulation of such themes as violence against woman (Betty Salomón and Lucia Villagrán), sexual violence, unfavorable working conditions (Mabel Filippini), and others. Cora Ferro traces the low concept of the woman operative in the church. Araceli Rochetti writes of the "internal debt" of Protestantism to women. Maria José Rosado emphasizes the important role of nuns and their difficulties as women in the pastoral. Graciela Uribe also deals with this theme. Alida Verhoeven rejects the language, imagery, and symbolism that excludes women, youth, the poor, and those of other races and other skin colors.[2]

The arrows shot at the woman are those we traditionally know as discrimination, submission, oppression, and violence— arrows directed with greatest accuracy against the poor woman.

Mixcóatl and the Theological Discourse

If we look at the themes that gather around the great warrior, we are able to make the connection between him and the traditional theological discourse.

If Mixcóatl has succeeded in imposing his power on other people, the traditional theological discourse has also shown an impositional spirit on all spheres of life. We can see this from a number of angles, such as in a spiritualized, abstract vision of the world. Separating concrete life and the daily experience of God from the theological discourse results in the dangerous dichotomy of the transcendent and the concrete, the material and the spiritual, the body and the soul. It is a concept of the world that has been prejudicial to woman, as Maria Clara Bingemer has explained so well in her chapter.[3]

The theology of liberation points to another way. Its methodology takes its starting point simultaneously in the praxis of liberation from the context of oppression and in the experience of God and the life of faith.

2. See *El Rostro Femenino de la Teología* (San José: DEI, 1986); and *La mujer en la construcción de la iglesia: una perspective bautista desde América Latina y el Caribe* (San José: DEI, 1986).
3. See "The Trinity from the Perspective of the Woman," p. 116 herein.

Women welcome this way of doing theology. To begin with the concrete is to begin with the daily relationship of man and woman. As a rule, traditional theology, if it touches daily reality at all, does so to apply what it has already thought, either to spiritualize or to marginalize it. The theology of liberation, from the perspective of woman, not only touches the daily reality but also makes us a part of the theological agenda as participant.

Therefore we affirm that the starting point of theology should be not only praxis on behalf of justice and the experience of God but also "the praxis of tenderness." That is, relationships between man, woman, aged, young, children, and all persons should be caring ones. The praxis of tenderness is lived out in daily reality. In this way, the theological horizons open to make place for other views, such as that of woman.

We say that the point of view of traditional theology is impositional, because it is often presented as the only way to see the world. If other ways of "speaking of God"[4] are suggested, they are rejected, as happens in our continent.

Fortunately, in recent years other ways of speaking of God have appeared, besides the theology of liberation, such as Asian, African, black, and feminist theologies. The women of Latin America welcome these theologies, but we especially welcome the Latin American theology of liberation as our theology, while we add to it the perspective of the woman.

One impositional aspect of Western thought, not only in theology but in general, is its logocentrism. It believes the only, or at least the best, way of speaking of reality is rational discourse, or in other words, Western systematic logic. It rejects as not very serious, or as secondary, a number of other ways of expressing real life: poetry, plays, painting, and others. Among women theologians, there is a search for new epistemological possibilities.

Let us return to the story. Mixcóatl is dedicated to war, so his daily relations are with his fellow soldiers (men). His horizon is always the same. His way of experiencing life is ruled by

---

4. A phrase of Gustavo Gutiérrez in his book *On Job: God-Talk and the Suffering of the Innocent,* trans. Matthew O'Connell (Maryknoll, N.Y.: Orbis, 1987).

one rhythm alone. This unilateral relationship leads him to see things in only one way. That which is, is that which should be. Mixcóatl needs other horizons, just as our theological companions need new accents to enrich them.

In response to the claims of forgotten sectors of the marginalized, the theology of liberation, because it is situated in a given place and time, considers history as one of its axes. It opens new horizons by the renewing incorporation of other subjects in its theological agenda, such as women, the indigenous, and the blacks of Latin America. The theological perspective is broadened because they are added not only as themes but as theologians (*teólogos* and *teólogas*).

Mixcóatl has values to be not despised, but accepted. He is courageous, able to bear the hardships of battle or the burning sun of the plains. He is not easily frightened and knows how to face other warriors. He is combative, but in some moments can be compassionate with his fallen companions.

In the same way, women need a combative and militant theology, that is, one which lays bare from their roots the causes of marginalization, from a biblical and theological perspective. So woman must demand with vehemence the right to be a creature in the image and likeness of God. She must reject the authority of all biblical readings that try to show her inferiority as the will of God. She must struggle to point out new hermeneutical guidelines, upon which a liberating biblical reading can be elaborated.

The difference between the combativeness of Mixcóatl and of women is that the former had as his purpose the enslavement and conquest of others. The combativeness of women is employed in the search for justice, with the victims themselves as protagonist. The great chief represents the dominators. His war-making has as its purpose the subjugation of others. This is why traditional theological discourse is impositional and monolithic.

Chimalman also had arrows, but she did not shoot them against the man, as Mixcóatl did against the woman. Her armaments are those of denunciation. Here is a new way of being woman or being man, and consequently of being companions before God and other persons.

Chimalman Faces Her Nudity

The word *Chimalman* means "hand-shield" (shielded by her bare hand). Chimalman was not called Chimalman before her encounter with Mixcóatl. The name was given to her later because of her unheard-of action of catching the arrows Mixcóatl hurled at her. Before this event, Chimalman did not have a name. She was an unknown woman, no-Toltec, and therefore, no-Chimalman. She had to appear in history, by stripping herself and facing the arrows of Mixcóatl, to be able to have the name, to call herself Chimalman.

Chimalman had beauty (covered by clothes), youth, and arrows, but she did not have a name. This is a curious thing: she existed and did not exist at the same time. She was alone with her beauty, her youth, and her arrows; hidden, ignored, silenced by history. She was always the absent one among the present or always present but invisible.

In the story we learn what it is to be Chimalman, but we don't know exactly what it was to have been no-Chimalman. We may elevate her and admire her for her beauty and youth, or abase her in a vulgar or immoral manner. There is a cloudiness that makes it difficult to define a no-Chimalman.

What does it mean to be woman? This is one of the central questions of theology today, theology from the perspective of woman. We must try to discover her identity, her experience of God, and her manner of the daily living of her religiosity. Carmen Lora and Cecilia Barbechea provide presentations about the identity of woman from the viewpoint of her sexuality; Consuelo del Prado, in "I Feel God in Another Way," shares woman's spirituality, a theme also taken up by Beatriz Arellano from the present Nicaraguan reality. Consuelo Lapiedra speaks of popular religiosity in the daily experience of the Andean woman, and Teresa Porcile has written of the right to beauty in Latin America from the perspective of woman.[5]

Each of these women theologians has a fundamental concern for the meaning of being woman, something extremely difficult to define because the imposed stereotypes are interwoven with the special longings of the women we want to be.

---

5. Cf. *El Rostro Femenino de la Teologia*.

We reject the macho ideology of our society, with all its access to the means of communication, which defines our feminine identity. But we cannot stop with the cloudiness of being no-Chimalman. Our identity must be given a name, not in the sense of exclusive feminist qualities, but in the discovery of nuances more predominant in the woman.

To have a name and enter history, no-Chimalman, the woman no-Toltec, needed an encounter with Mixcóatl. Alone she could not do it, nor could she alone give birth to a culture in which she was also a participant. In the confrontation she had to be the "hand-shield," that is, she had to be able to face the warrior's attacks, to stop his arrows, to break them. Chimalman did not attack the warrior. She put her arrows on the ground. Above all, she invited Mixcóatl to nakedness also, that is to say, to know himself, to share himself on a level of equality with her.

Our intention is not to eliminate our male companions, nor to wipe out present theological discourse. Our struggle, which should be vehement, is against male-dominated theology, whose victims are men as well as women. We are against all oppressive warrior systems that lead to the death of thousands, especially among the poor. Our concern is to join the feminist movement to the popular movement, as stated by Itziar Lozano and Maruja Gonzalez.[6] On the theological level, our intention is to recreate Latin American theology with a deep perspective of "the woman-shield," and to invite our male theological companions to intercourse with us and this theology.

Chimalman's first attempt was timid, because when Mixcóatl fled, she also ran away and hid in "the cave of a great cliff." Mixcóatl's confusion and his desire to find her again proved to be a calamity for "the little women," as he began to mistreat them. This negative fact, however, led to the solidarity and organization of the women of Cuernavaca, when they decided to go looking for Chimalman. In face of the demands of these women, Chimalman had to return and face Mixcóatl, leaving her hiding place forever.

Many Latin American women know that when they take their first step to join history and to be protagonists, they cannot turn back. They lose the ground on which they had stood, and

6. Cf. *El Rostro Femenino de la Teologia.*

187

more. The popular movement of women is moving forward, though slowly, as Rosario Saavedra has shown.[7] We are in search of a name. We want to pass from the invisible to the visible, from object to subject, from no-Chimalman to Chimalman.

The Strength of Nudity

Chimalman was given this name after she had dared to come out to meet Mixcóatl, with the courage to strip herself before him, and the ability to stop the chief's arrows. Her behavior was wise and without precedent: highly symbolic.

What set things in motion was her daring to be naked. The power she acquired in this act was such that it surprised, confused, and disturbed the hostile force, made it withdraw, and later return.

On the other hand, it can be said symbolically that this free initiative of the young woman gave her strength to face the darts of the man. It presented an energetic and exquisite invitation to come back and start over. Let us look at some of the courageous aspects of Chimalman and of Latin American women today.

In the first place, this beautiful woman appears on the road in the midst of a difficult era: Mixcóatl and his people are founding an empire. They have recently settled in Culhuacán and begun the conquest and domination of other neighboring peoples. Mixcóatl meets her on his way to take Morelos. She is courageous and adventuresome to appear in this violent situation. She is not a Toltec, as the dominator is. So her valor is even greater. She has two weapons: arrows and nudity; both are important. The arrows are to be shot to protect herself from those who want to strip and violate her (or torture her, as is done by our repressive governments). Her nudity—keeping to the symbolism—is used to know her own self and to invite the other also to nakedness. This means to lay aside all his privileged tradition, which society had given to him as the great chief, so he may also know himself as man. Woman and man on the level of equality may give birth in justice, love, peace, and pleasure

7. Cf. *El Rostro Femenino de la Teologia.*

to a new culture under the benediction of the god of life: Quetzalcóatl.

Faced with the naked woman, Mixcóatl's attitude is one of confusion, perhaps mixed with fascination: he feels threatened. He does not know what to do. The first thing that comes to his mind is to attack her, in other words, to behave according to his warlike and impositional customs. He is even more confused when Chimalman is not wounded because her magical speed stops his arrows. Confused by the nudity and bothered by the defense, Mixcóatl is disarmed. On this first occasion, his response is to retreat. At this point he is not capable of nakedness. This is one of the most difficult steps. It implies a new birth, but also the death of an old way of living. It takes time and many confrontations. So Mixcóatl and Chimalman meet again and repeat the previous scene.

Women of Latin America today share their experience in becoming aware of many things: of themselves as women, of pleasant discoveries, and of difficulties with their male companions. Nakedness means laying aside the "clothing" that society, the church, and theology have designed for women—clothing made at the will and convenience of the male-dominated ideology that permeates all of our institutions, as well as the mentality of many men.

Collaboration with other women in the base community, in the church, and in popular movements encourages us also to achieve "nakedness." For example, Mercedes Pereira has pastoral experience with peasant women, and Amparo Ferrer tells of the creative practice of women in feeding programs for children in Peru. Ivone Gebara, Beatriz Melano Couch, Maria Tereza Cavalcanti, and Leonor Aida Concha show us how women speak of God, the kingdom, the Bible, and Mary the Mother of Jesus as a woman of the people.[8]

Their attitude is similar to that of Chimalman, the woman-shield. We lay on the ground the weapons that injure us. We strip off our imposed clothing. We seek to recreate a theological discourse beginning with our daily experience of discrimination and liberation, and our own special way of experiencing God.

8. Cf. *El Rostro Femenino de la Teologia.*

Liturgy and worship are the food that reinforces us on the road on which "we have dared to appear." It is a hard road, a cruel moment in the male-dominated capitalist system, but at the same time it is very stimulating because a growing number of women are taking it. We journey out of the joy of finding ourselves as women, concerned about the lack of justice and peace in our continent. We are women who have committed ourselves to the struggle for the realization of the kingdom of God.

Nudity That Recreates History

Mixcóatl and Chimalman couple after two meetings. The same day they conceive their son, Ce Actl Topiltzin. A short time later, before the birth of his son, Mixcóatl is assassinated by one of his captains. Chimalman takes refuge in her native land. A usurper takes Culhuacán, and Chimalman dies giving birth to her son.

The child is born and grows in exile and is cared for by his maternal grandparents. There he assimilates a maternal culture and accepts the creed of his mother: devotion to the god Quetzalcóatl. He serves as priest and assumes the same name, according to the indigenous tradition.

Years later, when he is already using the name Quetzalcóatl, a group of people call him to retake the leadership of his father's people. The young Quetzalcóatl comes back to Culhuacán and overthrows the usurper. He then moves the capital to Tula and initiates a new way of life, founding the much-appreciated Toltec culture. He introduces such benefits of the maternal civilization as the god Quetzalcóatl, the most caring god of ancient indigenous culture. Over the years myths began to gather around his history. It was said he was cultured, the inventor of all benefits the world enjoyed. It was said that he gave corn to the human race. He stole the corn in the kingdom of the dead from the old god of the inferno. He was the father of agriculture, the ritual calendar, scriptures, astronomy, medicine, and so forth.[9] There was abundance for everyone; the narrative says they "were very rich and lacked nothing, there was neither

9. Bernal, *Tenochtitlán en una isla*, p. 90.

hunger nor lack of corn, they did not eat the smaller ears of corn, but used them as fuel to heat the bath water."[10]

So, then, Chimalman invites Mixcóatl to become naked also, and if he accepts, this means a reinventing of history. In other words, to lay down arms along with the clothes conditioned by society is to inaugurate a new way to live. It is to fecundate history with new life.

Unfortunately, this practice is so risky it can be fatal. Mixcóatl is assassinated by his society because of others' ambition to power. Chimalman dies in childbirth. Both die: one killed by the knife, the other to give life. But both make possible Quetzalcóatl, so he may live and recreate history. On a symbolic and on the real level, life generally comes after death and always in tension with it. The fifth Sun appeared with Quetzalcóatl, representing the new humanity, according to the legend. They are the perfect people who possess, thanks to the god Quetzalcóatl, the perfect food, corn.

It must be remembered that without the appearance of Chimalman, Toltec history would have been very different, for they would have continued to follow the semibarbaric hordes of Jalisco or Zacatecas. Topilzin, born of Chimalman and Mixcóatl, reinvented history because of the vision of the world he inherited from the maternal region.

Latin American women along with our male companions want to recreate cultural, ecclesiastical, and theological history. We want to cultivate with new hands, new seeds, new care, and new weapons. We want to produce new fruits: new daily relationships, new ways to practice faith in the church, and new theological discourse. In short, we want to lead to the dawning of "the sixth Sun" with the help of our Lord Jesus Christ. As men and women together we want to cure the "open wounds of Latin America."

There are always dangers in this. Quetzalcóatl is born and raised in exile, suffers pain, first from the death of his father and later from those who worship other gods, who demand human sacrifice. In the same way, our Latin American theology is born and raised under the gaze of hostile forces that resist the

---

10. Bernal, *Tenochtitlán en una isla*, p. 91.

procreation of this new history, culture, and society for which we long.

One of the great gifts of the priest Quetzalcóatl is precisely his propagation of the faith of the god Quetzalcóatl, god of life, creator of men and women with his own blood, according to the legend. What kind of god is this? A god who takes the form of an ant to enter Tonacatéptl and steal a grain of corn in order to give it to human beings so they may eat and live. A friendly god who teaches his creatures to sow this seed corn, to carve jade, to build houses. A god who voluntarily dies along with other companions so that men and women, aged and young, may have living and breathing space. It is a god who rejects human sacrifice, who struggles against other gods and priests who need human blood for their survival.

This god of the indigenous Mexican culture is the one who enters into coalition with our God of the Bible—the God of life, our creator and liberator, who through the Son, Jesus Christ, (incarnate in history, dead and risen to give abundant life) shows us the way to follow in the task of recreating history and culture, to make his kingdom visible. It is a coalition of Jesus and Quetzalcóatl—both born in exile, persecuted by enemies, loving humanity, entering into an alliance against strange gods who enslave men and women, such as Mammon the god of riches, or the gods who demand human sacrifice, such as Huizilopostli, God of the Aztecs and Molok, deity of the Ammonites.

All of these gods are still alive today, incarnate in our system. Therefore, the struggle of the gods continues. So does the human struggle.

PART II
THE ORIGINAL LEGACY—
DISTORTIONS IN ITS TRANSMISSION

Luther, the Reformation, and Liberation

LEONARDO BOFF *(Catholic, Brazil)*

Relevance and Limitations of the Theme

We begin with the theology of liberation as the horizon from which we will interrogate Martin Luther and the historic movement generated by the Reformation. To what degree does Luther contribute to the understanding of our situation of oppression and support the efforts of the poor? His message continues to demand a hearing despite the fact that we are five centuries from its formulation.

We recognize from the outset that we have sparse specific knowledge of the immense theological production provoked by the Luther phenomenon.[1] However, we dare to express some opinions from the viewpoint of our social and ecclesial place, that is, beginning with the believing poor of Latin America inserted into a church committed to their yearnings for liberation.

Theology Beginning with the Oppressed Poor: The Theology of Liberation

Liberation: A Concrete, Sociohistorical Process

The subjects of this liberation are the popular sectors and their allies (those who take an option for the poor). These movements

1. Important for our reading are W. Becker, *Reformation und Revolution* (Münster, 1983); *Reformation oder frühbürgerliche Revolution*, ed. R. Wohlfeil (Munich, 1972); J. Delumeau, "Las causas de la Reforma: la explicación marxista," in *La Reforma* (Barcelona, 1977), pp. 181-91; O. H. Pesch, *Hinführung zu Luther* (Mogüncia, 1983), esp. 304-7; and P. Chaunu, *Eglise, culture et société: Essais sur Réforme et Contre-Réforme, 1517–1620* (Paris, 1981).

have become aware of the levels of exploitation and have identified the mechanisms that cause their impoverishment: oppression is the other face of world capitalism; our countries are violently maintained in underdevelopment through economic domination, political control, or ideological subjection.[2]

Awareness of this situation brought into being popular organizations (labor unions, political parties with roots in the popular classes, associations for action/reflection) with practical social alternatives. This provoked a social rupture that led to the emergence of regimes of national security, with enormous and effective repressive apparatuses producing thousands of disappearances, tortures, exiles, and deaths in macabre torture chambers.

Yet this repression did not succeed in drowning out the yearnings for liberation, nor did it totally destroy the freedom movements. In all parts of Latin America there is a significant force of resistance to domination.

Christians in Solidarity with Liberation

The church in Latin America was undeniably an accomplice in the historic process of domination. Despite this complicity, at the same time there were always persons for whom the gospel was the central reference point. In its name they protested, defending the Indians and denouncing the iniquity of slavery. In modern times, many Christians have participated in and suffered and given their lives for the process of liberation. Especially after Vatican II, significant groups of priests and religious have learned how to come closer to the people, to ally themselves with the movements of popular mobilization. They have begun to evangelize by delving systematically into the liberating dimensions of faith.

The Christian Faith as a Factor in Liberation

The commitment of Christians to historic liberation has helped to free the Christian faith from its captivity to the dominating

2. P. Negre, *Sociologia do Terceiro Mundo* (Petrópolis, 1977), evaluates various interpretations of underdevelopment.

hegemonic powers.[3] In its effort to guarantee its hegemony, the ruling class tries to direct the church to favor the interests of the dominating power. When this happens, the church is changed into an ideological apparatus of the state (L. Althusser). But the co-opting of the Christian faith was never total. The subversive memory of Jesus and of his humble origins linked to the yearnings of the poor for liberation always remained alive in Christians at all levels.

With the participation of Christians in liberation, the gospel more and more came to be reread through the eyes of the poor. Important sectors began to project a certain image of Jesus and of the mission of the church as it is articulated in the struggle of the poor. Thus began the creation of social conditions for a liberating practice under evangelical inspiration, the preconditions for a theology of liberation.

Reflections of Christians from the Perspective of Liberation

Many Christians underwent a profound spiritual experience; they met the Lord as Suffering Servant in an entire social class of exploited people. They found that holiness is political and that virtues are those things that lead to solidarity in the struggle against deadly social mechanisms.

This meant that Christians had to make a more critical reading of capitalist society, manage concepts that unmasked the dominating ideology, project at least an outline of the society they were seeking, and mobilize for political advancement. Finally, beginning with praxis and social analysis, Christians began to reflect on the Christian faith and the themes of the theological agenda.

We must emphasize this decisive fact: the point is not to reflect on the *theme* of liberation, as one would reflect on any other theme (work, human sexuality, secularization) without changing the way in which theology is done. Rather, it is to think about faith from the starting point of the praxis of liberation,

---

3. Cf. Otto Maduro, *Religion and Social Conflicts* (Maryknoll, N.Y.: Orbis, 1982); P. Bourdieu, "Genése et structure du champ religieux," *Revue Française de Sociologie* 12 (1971): 295-334.

from the center of a commitment illuminated by faith in solidarity with the oppressed, and of social transformation.[4]

From this theological praxis there always emerges another type of Christian theologian. More than an intellectual, he or she is a militant, allied with the conscienticized people.[5]

Fundamental Intuitions of the
Theology of Liberation

It is impossible to do liberation theology without a previous option for the poor. Liberation theology has theological content because God, who is the God of life, shows in the history of salvation that the Divine hears the cries of the oppressed.

The poor in this context are not seen as needy individuals but as a whole class of workers who are deprived of life and dignity by an unjust social process. The kingdom of God in the theology of liberation constitutes a fundamental axis. It is more than each one of the concrete liberations, because it embraces all of them, but it would not be complete if it did not include economic, political, and social liberation.

It is fundamental to understand the christological mystery in terms of liberation. Jesus was liberator of the poor, the sick, and sinners (Luke 4:17-21; Matt. 11:4-5). His death was a consequence of his message and practice, which conflicted with those of the holders of political and religious power in his day. His resurrection is the apex of integral liberation.

The church's prolongation of the mission of Jesus is situated within the world, beginning with the demands of the marginalized. The church in Latin America has dedicated itself, more than any other social institution, to the defense of the oppressed.

So this is a two-way road: on the one hand, the practice of liberation helps in a rereading of the sources of faith, the figure of Jesus, and the mission of the church. On the other hand, the faith helps in the commitment of the poor against their poverty and toward their liberation.

---

4. P. Richard, "Teologiá da liberação latino-americana," in *A Igreja latino-americana entre o temor e a esperança* (São Paulo, 1982), pp. 13-34.

5. Clodovis Boff, *Theology and Praxis* (Maryknoll, N.Y.: Orbis, n.d.).

Historic Protestantism, Promoter of Bourgeois Freedom

How are the Protestant churches in Latin America related to the popular process of the liberation of the poor?[6]

Protestantism arrived in our countries with the ideals of liberalism. These ideals in their economic aspect reinforced modernization and industrialization against the old oligarchic land holders. In their political dimension they raised the banner of representative democracy. Culturally they disseminated schools and promoted individual liberty.

With this purpose, historic Protestantism wanted to reproduce in Latin America conditions similar to those in its countries of origin. Therefore, it made a structural alliance, within the play of social forces, with the most advanced sectors of Latin American society influenced by the ideals of the U.S. and French Revolutions, of enlightenment, of positivism, and even of Masonry.

This took place in the precise moment of the transition of traditional and colonial Latin American society to a modern and liberal society. The Catholic church was aligned with the historic land-holding colonial bloc. For historic Protestantism, "Roman Catholicism is . . . an anachronistic Hispanic order implanted in Latin America, which needs to be swept away to give place to a new, democratic, liberal, enlightened, dynamic order—which historically Protestantism has inspired."[7]

On the other hand, we must recognize that Protestant theology is tied to the historic liberal subject. Liberalism becomes the ideology of the dominant imperialism, creator of a

6. Lutherans and Presbyterians are of a confessional orientation, Methodists and Baptists are of an evangelical *revival* orientation. Cf. Vários, *Protestantismo y liberalismo en América Latina* (San José: DEI, 1983); W. Willems, *Followers of the New Faith: Culture Change and the Rise of Protestantism in Brazil and Chile* (Nashville, 1967); W. R. Reed, V. M. Monterroso, and H. A. Johnson, *Avance evangélico en América Latina* (Dallas, 1970); Christian Lalive d'Epinay, *Haven of the Masses: A Study of the Pentecostal Movement in Chile* (London: Lutterworth, 1969); W. A. César, *Por uma sociologia do Protestantismo brasileiro* (Petrópolis, 1973).

7. Cf. J. Míguez Bonino, "Historia y misión" (historical studies of Christianity in Latin America with reference to the search for liberation), in *Protestantismo y liberalismo en América Latina*, p. 25.

center and of a periphery. From the middle of the nineteenth century a neocolonialism has been established in Latin America. Protestantism, with its liberal ideals, is transformed into a legitimating factor of this neocolonialism.

The social change Protestantism favored was only reformist. It directly benefitted the middle and high strata and gave very scarce benefits to the popular sectors. Religious transformation centered in the conversion of the heart, in ethical practices.

The truth is, there is a Protestant liberating force of great significance in the global process of liberation and of a reflection built on it. Now we need to ask to what degree Luther can give strength to this mission.

Luther: Liberator in the Church, Reformer in Society

To what extent does Luther have a liberating function in the historic-social-religious process? Conversely, to what extent does he give legitimacy to a modernity that brings so much oppression to the majority of humanity in our time?

To reflect on this with a certain hermeneutic sense, we need at least a minimal reference point. I assume the hypothesis that a religious phenomenon, such as that of Luther, cannot be analyzed with religious categories alone. Anyone who tries to make a purely religious analysis ends up not even making a religious analysis. This is true because the religious factor (like culture, ideologies, values) is never built in isolation, but always in articulation with concrete history and economic-political structures of a society.

Beyond its specific character, each factor has its index of efficacy over the others. There can be moments in which the religious factor appears to be dominant.[8] This may be the case with the Reformation and Luther. The Reformation is above all a re-

8. For this whole question the fundamental work is O. Maduro, *Religião e luta de classes* (Petrópolis, 1981); also M. Godelier, "Marxisme, anthropologie et religion," in *Epistémologie et marxisme* (Paris, 1952), pp. 209-65; H. Portelli, *Gramsci y la cuestión religiosa* (Barcelona, 1977), pp. 58-64.

ligious phenomenon, but it is not only religious. All of the levels of conflict that touched society and the European conscience of that day are revealed in the religious field. Henrique Hauser said:

> The Reformation of the 16th century had the double character of social and religious revolution. The popular classes did not rise up only against the corruption of dogma and the abuses of the clergy. They also rose up against misery and injustice. They did not seek in the Bible only the doctrine of salvation by grace, but also the proof of the original equality of all human beings.[9]

The question of the causes of the Reformation is very complicated.[10] No one would dare reduce it to just a few factors, but we can say with certainty that the Reformers, especially Luther, responded to the great yearnings of their time, resulting in profound transformations. The discovery of new continents, the colonization of new lands, the invention of the printing press, the introduction of new financial methods, the emergence of humanism, and especially the cry from all Christendom for deep reforms were some of the causes.

Within his specific field (religion), Luther brought about a grand liberating process. He will forever be an obligatory reference point for all who seek liberty and know how to struggle for it. Hegel rightly considered the Lutheran Reformation as a *Hauptrevolution* (a fundamental revolution), because "the liberty of spirit begins with Luther," liberty that is "not only recognized, but vehemently demanded."[11] This liberty is achieved by breaking with the "Babylonian Captivity" to which Christianity was submitted under the hegemony of Rome.

For a better identification of the liberating significance of Luther within the religious field, and therefore within other fields of reality, it is important to place the church within the feudal and seignorial formation of that era.

9. *Etudes sur la Réforme Française* (Paris, 1909), p. 83.
10. Still classic is the work of J. Lortz, "Wie es zur Spaltungkam: Von den Ursachen der Reformation," in *Die Reformation als religioeses Anliegen heute* (Tréveris, 1948), pp. 15-105; or in *Die Reformation in Deutschland* (Freiburg, 1949), 1:3-20; *Luther und die Folgen,* ed. H. Loewe and C.-J. Roepke (Munich, 1983).
11. *Vorlesungen über die Geschichte der Philosophie,* Suhrkamp, Werke 20 (Frankfurt, 1971), 3:49, 50, 51.

Liberation from the
Babylonian Captivity of the Church

In the semifeudal and mercantile Europe of the fifteenth and six-teenth centuries, the church was a fundamental part of the structure. The Roman See and the bishops—especially in Germany—had great economic, political, juridical, and military interests. We should not forget that the pope exercised vast temporal power with innumerable treaties and benefits. There were the relationships of vassals and subjects, of masters and servants, of colonizers and colonized. Despite the many uprisings in Bohemia, Swabia, France, and other parts of central Europe, the peasants were kept in submission not only through armed coercion, but also through religious persuasion.[12]

Feudal aristocracy and bourgeois mercantile society made an agreement with the clergy (who also had secular power) so that the church became the central force for the reproduction of the semifeudal and mercantilist society. Thus, the church, in its multifunctional nature, consecrated and solidified the relationships of the *status quo*, of domination. This special function of the church was exercised with effectiveness through a thousand kinds of pious works, devotions to saints, and lucrative indulgences.

In the face of such a situation, Luther (coming from a profound spiritual crisis, allied to a deep desire for reform in his religious order and the entire church) raised his prophetic cry. He rose up against what he—many times—calls the "tyranny of the Pope."

He opposes justification by works with justification by faith.[13] He makes the unheard-of discovery of the unlimited mercy of God in the crucified Jesus Christ. Human beings are not condemned to fulfill laws and to seek salvation through good works. With the basic thesis of justification by faith, Luther introduces a radical liberation because the human being is free

---

12. Cf. O. Maduro, "A religião no regime semifeudal da Colónia," in *Religião e luta de classes*, pp. 87-90.

13. Cf. O. H. Pesch, *Theologie der Rechtfertigung bei Martin Luther and Thomas von Aquin: Versuch eines systematisch-theologischen Dialogs* (Mogüncia, 1967); also *Hinführung zu Luther*, pp. 264-71.

from all these demands, and free *to* receive grace and mercy as a pure gift and free offering.

Justification by faith is the expression of the incredible inner freedom achieved by Luther and waved as the banner of freedom for other Christians. April 16, 1521, when Karl V convoked the Diet of Worms and invited him to abandon his proclamation, Luther answered: "I neither can nor wish to retract because it is neither good nor sincere to act against one's own conscience. May God help me! Amen!" Urged for the last time by the official who said, "Lay aside your conscience, Brother Martin. The only thing which does not offer danger is to submit yourself to established authority," Luther definitively refused.[14]

The texts Luther had produced in 1520—*The Papacy of Rome* (June), *Appeal to The Christian Nobility of the German Nation* (August), *The Babylonian Captivity of the Church* (October), and *The Liberty of the Christian* (November)—created an undeniable aura of liberation. Obviously the theme of these texts is religious. Although they have social, political, and economic effects, the church was the basic institution for the coordination, hegemony, and reproduction of the existing system.

In *The Papacy of Rome*, Luther defines the fundamental intuition of Protestant ecclesiology. The visible church is purely human and cannot be identified with the mystic body of Christ. The church of Christ is like the kingdom, which is within us: it is invisible, spiritual, and inner.

In the extremely virulent work against the clergy and the pope, *Appeal to the Christian Nobility of the German Nation,* from the perspective of the convocation of a Council for the Reformation of the Church, he denounces the three walls of the Romanists which impede the liberty of Christians:

1. The superiority of the religious state over the civil, through which the pope intends to dominate all. The power of the church is only spiritual and its function is one of service. It remains only as long as it carries out that function. Beyond this diaconal insertion it continues to be lay. The "indelible character" is "just contrived talk and human regulation."[15] Here

14. Quoted by J. Delumeau, *La Reforma*, p. 35.
15. *Luther's Works*, vol. 44 (Philadelphia: Fortress, 1966), p. 129.

Luther defends the permanent validity of the universal priesthood of all laity.

2. Another wall is the right the pope assumes to an exclusive interpretation of Scripture. Luther, who had a marvelous
expertise in the sacred texts (his translation of the Bible, brilliant in its correctness and simple in style, had 84 editions during
his life and 253 after his death), affirms the right of individual
access to the text and to the illumination of the Spirit in its interpretation. This breaks the monopoly of legitimacy of interpretation and opens the way to free examination.

3. The third wall is the pope's pretension that only he can
convoke and recognize a council. On the basis of Scripture texts
and the witness of tradition, Luther asserts the right of the
princes to call a council and urge the reformation of the church,
even to "teach the Pope that he, too, is a man, and not more than
God, as he sets himself up to be!"[16]

In *The Babylonian Captivity of the Church*, Luther denounces the ways in which the priestly body had taken possession of the sacraments, through which it maintained the subjection of the loyal members of the church. They "have been
subjected to a miserable captivity by the Roman curia and the
church has been robbed of all her liberty."[17] He accepts and
defends three sacraments as such: baptism, penitence, and the
bread. The others are ecclesiastical rites related to the life and
the organization of the community, with legitimacy as human
religious constructions but not as expressions of the Divine will.

For Luther the sacrament is also *Evangelium*, that is, concrete expression of the Word of promise. Without the sacramental element, the promise remains "a naked promise." The sacrament is never just a sign, but a sign that contains the promise.
Therefore, according to Luther, it is not the sacrament (sign) that
communicates salvation, but faith in the sacrament (which contains the promise).[18]

With regard to the Mass, Luther demanded both bread
and wine for the people and regretted the fact that the Mass was
said in Latin, an incomprehensible language. The minister does

16. *Luther's Works*, vol. 44, p. 169.
17. *Luther's Works*, vol. 36 (Philadelphia: Muhlenberg, 1959), p. 18.
18. *Ibid.*, p. 124.

not renew the sacrifice on the cross, but commemorates the promise of forgiveness of sinners,

> the divine promise or testament of Christ, sealed with the sacrament of his body and blood. If that is true, you will understand that it cannot possibly be in any way a work; nobody can possibly do any thing in it, neither can it be dealt with in any other way than by faith alone.[19]

The captivity Rome imposed on this sacrament converted it into a business with votive masses, honors, and prayers for the dead.

Luther is especially hard on ordination as a sacrament (despite accepting the ecclesiastical right to introduce ministers into the community):

> Here, indeed, are the roots of that detestable tyranny of the clergy over the laity. Trusting in the external anointing by which their hands are consecrated, in the tonsure and in vestments, they not only exalt themselves above the rest of the lay Christians, who are only anointed with the Holy Spirit, but regard them almost as dogs and unworthy to be included with themselves in the Church. Hence they are bold to demand, to exact, to threaten, to urge, to oppress, as much as they please. In short, the sacrament of ordination has been and still is an admirable device of establishing all the horrible things that have been done hitherto in the Church and are yet to be done. Here Christian brotherhood has perished, here shepherds have been turned into wolves, servants into tyrants, churchmen into worse than worldings.[20]

The Freedom of the Christian is one of the most beautiful texts of Christian tradition. Luther sent it along with a letter to Pope Leo X. All of it can be summed up in two propositions:

> A Christian is a perfectly free lord of all, subject to none.

> A Christian is a perfectly dutiful servant of all, subject to all.[21]

The book is a defense of inner freedom: the person of faith feels free of all concern for salvation through obedience to precepts and other imperatives, because salvation is freely offered by

19. *Luther's Works*, vol. 36, p. 47.
20. *Ibid.*, p. 112.
21. *Luther's Works*, vol. 31 (Philadelphia: Muhlenberg, 1957), p. 344.

God. By function of this gift, hands, eyes, and heart are free to work for pure love on behalf of all.[22]

Near the end of this Treatise he adequately sums up his perspective:

> We conclude, therefore, that a Christian lives not in himself, but in Christ and in his neighbor. He lives in Christ through faith, in his neighbor through love . . . it is a spiritual and true freedom and makes our hearts free from all sins, laws and commands. . . . It is more excellent than all other liberty, which is external, as heaven is more excellent than earth.[23]

In *The Servant Will* (written in 1525, against Erasmus's *Of Free Will*), Luther shows that human liberty cannot be affirmed before God. Rather, its function consists in receiving the saving action of God; within itself, the human will cannot nor ever will succeed in sustaining a relationship with God.[24] This comes from the free initiative of Divine mercy, but in the life of this world human determination is exercised and, once touched by grace, can freely collaborate with God in the building of the kingdom.[25]

To conclude this discussion, we must recognize that despite his verbal excesses, his partial and sometimes erroneous judgments, Luther represents the presence of authentic prophecy, demanding conversion and reform in the whole church. He knew how to place the gospel and the cross as basic reference points to free the church of every kind of abuse of sacred power and manipulation of the doctrines in the service of the *dominium mundi*. An undeniable aura of liberty pervades his principal texts and is transformed into the yeast of liberation in the *corpus christianoram*.

22. For this whole question, cf. W. Maurer, *Von der Freiheit eines Christenmenschen: Zwei Untersuchungen zu Luthers Reformationsschriften, 1520-1521* (Göttingen, 1949).

23. *Luther's Works*, vol. 31, p. 371.

24. For Luther, the understanding of free will defended by Erasmus of Rotterdam leads to an excessive autonomy before God. Erasmus defined *liberum arbitrium* thus: "The force of human will through which one can direct himself toward those things that lead to salvation, or away from them" (*Diatribe seu collatio de libero arbitrio* 1b, 10, 7-10).

25. With regard to this point, cf. *Luther's Works*, vol. 33 (Philadelphia: Fortress, 1972), pp. 155, 242-43; M. Seils, *Der Gedanke vom Zusammenwirken Gottes und des Menschen in Luthers Theologie* (Gütersloh, 1962).

We know that Luther never intended to create a parallel Christian confession. This was the work of the German princes (beginning with the Alliance of Torgau, 1526), to face the league of Catholic princes, finally sealed in March 1531 by the Schmalkaldic League. When the Peace of Augsburg was signed in 1555, Germany was already divided between Lutheranism and Roman Catholicism under the principle *cujus regio, hujus religio* (who rules, his the religion).

The Appropriation of the Protestant Spirit by the New Lords

Luther's activity was liberating within the religious field. The same was not true within the political field.

The Roman Catholic church lost its religious monopoly and began repositioning itself within a divided religious field. Its social influence diminished. It had to face competition in the confessional and political arena from the princes who took up the banner of Lutheranism (a sizeable part of the northern regions).

Luther himself was not able to control the movement he unleashed. He was not even aware of its sociopolitical implications. Nor should this be asked of him, because it goes beyond the limits of "possible conscience" of those distant times. Thus Luther clearly said:

> My gospel has nothing to do with the things of this world. It is something quite apart which touches only the souls and it is not my business to solve and manage temporal affairs; for this there are persons who have the calling, the emperor, the princes, the authorities. And the source from which they should take their wisdom is not the Gospel, but rather reason, customs and fairness.[26]

The lack of a conscious political articulation is apparent with the outbreak of the Peasants War, led by the preacher Thomas Müntzer (1489–1525).[27] The uprising took place within

26. *WA*, 17:321, edition by Wilhelm Goldmann Verlag (Munich, 1967).

27. Cf. M. M. Smirin, *Die Volksreformation des Thomas Müntzer und der grosse Bauerndrieg* (Berlin, 1956); P. Althaus, *Luthers Haltung im Bauernkrief* (Basileia, 1953).

a larger movement that began well before the Reformation. The situation of peasants at the beginning of the sixteenth century was quite good.[28] They were active in their demands for the most fundamental sociopolitical rights, as can be seen in the document, *Twelve Articles*. Therefore, not only small landowners but also abbots, princes, and bishops (Fulda, Bamberg, Espira) associated themselves with the movement.[29]

Needing to take a position, Luther wrote an *Exhortation To Peace* (1525). He said clearly to the lords: "It is not the peasants who rise up against you, but God Himself"; and to the rebels, "The one who lives by the sword will die by the sword; even though the princes may be unjust, nothing gives you the right to rebel against them."

At the political level Luther is not a revolutionary.[30] Fundamentally, he respects secular power, because he sees it instituted by God, to be obeyed. In 1521, in Wartburg, he expressed himself very explicitly against rebellion and sedition: "I am opposed, and shall always be opposed, to those who use violence, however just it may be, because rebellion is never satisfied, except with the shedding of innocent blood."[31]

28. Lortz, *Die Reformation in Deutschland*, 1:322.
29. Ibid., 1:324.
30. G. Casalis, *Luther et l'Eglise confessante* (Paris, 1983), p. 82.
31. Quoted by G. Casalis, ibid., p. 82. Luther was a friend of the leaders of the repression against the peasants, such as Philip of Hesse, and said to them: "It is necessary to strangle them. It is necessary to kill the mad dog which comes against you. If not, he will kill you" ("Against the Gangs of Thieves and Murderers among the Peasants"). This position will never be forgotten by the oppressed who do not have a clear sense of the articulation of religion in a class society, religion that can be co-opted to function in the interests of the dominant class. In his *Commentary on the Magnificat*, Luther presents a spiritualist interpretation, referring to the poor and humble in these words: "The hungry are not those who have little or nothing to eat, but those who voluntarily suffer deprivation principally if they do this for others because of the love of God or truth." And he gives his motives for not considering the differences between the rich and the poor: "God does not judge people by their appearances. It is of little importance to him whether they be rich or poor, whether they occupy positions of importance or have lesser social situations. What God sees is the spirit which moves them. In society there will always be the privileged and the disinherited. The former should not grasp advantages which they enjoy and the latter should remain tranquil" (*Luther's Works*,

Jean Delumeau correctly concludes:

> The peasant revolt showed clearly the political incompetence of the Reformer. Especially it made him lose faith in the people organized in communities. From the moment he asked the princes for the reform of worship the Luther of the "State Church" replaced the Luther of "Christian Freedom."[32]

To verify his putting the religious over the sociopolitical, we need to ask about Luther's allies in the religious movement. In this case we can say with certainty that—more than the poor people, the peasants and serfs—his allies were the princes, the humanists, the artists (Dürer, Cranach, Holbein), the urban bourgeois.

The historic project shaped by his practices was not oriented to the line of liberation but to the accumulation of wealth and privilege. Max Weber has shown the logical identification between Protestantism and capitalism.[33] A faith lived in accordance with the Protestant pattern results in the establishment and expansion of the capitalist mode of production.

> So to the extent that the Western world is ruled by the logic of capitalism, we can conclude that Protestantism feels at home in that world whereas Catholicism does not. The Protestant ideology brings together individual freedom, liberal democracy, and economic progress as expressions of the spirit of Protestantism. In short, the modern world is a fruit of Protestantism.[34]

The historic association of Lutheranism with the princes and the victorious bourgeoisie led to the incorporation and legitimization by Protestantism of the interests and social ideals of this class.

The famous Protestant individualism finds itself impotent and mute before the structures of injustice. To the degree

---

vol. 21 (St. Louis: Concordia, 1956), pp. 343-46, the spiritualized commentary of the verse: "he has thrown down from the throne the powerful and exalted the humble").

32. Delumeau, *La Reforma*, p. 45.

33. *The Protestant Ethic and the Spirit of Capitalism*, trans. Talcott Parsons (1930; rpt., New York: Scribner's, 1956).

34. Rubem Alves, *Protestantism and Repression: A Brazilian Case Study*, trans. John Drury, rev. Jaime Wright (Maryknoll, N.Y.: Orbis, 1985), p. 15; cf. "The Protestant Principle and Its Denial," p. 213 herein.

that it does not reflect evangelically on this challenge, it runs the risk of masking the conflicts that torment the poor and thereby failing to collaborate with the messianic task of the liberation of the condemned of the earth.

Therefore, returning to the question we have raised regarding Protestantism in Latin America, we must say that our suspicions are confirmed that there does not exist any meaningful communication on the social level between Protestantism and the liberation of the poor. This linkage should come from some perceptions of Luther, especially from his open spirit of liberation within the church.

Protestant Evangelism as a Factor in the Liberation of the Oppressed

In the first place, we should note carefully that the situation today is profoundly different from that of Luther's time. In those days the church was the principal factor in shaping the social system, so the changes Luther introduced in the religious field could have immediate repercussions in the social. Today religion occupies a subsidiary role.

In our capitalistic societies, whether peripheral or elitist, economic activity is central and dominates all others, causing extensive marginalization of impoverished people. This means that a possible liberation does not come with changes in the religious field, unless there be an explicit link with other areas which in our situation are more determinant and dominant.

The religious factor can be seen as a liberating factor only by beginning with the sociopolitical and in permanent connection with it. I would like to identify some points rich in liberating content within Protestant evangelism.

The Protestant Principle

Paul Tillich coined this phrase[35] to express the basic intuition of Luther: he rebelled in the name of the gospel against the over-

35. *The Protestant Era* (London: Nisbet, 1955).

whelming power of the clergy, against usurpation by the dominant of the rightful place of the dominated, against the historic that presented itself as divine.

The Protestant spirit unmasks the religious and political idols and refuses simply to legitimize the status quo. Everything must be changed in the process of conversion. That means, there must be total freedom from every type of oppression: enlarged space for the free action of God and for the human being to be fully human.

The Protestant principle will help Protestants themselves to be freed from their bourgeois moralism and to find support in evangelical radicalism, as Luther did.

Recovery of the Liberating Potential of the Gospel

The preeminent significance of Luther was his profound linkage of the biblical and the evangelical.

In a day in which the gospel was imprisoned by educated and clerical elites, Luther redeemed it as *viva vox* and gave it into the hands of the people. In Latin America the gospel is read and meditated on in tens of thousands of base Christian communities as the great source of prophetic challenge to a system of exploitation and the source of liberating commitment.

The liberating potential of the Scriptures emerges when they are read in the light of the questions that come from social conflict and the cry of the oppressed. This interchange between the Word of God and the words of the impoverished and humiliated recovers the permanent reality of God's revelation and saving act in the installation of the kingdom against the strategies of the anti-kingdom.

Faith Which Is Fired by Works of Liberation

Luther helps us all understand that liberation is fired by the gift of God, who takes the initiative before any human, historic act. This awareness does not immobilize persons in their engagement in the struggle. On the contrary, it stimulates them with greater strength to throw themselves into good works that free their neighbor. In this sense Luther contrasts *fides abstracta vel absoluta* (outside of good works) with *fides concreta, composita seu incarnata* (active in good works).[36]

In line with this, Luther can speak of the Christ who is "contemporary to the nth degree" with his members who assimilate the acts of Jesus Christ and lead a converted and liberated life.[37] He emphasizes that faith is energized by works done as a result of the gift of God and of mercy. Today these works cannot be reduced to the subjective level without having repercussions on the structures of society.

To guarantee that action which is born of faith will be efficacious, first there must be an analysis of the mechanisms that produce oppression and a definition of the concrete steps toward liberation. In this, we, Catholics as well as Protestants, must learn to become disciples of a different theological practice, one that knows how to articulate the discourse of evangelical faith with the social sciences. It is within this context that the liberating potential of the Christian faith emerges.

Finally, I would like to make my own the words of the Joint Catholic–Lutheran International Commission in its document of May 1983: "We unite in considering Luther to be a witness to the Gospel, a master of the faith and a voice which calls to spiritual renewal."[38]

For us who live in Latin America, the gospel must be lived in a liberating form, a faith in commitment with the neediest, beginning with the experience of the primary mercy of God and spirituality as a mystique that brings together faith and politics, builds community from below with the humblest, full of the spirit, that they may truly be the messianic community that is the prolongation of the redeeming and liberating mission of Jesus Christ, the Messiah.

36. *Rhapsodia de loco iustificationis* (1530): *WA* 30: 2, 659, 13-21; P. Manns, "Fides absoluta—fides incarnata. Zur Rechtfertigungslehre Luthers im Grossen Galater-Kommentar," in *Reformata Reformanda*, Fest. H. Jedin (Münster, 1965), 1:265-313.

37. *Luther's Works*, vol. 31, pp. 56, 26; cf. J. Wicks, "Il cuore della teologia di Lutero," *Rassegna di Teologia* 24 (1983): 110-25; 219-37; "Fede e giustificazione in Lutero."

38. *Martinho Lutero: Testemunha de Jesus Cristo, na secção "Documentação" deste fasciculo*, pp. 830-36 (Spanish edition *Ecclesia*, August 1983, pp. 15-19).

The Protestant Principle and Its Denial

RUBEM ALVES   *(Presbyterian, Brazil)*

Preliminary Questions

I agree with Nietzsche, who said with corrosive irony that the historian is so involved in the past that he becomes a crab thinking from front to back. It so happens that a personal idiosyncrasy, possibly a result of my Christian upbringing, compels me to read the past from the point of view of the future's need for redemption. Memory is subordinated to hope.

It is obvious that I am selective. I am looking for *ideas:* ideas to the degree in which they *express* or *determine* the way of being Protestant in this more than a century of the history of Brazilian society.

In the specific case of the Reformation there are brilliant visions and grotesque mistakes. If we are aware of them, we may avoid repetition of the past. We may even understand some of the historic developments generated in that era: from Luther to psychoanalysis, from Calvinism to capitalism, from Müntzer to Marx and Engels.

Leaving aside the European ancestry of Protestantism, I look for the thoughts and actions the Protestant communities generated, not from the beginning, but as we have lived in a Brazilian cultural space.

Look what happened to the uprooted Catholics, scattered all over Brazil, living without a priest or a bishop. The memory almost disappeared, but even so (or perhaps because of this) there arose from Catholic devotion a popular religiosity that could call by their right names things that erudite traditional theology rejected: the savage, the magic, the festival, that which was less or more than morality, the exotic. Yes, exotic, in the precise sense of the term, ex-otic, out of sight, strange, offensive, and surprising. So much so that many efforts were made to eliminate or commercialize it.

This is not what we find among Protestants. However humble they may have been, they always stayed within the rigorous limits of the rational. On one side is the cultivation of family values, blessed by a benign patriarchal system, protector of conjugal fidelity, of the education of children, and of a hierarchical order which ties the mother to the father as head of the family, and the children to both.

On the other side are the petite bourgeoisie values, so distinctive of the poor who want to rise in life: individual effort; hard work; personal discipline; thrift; the rejection of any and every form of irresponsible dissipation through alcohol, smoking, gambling; the love of cleanliness; honesty—the basis of any social contract; obedience to authorities—the guarantee of everyone's rights. This becomes real at the level of domestic life and individual conscience.

I might have hoped that Protestantism should have made some contribution to Brazilian literature. I look for a great romance, a great novel . . . in vain. It is necessary to remember here that if Catholicism gives highest value to the eyes, in Protestantism the ears are predominant.

But what should be heard? The Word of God, preached in its purity. The Word that is the *rule* of faith and practice, imposed as an imperative. It is selective hearing, hearing that knows where the *authority* is and where *truth* comes from. This is the reason for the architectural austerity of Protestant churches, reduced to a kind of classroom, where the preacher-teacher speaks while the believer-student listens. It so happens that literature cannot survive this didactic obsession, because literature is aesthetic, contemplative. Its value is in direct relationship to its capacity to produce structural paradigms through which the hidden fractures and daily links are seen.

Protestant literati cannot escape the witchery of their habits of thought. Their novels are disguised sermons or Sunday school lessons. In the end the grace of God always triumphs, believers are rewarded, and impiety is punished. There is no need to read the last chapter. Protestant didactic has the moral of the story ready even before it happens.

We produce good grammarians, respected philologists, and even good educational literature. Here Protestants feel at home. Philology is linked to exegesis, to the demand for a rigorous reading of the sacred texts. The didactic concern has always been dear to the Protestant soul: pure hearts, clear ideas, logical thought. Action follows thought: this is the rule for all those who have been reached by saving grace.

Finally, I think that not only the Protestants but anyone who analyzes the ideas in our inheritance has the right to know the relation of all this to politics. What ideas were raised? Which became horizons of struggle or inspiration for sacrifice? Without doubt, there were many sacrifices, solitary sacrifices, of heroic individuals who struck out along unknown trails, to preach, heal, and teach. But this is not the kind of sacrifice I am asking about. I ask about political sacrifice to change the destiny of entire peoples, such as happened in Geneva in the iron hands of Calvin, or in the United States which found in Protestantism the blessing for its epic.

And here?

Protestantism, the religion of foreigners and of marginal Brazilians, put on the defensive by Catholic intolerance, is in search of a place in the sun, and of air to breathe. It is understandable that it should have weighed and measured its words, applauding with enthusiasm the republican cause, the separation of church and state, as well as all similar initiatives to lessen the power of a Catholicism that threatened it.

It achieved nothing beyond this limit of its political awareness. Rather, it was dragged along by the wave of liberal capitalism, which to its eyes appeared to be nothing more than a secularized version of the Christian faith. Protestantism could not have thought in any other way, because it came to us from the center of liberal capitalism.

No, we have not told the whole truth. There are also memories of aborted attempts to raise banners. The fact that they were aborted does not make them less Protestant. It is even possible they still survive in tombs from which they may be resurrected. The fact is, the Protestants dared to talk about social justice and were able to see a depth of capitalism hidden to naive liberalism. We will return to this later.

Now we can look at the past and ask *how?* and *why?*

215

Origins and the First Century (1820–1950)

The first Protestant groups arrived in Brazil at the beginning of the nineteenth century, German immigrants who settled in Friburgo, in the state of Rio de Janeiro, about 1823-24. They were Germans rooted in the traditions of their people, suffering the agonies of cultural shock. They brought Protestantism as a sacrament of the fatherland they had left behind, and as a promise that the fatherland would continue here.

It is understandable that the Germans would not show any interest in integration into Brazilian culture. Protestantism was part of their secret, their mark of identity, which, along with their language, formed a Germanic space here. It is not surprising that they continued to speak and worship in German, did not mix with Brazilians, did not enter into evangelistic ventures, and that their pastors received their theological training in Germany.

When, about 1930, the first young Lutherans born in Brazil began to be interested in theology, they were sent to Germany for their training. Their own theological themes? There were none, because the theological space and time were found on the other side of the Atlantic. According to the witness of one leader of the Lutheran Protestant Church in Brazil, the theme that "appears to have been the great concern of the communities and pastors for most of this century" was "evangelical faith and Germanism."

The discussion sharpened during the Nazi period, when there were a series of conflicts and confrontations in Germany itself, with the active participation of Karl Barth and Martin Niemöller. The name of Bonhoeffer remains the symbol of innumerable martyrs who died at that time. Only after the war, considering the enormous risks to a church that called itself by the name of its country of origin, would "The Evangelical German Church" accept the fact that it was living in Brazil.

A different kind of Protestantism came from the United States. It was not a case of creating a cultural space for a population of immigrants, but of invading the culture of the natives to convert them to a new faith.

What were the theological themes of this missionary invasion?

Above all it is necessary to recognize that Catholicism and Protestantism, at the deepest levels, lived in the same world. This is the only thing that makes polemic and the easy transit of converts possible. To pass from Catholicism to Protestantism is not to pass through two incommensurable worlds. I agree completely with Ernst Troeltsch when he says:

> The basic point to be noted is that from a theological and historical perspective Protestantism was above all a simple modification of Catholicism, in which the Catholic formulation of the problem was maintained, but a different answer proposed to it. . . .
>
> From the beginning Protestantism was concerned with answering the old question about the *certainty of salvation,* which has as its assumptions the existence of God, with ethical and personal character, and, in general, the medieval biblical cosmology, and has as its only and urgent problem absolution in the Final Judgment, seeing all persons are condemned to hell as a consequence of original sin.[1]

What Troeltsch points to here as the center of Protestant religious thought was also the thought of the missionaries and of the early congregations they formed.

Emile Leonard thinks that in its first moments the situation of Brazilian Protestantism replicated the conditions existent in Europe at the time of the Reformation. He became interested in the study of young Protestantism in Brazil, because he thought such study would help him understand "European spiritual history."[2]

Even in 1950 Leonard saw Brazilian Protestantism of the missionary frontier as a contemporary of the age of the Reformation, which in other places he found in the early periods following the Reformation (p. 16). What the North American missionary or Brazilian evangelist is going to do is simply announce the sufficiency of the Bible as an inspired book, the need for repentance and surrender to Christ, the unique and sufficient efficacy of his vicarious sacrifice, the imperative to give up

1. Troeltsch, *Protestantism and Progress: The Significance of Protestantism for the Rise of the Modern World* (Philadelphia: Fortress, 1986), pp. 59-61.

2. Emile Leonard, *O Protestantismo Brasileiro* (ASTE), p. 15.

idolatry and the saints, the demand for personal responsibility, and the sanctified life.

It is necessary to point out the very unusual aspect of the missionary situation in Latin America. In 1910, in the first ecumenical missionary conference in Edinburgh, Latin America was not included as a missionary frontier, because it was said a Catholic continent should not be considered pagan. In fact, unlike missionary penetration into Asia and Africa, the Protestants broke ground here in the midst of others who called themselves Christian.

For Protestants there was only one way of justifying their work: to define Catholicism as disguised paganism. This was not new, because the Presbyterian *Westminster Confession of Faith* had already defined the Pope as the Anti-Christ.

Protestantism, child of North American missions in Brazil, (unlike the German Lutheran Church, which had no proselytizing concerns), in order to justify itself to the world Protestant community, *had* to define Brazilian Catholicism as paganism, that is, as a mission field, where proselytizing should be carried out to gain lost souls for Christ.

The Catholic church, for its part, made an active contribution to this definition, through its intolerant attitude and its persecution of Protestants. From my point of view, this was the most important theological crystallization of this period, which continues until now. In the final analysis what is in play is the Protestant identity and the church's sense of mission. If Catholics are considered to be brothers and sisters, what is left to us as a mission field?

It would be a mistake to interpret the missionary invasion as a simple transplanting of North American Protestantism. The need to define Catholicism as a threat and enemy set the preaching of salvation in a framework of polemic bitterness that marked Protestant thought until the middle of this century and still survives in the more conservative circles. I think it would not be wrong if we said the energies of Protestant thought were channeled almost exclusively into polemic, with no advance in the field of theological production.

The presupposition was that Protestant theology had completed the codifying of biblical truths. The system of doctrine in harmony with the Scriptures was already perfected. Pastors may have studied theology, but the idea of an original theological production was inconceivable. The open field of Protestant creativity was preaching. Ministers distinguished themselves here with an easy and direct rhetoric, sprinkled with illustrations taken from daily experience, in the "revival" tradition in which D. L. Moody[3] had a profound and permanent impact on North American churches. In this context we can understand the statement made in 1959 on the occasion of the centennial of a Protestant denomination, "Our pastors are not like Karl Barth, who does theology through his pipe smoke. Our pastors are men of action."

The truth is that the religious scenario of the United States during the second half of the nineteenth century was dominated by an obsession with action, a sense of urgency tied to an enormous optimism about the fruits of that action. Within this cluster there were three complementary tendencies: revival, the missionary movement, and the social gospel movement. The significance of these should be kept in mind in order to understand some peculiarities of our historical development.

The revivals were marked by warmth of emotional experience, and turned on an intimate sense of the new birth. These characteristics marked the religion of the United States of the past century. They make North Americans perhaps the most religious people in the world, activist and perfectionist, propelled by the fervor of social reform and missionary vision. All of this fit well into imperialist expansion.[4]

It is interesting to note that the spiritual awakening and the experience of conversion that accompanied it led to a whole series of organizations dedicated to personal renewal, social reform, and missionary advance. This dove-tailing of personal, individual, intimate fervor, on the one hand, with social concern on the other, is very suggestive. It is so because, in the present moment, these two tendencies are often broken into opposing camps. The fact is that in the nineteenth century the search for perfection was linked to compassion for the poor and needy, along with millennial expectations.

3. *Livro de Confissões* (Missão Presbiteriana do Brasil), n. 14.

4. Ronald C. White, *The Social Gospel: Religion and Reform in Changing America* (Philadelphia: Temple University Press, 1975), p. 5.

The rapid growth of urbanization, a result of industrialization, led to the rise of serious social problems that affected the working classes especially. This was a challenge to the churches, and it was in this context—the same context of revivals—that the social gospel appeared with the intent of fomenting "the application of the teaching of Jesus and the total message of the Christian salvation to society, the economic life, and social institutions . . . as well as to individuals."[5]

The writings of Walter Rauschenbusch, Baptist historian, became classics. Two examples are *Christianizing the Social Order* (New York: Macmillan, 1914) and *The Social Principles of Jesus* (New York: Association Press, 1916). The titles of some of their chapters are significant: "A Religion for Social Redemption," "What Do We Mean by Christianizing the Social Order?," "The Profit Motive," "The Moral Values of Capitalism: Profit vs. Life, Commerce vs. Beauty," "Christianity vs. Capitalism," "Socialization of Property," and so on. The style is direct and clear; these are books to be read by everybody. They are manifestos of action. In sum, one could call the social gospel movement the theology of liberation of the nineteenth century, actively espoused by the pious sectors of the church (e.g., Sunday School Council of Protestant Denominations).

Out of this bubbling caldron arose missionary vocations. The missionary was understood as agent of transformation of the world, in face of the demands of the gospel. To link the missionary movement purely and simply to imperialistic expansion is to transform it into a cynical appendage of economic interests. It happens that behind all this there was an erupting volcano, where individual fervor was mixed with moral indignation, love for those who suffer, and hope for the transformation of the world. If in the polemic with Brazilian Catholicism, Protestants insisted on the complicity of Catholicism with economic backwardness, neglect of popular education, and the development of totalitarian political institutions, it was because behind it burned hope for the regeneration of the social order, impelled by ethical Protestantism, in contrast to magic Catholicism. Needless to say, since Protestantism did not have the human

---

5. Shailer Mathews, "Social Gospel," in *A Dictionary of Religion and Ethics* (New York: Macmillan, 1921), p. 416.

mass that could take on the cause of social regeneration, it tried to achieve the purpose through schools and hospitals.

In the course of North American history, however, the churches had come to experience profound schisms, which were reflected in Brazil. Their most conservative sectors identified dangerous, modernist tendencies in operation, among them the "Social Gospel." Its heresy consisted in the tendency to *horizontalize* the *verticality* of the kingdom of God. Even today in Brazil the words *modernist* and *social gospel* are used as epithets. Out of these conflicts even missionary societies began to split institutionally: the "verticalists" occupied a given field while the "horizontalists" worked in another. In Brazil social involvement was practically reduced to education and the founding of schools.

For about a hundred years Protestant thought did not experience significant crises. Taking the theological task as completed, it remained only to combine certain basic themes, in the face of two fundamental necessities.

The Anti-Romanist Polemic

The word *romanist* was used especially of the Catholic, for obvious reasons. Anti-catholicism came to be the most important mark of Protestant identification. This is necessary information for the historian, who must be able to interpret the ascetic nature of Brazilian Protestantism, which goes far beyond that of the Europeans and North Americans.

This also helps us understand the relationship between Protestantism and Brazilian culture. To the degree in which the culture is intertwined with the Catholic liturgical calendar, Protestants considered it necessary to keep their distance from it.

The Growth and Strengthening of the Congregations

We are here on the level of the sociology of institutions.

In dealing with his congregation, the pastor has a serious problem to resolve: his own survival. Unlike the celibate priest whose decisions affect only himself, however, the pastor usually has a wife and children.

It is necessary also to understand that the institution prepares its servants carefully, demanding of them "exclusive dedication" to their flock and the affairs of heaven. This means the pastor should be a *man without alternatives.* Men without alternatives tend to be faithful to their superiors. Even without vows of monastic loyalty, the pastor is condemned forever to the church, because it is the only institution where what he knows can be transformed into a salary.

It happens, however, that in practice pastors are not employed with the institutional church but with a local congregation. In most Protestant denominations a pastor is elected; even in episcopally governed churches the bishops are sensitive to the desires of the congregation.

How is one to judge the success of a pastor's work?

1. He must be a good preacher. Let us not forget that for Protestants the power "ex opere operato" of the sacrament is out of the question. They do not go to worship for the magic of the sacrament, but to be edified, instructed, consoled. Bad preachers only produce sleeping members and empty pews.

2. He must be able to establish relationships of confidence, friendship, and spiritual influence with his parishioners. People need to be consoled. The words of the pastor should be spiritual balm. He soon learns that prophets are not reelected. The same things happen to prophets that happen to striking workers: besides losing their job, they have difficulty in finding another.

3. The church must experience an increase in giving. A pastor who is a good preacher and impressive as a person inevitably increases the number of members in his congregation, which also implies an increase in financial contributions. Consequently, a better salary.

4. The criteria in the selection of pastors are clearly drawn from business categories. When the big churches, for any reason, lose their pastors, they go out to search for a replacement among the most promising, those who have distinguished themselves by their ability to preach, convince, make friends, cause the flock and the budget to grow, and build churches.

The pastor is really at the mercy of the members of his congregation. The maximum limits of their ideas are the limits within which the pastor can safely work. It is clearly a situation that leaves little space for prophetic ministry.

There is, then, an enormous gulf between the seminary and the situation of the pastor in a congregation. Ideas that circulate in seminary have nothing to do with the ideas that circulate in the parishes. This explains in good part the conservative, pietist, and charismatic stance of individuals who were at least liberals in the days when they were theological students.

We have here a generalized Darwinism. The fittest survive and rise. Others, less fit, are condemned to the lower levels. This means smaller congregations, in small cities or working-class neighborhoods (when not in slums), without prestige and with minimal salaries. In this context, institutional continuity calls for the absence of conflictive ideas. The institutional organization of Protestant churches inhibits the emergence of new ideas, in face of the threat to the security of the pastor under the shelter of (and obligation to) the church.

On the other hand, when such ideas do appear, they do not remain within the great ecclesial body, as happens in the Catholic church. They are expelled and form new denominations. This is an extremely efficient mechanism to make each group immune to invading intellectual germs.

We should note that during this first century (1820-1950), our theological institutions succeeded in isolating all European thought. Theological texts were imported from the United States—with the exception of those for the Lutheran church. The truth is that Brazilian Protestants always had a serious suspicion of Europeans—cold churches, without missionary zeal, and above all, worldly: they smoke, drink, and some even dance. With the exception of some isolated individuals, who did some reading on their own and paid dearly for it, nothing was known about Barth, Brunner, or Bultmann until the decade of the fifties.

I am not referring here to what the laity knew, but rather to the seminaries, which preferred a metaphysical theology that opened with proofs of the existence of God. Kant had not even been born. Theology had no relation to the life of the congregations because, as we have said, the rules of institutional circulation of ideas in the seminaries were different from the operative rules in local churches.

If I had to choose one word to define the dominant tendency of Protestant thought in this period, I would say it was marked by *parochialism:* separated from the world currents that inspired other churches; separated from the universal political questions; separated from national culture and life.

Protestantism moved in accord with the demands of the parish. As a result of its specific institutional organization, the survival of intellectual leadership depended (as it still does) on support from the parish.

Turbulence: The Nineteen-Fifties

The decade of the fifties marks an intellectual convulsion in Protestant circles. On the one hand, the entire country passed through a political-social ferment, as a result of the rapid social transformations coming from industrialization and urbanization. Developmentalist programs made large segments of the population aware of the immense misery and the enormous backwardness of the country. On the other hand, it also suggested alternatives available to them.

For a long time the churches had organized youth movements, whose objective was to create a place for young people. In the beginning these operated as pietistic associations that offered "wholesome recreation" (sports, necessary to sexual sublimation; parties, in which dancing was prohibited; and folk games, chiefly imported from the U.S.) and were intended to become a "spiritual incubator" to keep the youth from contamination by the world.

Gradually, however, the leaders of the movement became more mature, and this led to a radical change in orientation. The objective now became to create a space in which to work. By the middle of the decade one of the most important activities was the "work camp." Youth of various denominations dedicated their vacations to living in a poor locale, frequently *favelas* (slums), to carry out some kind of manual labor such as building a road, a reservoir, or something similar.

Such a movement was already the fruit of the penetration of ecumenical ideas into Brazil, and duplicated things European and North American youth were doing. New ideas provoked ferment everywhere: the ecumenical idea (basically Protestant), a new liturgical concern (which would make Protestants more sensitive to Catholicism), a new kind of Bible study (far from the polemic and moralizing ideas of pastoral preaching) and, above all, social concerns.

The movement had two important results: (1) a radical theological influence that separated the youth from the classic pastoral leaders, and (2) the formation of a lay leadership, free of the parochial controls to which pastors were subject. Youth had little to lose because they did not receive their livelihood from the church, as did pastors and lay church professionals. Therefore they enjoyed an immense freedom. The theological rupture resulted in conflicts that eventually crushed the movement. Out of their experiences arose a wave of students eager to choose vocations in the pastorate (myself included).

We should note that this is typically a middle-class movement, which used a new theological instrument imported from Europe. Popular Protestantism, of the pentecostal type, remained on the margins.

Parallels with the conditions that led to the rise of the social gospel are suggestive: rapid social changes, the formation of voluntary (nonclerical) movements, especially among youth and students, a rereading of the faith in terms of its political-social effectiveness, and the inevitable appearance of crises. It would not be wrong to identify the social gospel as the precursor of the theology of liberation.

The Purge: Beginning at the End of the Decade of the Fifties

Following the military coup of 1964 the dissidents found themselves accused by the church of being subversives. Their reaction was violent and radical. The youth movements were dissolved; the seminaries went into ecclesiastical receivership; dozens of students were expelled; professors were fired; church journals were closed. In return, those who defended the new ideas were piteously denounced as modernists, heretics, adherents of the social gospel, ecumenist-romanists. The sector of the Social Responsibility of the Church of the Evangelical Confederation was dissolved and its directors dismissed.

The climate of "witch-hunts," which is often present in crisis situations and is useful to those in power, makes it impossible to maintain the warmth and spiritual devotion of a community. When this takes place, spiritual warmth can find fuel only in some alternative source of energy.

In this situation just such a new phenomenon occurred: the pentecostalization of the middle-class churches, a movement that emphasized the gifts of the Spirit, such as speaking in tongues, prophecy, and healing. It took the name of "spiritual renewal." It was no longer the proletariat speaking in strange tongues, but the respectable and well-off middle-class families who would never think of joining a Pentecostal congregation. They preferred to live their extraordinary experiences within the respectable space of their traditional congregations.

Spiritual renewal obviously created parallel leadership. The institutional and bureaucratic leadership did not subdue the charismatic leadership. Conflicts arose, but the pastors soon learned that the best policy was peaceful coexistence. Now the danger was no longer the loss of a few youth, who made no difference in the church budget, but the catastrophic desertion of entire middle-class families, without which prosperous congregations would be reduced to caricatures of what they had formerly been.

What happened to the generation that convulsed the church in the fifties? This research still must be done. Many simply abandoned the church. Others joined more liberal congregations, carrying on their activities as ordinary members with a certain amount of daring. Some adapted under the institutional pressures to which we have referred. Another group tried to create alternative space, ecumenical and para-ecclesiastical, as instruments of their ideas.

This causes us to face the crucial question of the purposes of the writing of history. A positivist perspective would say that history is written simply because it is there, in the past, and is offered to us through documents and monuments. The historian is someone who recovers lost memories and distributes them, as though they were a sacrament, to those who have lost memory. In fact, what better communitarian sacrament exists than the memories of a common past, marked by the experience of pain, sacrifice, and hope, gathered up to distribute? A historian is not just an archeologist of memories; he is a planter of visions and of hope.

This is why scientific concern bores me when it invades history. Can a historian be objective and dispassionate? Does he not go about his research like someone searching for a lost love letter that will make the loved one forever happy? Does he not go about as someone who searches for a lost will that will enrich the poor one who looks for it?

Every work of history should begin with a confession of love—which would save it from antiseptic, scientific character, and give it political significance.

Look how difficult it is to know and to say what Protestantism is. History gives us a complex of conflicts and oppositions that we are not able to separate. Both the inquisitors and those who suffer the inquisition are called Protestants. If I still call myself Protestant, it is because I make a selection of materials, beginning with love—in the same way the lover ignores the temper tantrums of the one beloved. The loved one is always sweet. The shrew that inhabits her or him is ephemeral, caused by hormonal chemistry.

There is a rich tradition in Protestantism to be uncovered and distributed, beginning with Luther's believer free of law (which K. Holl affirms to be the precursor of the creative person of Nietzsche), passing through Kant, Hegel, Kierkegaard, Feuerbach, Albert Schweitzer, the eternal Bach; which reappears in an uncounted number of companions of the struggle with whom we pray—some alive, some dead (some assassinated)—for whom we would do anything out of loyalty and gratitude. I feel very comfortable in the company of these people. I carry on my dialogues with them. Maybe this is what it means to continue to be Protestant.

Without forgetting that Protestantism hanged and burned witches, enslaved blacks, and theologically justified slavery—with more recent frequency than we might like—still it offers inspiration to those armed for the liberating struggle.

I am saddened by the suspicion that Protestant thought is capable of handling only the well-ordained situations, without knowing what to do with earth-shaking or apocalyptic ones. Worlds need to be destroyed and created. This is what the past whispers to us.

It is consoling (yet irritating) to recognize that it was the Catholic church that took advantage of the best fruits of Protestant thought. And this suggests a strange possibility to us: could it be that a study of Protestant ideals must move beyond Protestant institutions to enter the heart of Catholicism?

As to the future, I have nothing to say. The question should not come up—unless the past is seen as the origin of prophecy. Can we agree with Nietzsche?

> The verdict of the past is always an oracle.
> Only as architects of the future and
> in knowledge of the present
> can we understand it.

Perhaps to talk of the future of Protestantism, it is necessary to remember the past of Catholicism. Which takes us to the Vision of the Valley of Dry Bones of the prophet Ezekiel, which miraculously becomes an uncountable living multitude. Who would have said that the Catholic church would pass through the metamorphosis it has experienced?

Nobody, especially not the Protestants. Protestantism may rediscover its own heritage, alive in Catholicism. This may lead to the miracle of the healing of the enmity between them and an openness to a common future.

Distortions in the Transmission of the Original Legacy of Wesley

MORTIMER ARIAS *(Methodist, Costa Rica)*

Three Initial Observations

The Protestantism we experience today in Latin America came to us through the faithful witness of others. It shows no lack of appreciation for their fidelity to analyze the distortions which resulted in the transmission of the original legacy.

The first "distortion" was the change of context or environment, as light waves are distorted when they pass through environments of different density. A familiar example is the "broken" spoon in a cup of water. The context of eighteenth-century England was not that of the North America of Independence, or the Western frontier, or the Civil War, or post–World War. None of these is the context of twentieth-century Latin America. It would have been a miracle if there were not distortions in the transmission of Wesley's legacy.

Second, in addition to the distortions were continuity and fidelity, even correction and enrichment. I think of three "corrective" and enriching contributions to our original legacy: the so-called social gospel, the ecumenical movement, and as a specific contribution of Latin America, the theology of liberation.

Third, we need a close look at what we consider to be the "original legacy of Wesley." I suggest we begin with the words of Wesley himself, with his definition of the mission of Methodism in the First Annual Conference of 1744:

Question: What can we reasonably believe to have been the plan of God in raising up preachers called Methodists?

Answer: Not to form a new sect, but to reform the Nation and especially the Church, and to spread scriptural holiness throughout the nation. (*Works,* 5:212)

Here we discover the first "distortion" in the North American transmission. In the First General Conference of 1784 in Baltimore, when the autonomous Methodist Episcopal Church was constituted, the answer to the same question was put in this way:

Answer: To reform the Continent and to spread scriptural holiness over these lands (*Discipline,* 1785).

Here we have continuity and discontinuity. Reform of the church is not mentioned because the reform movement is now a church. The note about "not to form a new sect" naturally disappears. However, the central nucleus of "to spread scriptural holiness" is maintained. "The Nation" is replaced by "the Continent." And the verb *spread* or *propagate* signals the missionary impulse so characteristic of the Wesleyan tradition.

Another basic statement of Wesley's suggests a nuance of his concept of "scriptural holiness" as related to the totality of individual and social life: "The Gospel of Christ knows no religion other than social, nor does it recognize any holiness other than social" (*Works,* 7:593).

From "Scriptural Holiness" to the Controversy over Sanctification

Wesley's thought was little known within North American Methodism except, among the pastors, through the *Sermons* and, at the congregational level, through the *General Rules.*

Theologically, sanctification became the most familiar Wesleyan doctrine. Transmitted through the works of Fletcher and Watson, second generation British Methodist theologians, it was later given a personalistic and liberal reformulation, notably from Boston Theological Seminary.

In the field of Methodist spirituality and practice, the doctrine of perfection in love (which José Míguez Bonino calls "human fullness") undergoes two fundamental reductions. One is the *puritan reduction,* concentrated in a negative ethic of prohibition of amusements, abstinence from alcoholic liquors, and in the observance of the Sabbath. Methodist publications and our own generational experience show how influential this puritan reduction was in the transmission of "scriptural holiness." It was a reduction not only of the biblical doctrine of holiness but also of Puritanism itself, with its rich biblical and theological heritage (the covenant, the kingdom of God, election). This heritage was of enormous importance in the genesis of modern democracy and in the reordering of society. The influence of Ritschl and his followers in North America helped to reenforce this moralistic tendency, although it also contributed decisively to the theological foundations of the social gospel.

With similar reservations, we may speak of the *pietist reduction* of "scriptural holiness." That is, the tendency to emphasize holiness as a personal religious experience comparable to conversion: unique and distinct, instantaneous and definitive, called the "second blessing."

This was not the distortion transmitted to Latin America, because the missionaries trained in the seminaries of Garrett, Boston, Drew, and Emory represented a gradualist view of sanctification. However, the little emphasis given sanctification in the Methodism transmitted to Latin America is notable, as is the almost total absence of references to "scriptural holiness."

The distortion, however, is neither total nor unanimous. There is a much richer and more dialectic context for sanctification in the thoughts of some persons and movements, such as the first dissidents who formed new denominations. For example, the Wesleyan Methodist Church separated in refusal to accept the episcopacy and in condemnation of slavery. The separation was basically in fidelity to "pure Wesleyanism," especially with respect to the emphasis on sanctification. The Free Methodist Church, parallel to the Wesleyan, with origins in the Tennessee (Pennsylvania) Conference, had a series of controversies with the Methodist Episcopal Church over forms of worship, episcopal authority, doctrinal emphases, participation in secret societies (Masons), paid pews, and tolerance of slavery. Wesleyan perfection was their objective and motivation.

Also within the Methodist Episcopal Church were men and women who took part in the movement to "promote holiness," who were militantly active in social reform movements.

Among them were Bishop Gilbert Haven, firm defender of racial and social justice, and Frances Willard, founder of the Women's Christian Temperance Union, also a leader in the abolition movement and in emerging feminism. While some, such as Phoebe Palmer, separated "holiness" and "world," others tried to maintain the unity of the two elements of the Wesleyan legacy: personal holiness and social reform.

Gilbert Haven opened Methodist work in Mexico. Therefore one might think that the results of this work would be representative of the Methodist passion for personal and social holiness. But it was not so. Even in the churches of Central and South America, founded by the Methodist Episcopal Church of the North, the social accent was almost unknown.

From Evangelical Renewal to the Anti-Catholic Polemic

Another distorting tendency in North American Methodism at the end of the century, also present in the entry of Methodism into Latin America, was a strong anti–Roman Catholic orientation.

In the Wesleyan tradition there is Catholic substance along with an accidental anti-Roman posture. For obvious historical reasons, from the time of Henry VIII and successive attempts at the restoration of Catholic monarchs in England, "romanism" and "popery" were real factors.

Wesley adapted the Anglican Articles of Faith, keeping those that were polemically defined against the Catholicism of the Counter-Reformation of Trent, including their combative language ("Of Works of Supererogation," "Of Good Works," "Of Purgatory," "Of the Use in the Congregation of a Language the People Understand," "Of the Sacraments," "Of Transubstantiation," "Of the Marriage of Ministers"). Of course he preached against the errors and deviations of "romanism."

Wesley's theology, however, is profoundly Catholic. His emphasis on sanctification along with justification was always a cause for suspicion among other Protestant theologians. Wesley was strongly attracted by the spirituality of the Catholic mystics. He learned Spanish to be able to read the works of the sixteenth-century Spanish mystics in their own language.

His quadrilateral criterion of authority in theology (Scripture, tradition, reason, and experience) is a mark of his catholicity. Committed to the renewal of his own church, based in the christocentric experience of salvation, he opposed the Roman "deviations" consolidated at Trent.

Catholicity is essential in the Wesleyan concept of faith. He did not want to convert Catholics to Protestantism, but wanted all to be converted to Christ, whether they were Catholics, nominal Protestants, or members of his own Anglican Church.

North American Methodism, like all Protestantism in the colonies, did not suffer the effects of Roman Catholic domination or intolerance so characteristic in the countries of the Counter-Reformation. On the contrary, Catholics were a minority, initially confined to the small state of Maryland. However, as Martin Marty notes in *Righteous Empire,* the missionaries of the "Protestant Empire" began in some way to lump "Catholics" along with "Indians" and "Pagans" as adversaries to be conquered.

A report on the "State of the World" in the Methodist Episcopal Church, South, in 1847 reflects, from that viewpoint, what was perhaps a more generalized attitude in relation to Roman Catholicism:

> The daring and aggressive movements of popery, the very clear purpose of the Pope is to colonize our lands, to people our happy land with a flood of European subjects . . . through the Jesuit instrumentality . . . hiding the doctrine of supremacy. . . . American Protestantism . . . trembles both for its country and its Christianity.

From this, the report drew arguments to reenforce missionary work within the northern nation itself, with a section entitled "The Importance of Home Missions as a Means of Resistance" (*Annual Report of the Missionary Society, 1846–1850,* pp. 67-68).

This motivation naturally penetrated the mission outside the nation, especially that in Latin America, the "papal lands" where romanism had ruled for centuries and kept the people in "abject darkness." The dominant impulse of nineteenth-century missions was to fulfil the Great Commission (Matt. 28:19) and take the light of the gospel to the people who lived in the "shadows of paganism."

In the case of Latin America, the "shadows of Catholic semipaganism" represented a "corrupt and idolatrous" Christianity, which denied religious liberty and made the Bible a forbidden and totally unknown book.

Of course, objective conditions in these countries actually confirmed these fears and prejudices. The Catholicism that reached Latin America was that of the Inquisition and the Counter-Reformation, not accustomed to ecumenicity. Popular Catholicism was highly superstitious, syncretistic, tied to the veneration of saints, holy places, and the Virgin Mary. All of this was immediately obvious to the first Protestant missionaries to arrive in these lands. In Rosario, Argentina, a missionary was disturbed when she saw "the spiritual ignorance of the masses . . . and a perverted and corrupt form of Christian faith" (Baker, p. 382).

Foreseeably, the preaching of the gospel in its Protestant version provoked violent Catholic resistance. There was rejection and hostility in every country. The reaction was out of all proportion to the presence of one or two missionaries distributing Bibles and holding meetings with believers. For example, in response to the presence of the first missionary, Justin R. Spaulding, Padre Luis Gonçalves dos Santos published a book, *O católico e o metodista*, in Rio de Janeiro in 1839. In it dos Santos said:

> Up till now no heretic has dared to raise his voice to pervert Catholics, because the Catholic Church of Brazil was a closed garden into which no dangerous animal could enter: a sheepfold protected on all sides which no wolf would dare approach. (Quoted in Long, p. 20)

Padre Luis regarded the Methodists as the most recent sect, concluding that

> [they] are, of all Protestants, the most lax and immoral despite the hypocrisy which they affect outwardly to deceive fools.
>
> These so-called missionaries have already been among us for almost two years trying to pervert Catholics, shaking their faith. (Ibid., p. 32; Reily, pp. 107-8)

But it was not just Protestant presence and evangelization that provoked reactions: there was a strong tendency among the first missionaries and their early converts—especially former Catholic priests—to an exaggerated anti-romanism in their preaching.

It is easy—and certainly distorting—to judge this missionary strategy almost a hundred years later from the point of view of our present ecumenical perspective. But the fruits show that churches do not come into being or grow on pure polemic. There is always the latent danger that the understanding of the gospel will be reduced to an "anti-." For example, I asked a young man in one of my Montevideo churches why he was a Protestant. He did not know how to answer except to say, "Because I'm not Catholic."

In this sense the Wesleyan legacy was distorted. The distorting tendency was already present in the first missionary motivation but it found on Latin American soil a highly propitious context for its exacerbation and perpetuation. A look at the list of Methodist publications at the beginning of this century illustrates this: the majority of the books and tracts are anti-romanist; of Wesleyanism and Christianity there was almost nothing. The most popular Protestant book in the first part of the century was *Nights with the Romanists,* loaded with anti-Catholic controversial ammunition.

From "World Parish" to "Manifest Destiny"

Wesley's statement, "the world is my parish," became the motto of Methodist missionary expansion. Through two hundred years in North American Methodism, the expression was reinterpreted out of context and impregnated with other elements of the spiritual and ideological atmosphere of the republic of the North.

The words were originally directed to those who said Wesley had no right to preach in their parishes. It was a question of canon law, which was on Wesley's side. As a "Fellow" at Oxford he had the right to preach in any episcopal jurisdiction. But Wesley went deeper and held that anywhere a person needed him, in any place where he was asked to preach, he would be there: "the world is my parish." The criteria are human need, the freedom of the spirit, and the nature of the gospel.

The missionary impulse, the mandate to take the "Gospel to the whole creation," which is part of the Wesleyan legacy, was distorted when interpreted in the context of North American "manifest destiny" as the need to carry the gospel in its North American version, with Anglo-Saxon instrumentalities, into all the world!

Manifest destiny originated in the Puritan interpretation of God's providence, which saw the North American experience of freedom, expansion, and progress as a blessing from God and the proof of being the "new Israel," the chosen people of God with a special mission. In fact, the deists (Franklin, Jefferson) who prepared the coat of arms of the new nation used the biblical scene of Moses leading his people to freedom.

Furthermore, manifest destiny was used to justify the conquest of the West—shoving the Indians out and finally shunting them onto "reservations"—and the annexation of Florida and Louisiana. The Mexican-American War, resulting in the consolidation of the Southwest, completed the occupation from ocean to ocean.

Again, manifest destiny served Theodore Roosevelt in the building of the Panama Canal, and permitted control of the Caribbean as a *mare nostrum*.

The religious version of manifest destiny, which reenforced the missionary motivation, was that the churches of the United States represented the purest form of Christianity (with those of England a distant second). Protestantism was the surest hope for Christianity and for the world. Some Methodists even came to believe that Methodism, in its turn, represented the purest and most advanced form of Anglo-Saxon Protestantism. This was the connotation given to missionary phrases such as "the Great Commission," the "evangelization of the world," "the salvation of humanity in Christ."

An extreme form of this manifest destiny, in its Methodist version, appears in the Annual Report of the Missionary Society of the Methodist Episcopal Church, South (1848):

> Methodism is Christianity in successful operation. Nothing that is not Protestant can be truly and legitimately American. All the other communities . . . supported and controlled by foreign influences [a clear allusion to Roman Catholicism

with its center in the Vatican] should be considered as strangers and foreigners in the community [commonwealth] of our Israel. We are destined . . . to be the honored instruments in the religious and political regeneration of the world . . . untouched and uncontaminated by worldly associations. . . . Here, in this land, nowhere else in the world, . . . we have been blessed with pure Christianity. (Pp. 10-13)

In the North, despite the onerous war with the South, there still survived a triumphalism, seeing God's providence in the defeat of the South and the end of slavery. It is also seen in the church's mission to the South and among freed slaves.

It is possible that during the decade of the 1880s this triumphalism may have somewhat thinned out. Methodist influence in the society at large had lessened. It is interesting to note, however, that J. Spaulding in his mission to Brazil had expressed the hope of contributing to the cause of freeing the slaves (1836–1838). In 1888 the Eastern Conference of South America had set up a "Protective Board for Freed Slaves" (Minutes of the Annual Conference East of South America, 1888, pp. 36-37). The magnitude of the task (a million and a half freed slaves in Brazil) is not seen as an impediment:

> The abolition of slavery in South America is a joyful event. . . . Our church in North America distinguished itself, excelling the other denominations . . . , impels us to act on behalf of these disinherited ones, our brothers with common human blood, following the same lines of action that our church made glorious in North America in analogous circumstances. (Minutes, 1888, p. 37)

The intentions were very good, but there is no doubt we were infected with the triumphalism of manifest destiny in its Methodist version. This was in faithful continuity and, at the same time, distorting discontinuity with our Wesleyan legacy.

From a "Religion of the Common Man" to a Middle-Class Church

Another distorting factor of the Wesleyan legacy was the evolution of the social component of the original Methodist movement. Wesley spoke to the masses, preaching to the miners and to the floating populations of the cities and industrial centers of Great Britain. The Methodist societies were made up basically of workers, artisans, domestic employees, and others with no social or economic status. This is what scandalized the Duchess of Buckingham when they told her she was on the same level as these "poor unfortunates." It is what made her look down on the "people called Methodists" and their "chapels" (they were not churches or sanctuaries).

The first generation of lay preachers was composed mainly of the sons of workers, artisans, sheepherders, and school teachers. From their ranks and from those of the Sunday school teachers came the first leaders of the English "labor" movement. Yet the Wesleyan church, which succeeded John Wesley, began to distance itself from the workers and their unions. It assumed an attitude of neutrality and declined to join the social struggle. The Primitive Methodist Church split from the original church precisely because of its attitudes with relation to the workers' movements.

In the United States, the phenomenal growth of the Methodist movement took place in the lowest social, cultural, and economic levels of the emerging society, through revivals and the sacrificial work of "circuit riders" who accompanied the people into new territories. Around 1850, however, the Methodist Episcopal Church began to take on the shape of a middle-class church, through the upward social mobility of its members. This was especially accentuated after the Civil War.

Interest in the evangelization of the North American Indians and the improvement of the conditions of freed slaves continues. Wesley's legacy is preserved with greater clarity, however, in the black Methodist denominations, among Methodists who participated in the "populist" movements in the South, and among those who were militant in the first attempts at a North American socialism.

But neither black Methodists nor the participants in these movements came to Latin America. The missionaries, graduates of liberal seminaries from the last quarter of the century, represented a middle-class church, principally of small landholders and ranchers in the rural areas.

Some large churches were beginning to be formed in the

cities. The Methodist "ethos," however, was still that of the countryside and small towns.

The Methodist Episcopal Church had already embarked on the creation of large universities and seminaries as breeding grounds for the leadership of the national church and of the missionary enterprise.

The motivation of reaching the "poor" was not lost, not even in the Methodist Episcopal Church, South. It was the basis for its own mission among blacks, Indians, inhabitants of all races in the "destitute areas" of their own states, although with strong individualistic and spiritualizing accents.

The consistent missionary strategy in Latin America was to "occupy" the principal cities, beginning with the ports and spreading along the principal access roads to the interior. The point of entry into a closed society, religiously controlled by the Roman Catholic church, was the migrant population of English, Germans, and French, among whom there were already Protestant families.

Methodism also found echoes among immigrant artisans, more independent with relationship to local and national traditions. Many Italian societies directed by Garibaldians and the new Masonic lodges were among the first to hear the preachers.

Education was a primary need in our countries, and was welcomed by liberal governments wishing to be free of the control of education by Catholic religious orders. New types of education, especially from North America (mixed, practical, scientific, and commercial, with the teaching of languages) were valued. The well-known educator-president of Argentina, Sarmiento, praised the "popular education" in Protestant countries and brought teachers from the United States. José Pedro Varela, of Uruguay, was pleased with the establishment of the first Methodist schools.

The same thing happened with the government of Bolivia, which stimulated the establishment of schools, even changing the constitution to incorporate religious liberty and to revoke the death penalty for non-Catholics, which had been in the Penal Code. These trends provided a foothold for the new missionary movement.

In Chile the schools and colleges were the indispensable

base for carring out William Taylor's strategy of founding self-sustaining missions.

Although there were always scholarships for poorer students, tuition was charged and the schools became elitist. The presence of well-to-do families, able to pay and interested in modernizing educational methods, influenced the philosophy and orientation of the institutions. An illuminating example is that of seventeen small schools for poor people in the barrios of Montevideo that were later concentrated into one school. And for many decades Crandon Institute has been one of the most exclusive secondary schools in Uruguay.

Education, which began as a necessity on the mission field, including the preparation of candidates for the ministry, ended as a distorting factor of John Wesley's original legacy. He too founded schools and orphanages, but for the poor of the mining centers.

In recent decades, Methodist schools have been used in support of a pro–North American policy. As Wilson Boots has said, while some missionaries saw schools as a form of Christian evangelistic witness, others saw them as a way to inculcate Christian ideals in the future elite. Still others justified them as an instrument for furthering Pan-Americanism. Ambassadors praised the schools for their effectiveness in developing good relationships with the United States. But using North American symbols and names, as well as North American personnel, led to many errors among friends and adversaries. A pathetic case concerned the Methodist schools in Bolivia. When they tried to change the word "American" in their name to another more faithful to national objectives and programs, the reaction came precisely from alumni who used their influence in the government to reimpose the old name.

Currently the basic question about the "educational apparatus" is whether it serves to carry forward or to distort the Wesleyan legacy. In a Latin American Methodist educational consultation in Bolivia in 1980, the delegates chose "an option for justice" in the schools. They were very aware of the difficulties of transforming middle-class institutions, oriented to the dominant class and to upward social mobility, into instruments of conscientization, popular education, and liberation. This is an agonizing problem; the distortions and contradictions are evident.

Missionary John E. Washburn, after working some time in the Methodist school in Cochabamba, laid out the situation in these terms:

> We have the lower class in the church and the higher class in the school. It is well known that these two cannot mix without provoking displeasure in the higher class. (Quoted in Barclay, 1957, p. 33)

This has been our dilemma and a distorting factor in our legacy, and a common pattern in other Protestant educational institutions.

We still have many "common people" in our Latin American Methodist churches—more than we suspect or want to believe. This is so because, in our mentality, our focus, our methodology, even if not in our own social class, we are a middle-class church. We need to see them as a gift of pure grace.

That is where we have to begin today in taking our own options. It is not simply a case of analyzing the distorting mediations of the "original legacy of Wesley," but of analyzing our own distortions!

Personal Conclusions

Allow me to end on a personal note. Recently I had the great joy of visiting in Uruguay an eighty-two-year-old man, who had been my pastor in the crucial years of my adolescence. He did not have a seminary education—and carried this complex through all his life—but he knew how to be a pastor. He transmitted to me "the Wesleyan legacy," which is nothing but the Christian legacy, the best he could, distortions and all. It was through him and his ministry that I came to know the gospel that has given meaning and value to my life.

Most of what I am, I owe to the Methodist church. Yes, this same one with the distortions we are analyzing. "Noblesse oblige"—gratitude obligates us. But gratitude does not exempt us from self-criticism, nor from corrections we should make. This self-criticism and return to the original legacy of Jesus Christ is also part of the "original legacy of Wesley" that we have received and for which we are responsible.

Works Consulted

Annual Report of the Board of Foreign Missions of the Methodist Episcopal Church (the years prior to the union of the Methodist Churches of the United States in 1939), New York.

Annual Report of the Board of Missions of the Methodist Church (1939–1968).

Annual Report of the Board of Missions of the United Methodist Church (since 1968).

Annual Report of the Board of Global Ministries of the United Methodist Church (since 1972).

Annual Report of the Missionary Society of the Methodist Episcopal Church, South. Louisville: Morton & Griswold's Power Press, 1846, 1847, 1848, 1850.

Arms, Goodsil F. *History of the William Taylor Self-Supporting Missions in South America.* New York: Methodist Book Concern, 1921.

Baker, Frances J. *The Story of the Women's Foreign Missionary Society of the Methodist Episcopal Church, 1869–1895.* New York: Eaton & Main, 1898.

Barclay, Wade Crawford. *History of Methodist Missions,* vol. 1: *1769–1844;* vol. 3: *1845–1895.* New York: Board of Missions of the Methodist Church, 1957.

————. *History of Methodist Missions—Early American Methodism, 1769–1844.* New York: Board of Missions and Church Extension of the Methodist Church, 1949.

Bixly, William. *An Outline of Foreign Missions of Methodist Episcopal Church.* Syracuse, N.Y., 1876.

Boots, Wilson T. *Cristianismo evangélico en Bolivia.* New York: Union Theological Seminary, 1966.

Butler, Mrs. F. A. (Sarah Frances Stingfield). *History of the Women's Foreign Mission Society—Methodist Episcopal Church, South.* Nashville: Smith & Lamar, 1904.

Cameron, James, III. *History of Southern Methodist Missions.* Nashville: Cokesbury, 1926.

Copplestone, J. Tremayne. *History of Methodist Missions*, vol. 4: *1895–1939*. New York: Board of Global Ministries of the United Methodist Church, 1973.

Leonard, Emile G. *O protestantismo brasileiro*. São Paulo: Aste, n.d.

Long, Eula Kennedy. *Do meu velho baú metodista*. São Bernardo do Campo: Junta de Educação Cristã, Igreja Metodista do Brasil, 1968.

Marty, Martin E. *Righteous Empire: The Protestant Experience in America*. New York: Dial Press, 1970.

Meno Barreto, Jaime Eduardo. *História do metodismo no Rio Grande do Sul*. Porto Alegre: Empresa Gráfica Moderna, 1963.

Montí, Daniel P. *Ubicación del metodismo en el Rio de La Plata*. Buenos Aires: La Aurora, 1976.

Reid, J. M. *Missions and Missionary Society of the Methodist Episcopal Church*, vol. 2. New York: Philips & Hunt, 1882.

Reily, Duncan A. *Metodismo brasileiro e wesleyano*. São Bernardo do Campo: Imprensa Metodista, 1981.

Richardson, Harry V. *Dark Salvation: The Story of Methodism as It Developed among Blacks in America*. Garden City, N.Y.: Doubleday, 1976.

Rocha, Isnard. *Histórias da história do metodismo no Brasil*.

Souvenir Book of the Golden Anniversary or Jubilee of the Methodist Episcopal Church in Mexico, 1873–1923, Mexico: Casa Unida de Publicaciones, 1924.

The Missionary Heritage of the Cuban Churches

Despite Everything . . . I Am Still a Protestant

ISRAEL BATISTA GUERRA   *(Methodist, Cuba)*

Twenty-five years after the revolution—this is a time for objective thinking, to discover not only the failures and successes of the past but also the way forward into the future.

My starting point is the tension I have experienced as a Protestant in a revolutionary situation. My experiences have been very mixed: experiences of being torn apart and of creativity; of pessimism and of optimism; of cursing the heritage we have received (after the manner of Jeremiah), and of thanking God for the educational blessings that are ours (after the manner of Paul).

Being a Protestant in a revolutionary situation has meant experiencing a crisis of meaning: What does it mean to be a Protestant, a member of a somewhat alienated minority, in the midst of a society in reconstruction? At the same time, there has been a crisis of mission: How can we ensure that Protestantism identifies with the people in their historic process and transcends the liberalism of its origins?

I should like first to examine what I have called "the heavy burdens of a heritage that obstructs progress"; then to consider "the factors that make renewal possible."

The Heavy Burdens of a Heritage That Obstructs Progress

What are the negative factors of the missionary heritage in which we were reared?

244

The Economic Factor

Protestantism has produced *homo productivus* rather than *homo ludens*, and we need to reconsider the economic factors influencing our thought patterns and modes of action. While not falling into a mechanistic Marxism, I feel it impossible to deny the economic implications of theological activity. In this regard, I mention three factors that show the connection between Protestantism and capitalist methods of production.

First, Protestantism in its origins, in addition to being a voice of protest and liberation, is the product of a particular period of history, that of the transition from feudalism to capitalism. Max Weber's description of capitalism and the spirit of Protestantism is a classic presentation. It is undeniable that capitalism has proved capable of co-opting Protestantism with the greatest of ease. We have unwittingly become part of the system; the market theory has become deeply imprinted on Protestant thinking.

In the Cuban experience we see two manifestations of this interrelation between Protestantism and capitalism: (1) during the early years of the revolution, many of our brothers and sisters, who were genuinely Christian, felt disturbed and confused in their faith when the capitalist structure of the society disappeared. Some still feel that. Many asked sincerely how it was possible to be a Christian in a socialist society. In some cases it was more a crisis of faith than of politics.

(2) Because Protestants are a minority, they have always felt threatened. Evangelism has thus been determined by the need to be successful rather than simply to engage in mission. Just as the criterion of success is characteristic of the market theory, it has likewise motivated us in our evangelism. At present, we are going through a period of neoconfessionalism, which is to a certain extent understandable as we search for an identity and a way to strengthen our institutions; but this runs the risk of becoming a proselytizing movement with success as its aim.

Second, the theory of dependence is a description of the relationship between development and underdevelopment. That is, historically, underdevelopment is the product of the development of capitalist countries that have been stripping Third World countries of their wealth.

In our Latin American region, Protestantism is seen as part of this economic dependence. The arrival of the missionary movement in Latin America coincided with the introduction of economic dependence, first on Europe and then on the United States. It is not simply that the entrepreneur and the missionary arrived together—as the conquistador and the priest arrived together in former days—but also that this economic dependence brought with it a very pronounced intellectual dependence. The ideal—of which U.S. society was an example—was that of a nation with a "manifest destiny."

Economic dependence creates intellectual underdevelopment. In the economic field, ties were formed almost unilaterally with the United States, and similarly the missionary movement has made us look exclusively to the churches in the United States. Thought patterns, styles of worship, moral standards, even customs and dress in Cuban Protestantism are clear evidence of dependence on missionary Protestantism.

The relationship of dependence in the missionary movement is evident in two ways. Protestantism found greater acceptance in the middle class and gave priority to its work among that class. In addition, the educational emphasis in our churches resulted in the setting up of staff training centers for foreign firms. In other words, the ties with the middle class and the education provided for them made economic dependence inevitable.

Third, the arrival of the missionary movement coincided with the redivision of the world among the developed countries at the end of the nineteenth century. In the case of Cuba, the missionary movement is the direct result of U.S. intervention. As U.S. economic interests gained a firm foothold in our country, Protestantism consolidated its position. There was between the two a mutually beneficial relationship and an undeniable natural affinity.

My point is that the economic influence of the capitalist model of production is so intrinsically present in Protestantism that it has become a factor of which we are hardly aware. In Cuban Protestantism, the market economy has become so much a part of our inner being that it is a major cause of the confusion often experienced by the churches.

The Cultural Factor

Latin American Protestantism has failed to recognize the importance of the cultural factor. There is an endemic cultural poverty in Latin American Protestantism, and in Cuban Protestantism it is a problem of the first order.

The missionary movement arrived on our shores when our countries were gaining independence from Spanish colonialism, and our societies were beginning to shape themselves on a liberal pattern, under the influence and example of the French and American revolutions. It was a time when we were seeking our identity.

The missionary movement set Cuban Protestantism in the modern world of "civilization," thus producing a cultural vacuum. Hence, one of the greatest problems of our Protestantism is its lack of cultural identity, which sets it apart from the people. For example, worship in Cuban Protestantism is an example of a subculture dominated by practices from outside the country. Despite our efforts to renew worship in recent years, the influence of these traditional practices asserts itself. The lack of cultural identity is so pronounced that it is seen in the most progressive parts of our church. Because of our cultural poverty, we tend to be a leftist elite, with few links with the people, very given to enjoying the privileges and refusing to pay the cost involved in adopting popular culture.

Our Cuban-ness is a mixture of Spanish and African elements, a mulatto culture. It is impossible to find it in a pure form. The greatest achievement of Cuban identity is this mulatto quality. The missionary movement brought us, however, a Protestantism claiming to be pure and fearfully eschewing religious syncretism. The claim was made that certain values and standards corresponded to the pure gospel. In fact some of these elements were products of the "blond Anglo-Saxon" tradition and did not even reflect the "black African" traditions of the United States. To promote a "blond Anglo-Saxon" culture in a land of mulattoes results in cultural castration.

I wonder why there is this fear of syncretism. Until Cuban Protestantism overcomes this fear and accepts syncretism creatively, we shall have no cultural identity. In our churches we will continue to be a minority far removed from the people. This lack of cultural identity is one of the greatest problems confronting Cuban Protestantism.

The Biblical and Theological Factor

The Reformation was a very creative and fruitful time for biblical and theological activity. In our origins, we found that this biblical and theological thinking was a channel for the aspirations of the people. But this initial impetus was gradually lost, and the first creative period was followed by a second period marked by accommodation to the system and manipulation by it.

The transition is an interesting process. We tend to generalize when we say that the problem of traditional Protestant theology lies in its dualistic Greek separation of the sacred and the secular. That is in part correct; but Protestant dualism has peculiarities of its own. It does not produce mystics and monks, but pietists and entrepreneurs.

What has developed is an entrepreneurial pragmatic dualism. That is, people work in society with a great sense of vocation and dedication. Work is not despised, but there is no bridge between human beings as producers and human beings as people of faith, between the worlds of politics and of faith. This type of Protestant dualism is easily exploited by a social, economic, and political system. The only link between faith and politics is the idea of success, understood as the sign of God's blessing.

The missionary movement was the bearer of this type of dualism, to which it added a touch of fatalism and a strong emphasis on the gospel as apolitical. It is amazing how missionaries from the United States, who were so imbued with the ideas of "manifest destiny" and "civil religion," failed to see them as ideologies and proclaimed total separation of faith and politics.

Our own Protestant tradition really got underway with the "patriotic missionaries," Cubans returning to Cuba at the end of the nineteenth century with the revolutionary fighters of Cuban independence.

Originally faith and politics were very much one for us, but with the missionary movement they became divided and separate. The missionary movement produced two types of biblical and theological thinking that characterize two types of

Christians: fundamentalist Christians with a ghetto mentality, very hard working, but alienated from reality; and liberal Christians who were more intellectually and academically open, but who corresponded to and consented to the modernization of the system. The typical graduate of the Evangelical Seminary in Matanzas was of this latter type. Since the revolution, about 85 percent of them have left the country.

These two types of thinking have been deeply rooted in our churches and are still present today. We have the fundamentalist approach, which produces a type of schizophrenic Christian who participates and works in society but is alienated within our churches. And we have the liberal-progressive approach, the followers of which sacralize change, thus producing a sort of masochistic Christian, for whom everything outside the church is good, and everything in it bad! Nevertheless, signs of a new liberating approach have appeared recently.

The Ecumenical Factor

The individualism produced by Protestantism, of which the missionary movement is heir, is one of the major heretical distortions of the biblical concept of the *oikumene*.

Individualism fragments the spirit of community and of solidarity, which are essential elements in ecumenism. Not only do we feel denominationally divided; our divisions are an attack on the human community itself. Individualism makes us ungenerous and selfish instead of altruistic and outgoing. In my secular work I must admit I have found it very difficult to break out of this individualistic pattern.

Protestantism has also made private property a tenet of the faith, and private property in market theory is the quintessence of individualism. The irrational dogmatic defense of private property is an indication of how anti-ecumenical Protestantism is.

This reductionist ecumenism is an attack against human spirituality. Our spirituality has been a sectarian one. It has been the spirituality of a particular place—my place of worship; with a specific name—my denomination; with a select group of people—my Christian brothers and sisters.

The most important element in ecumenism is not its organized structures but its spiritual dimension. The *oikumene* has to do with the whole created world, the whole inhabited earth, without exception. Ecumenism reveals to us a spirituality of life confronting death. When we remove ecumenism from the whole inhabited earth, its culture, its political life, its ethos, we make it sectarian. Sectarianism is antispiritual because it denies solidarity and the beauty of human relationships. It becomes incapable of discovering the spirituality of life in human history.

The most painful experience for many of us in these difficult but hopeful years has been our ambiguous feelings toward our spirituality. We have wanted to throw this sectarian spirituality overboard, but at the same time we have felt like shipwrecked mariners wanting something to cling to. This reductionist ecumenism that has prevented us from finding God in the "whole inhabited earth" has cost us much as Christians.

The Factors That Make Renewal Possible

What are the liberating elements in our Protestant tradition that were strengthened by our missionary heritage and that need to be revitalized in the revolutionary process?

In our Protestant origins we find an emphasis on *freedom*. It is true that there have been negative tendencies in Protestantism, such as excessive authoritarianism. Freedom is too often understood as a formal principle rather than as a liberating praxis. It is no less true that a rich part of our heritage has also been freedom as an expression of "not being conformed to this age," the perpetual search for what is new with a constant openness to renewal.

I am not speaking here of bourgeois freedom, with its successes and failures, but of the freedom that liberates the human heart from all sin, ordinances, and law. As Luther said, such freedom is not complacent but makes us dissatisfied with the present because we are seekers and builders of the kingdom. It is the freedom to be bound to Christ and our neighbor alone.

When a society decides to change its structures, the criteria of freedom are also changed—and even more so when, for its own survival before unjustified attack from outside, it must restrain individual freedom for the sake of the community.

In the Cuban experience, a Protestant contribution to this society in construction is that it sees freedom as a road being built, not as a finished work; freedom is not the attainment of perfection but the possibility of being open to it.

In the biblical story, human society is viewed as a society of workers. *Work,* with its element of vocation and creation of a new world, is the basic means of changing the created world. In contrast to the contemplative static ethos of the feudal world, capitalism arose as a world of work but it was quickly taken over by new masters. A high regard for work, however, still exists in Protestantism.

Work is another of the elements in our Protestant and missionary tradition that needs to be redeemed—not only because we live in a society of workers, but because there are two aspects of this to be considered in our society. On the one hand, the socialist system of production has not yet reached the efficiency of the capitalist system, which is based on inequality and oppression, in areas ranging from technical matters to the actual security felt by workers in our society. On the other hand, Cuban workers have a considerable spirit of sacrifice, but they sometimes find it difficult to see the importance of regular work day after day.

In this perspective we can contribute to the building of new men and women, instilling in them a deep sense of vocation, stressing the dimension of service to one's neighbor, regular commitment, the creation of what is new, and self-sacrifice as a sign of solidarity. This tradition of work in our Protestant heritage has its place in our society.

Because we had become somewhat weary of pharisaical *morality,* we attempted to throw out a whole series of moral concepts. But we soon discovered that morality cannot be changed as one changes a suit of clothes. Morality has to arise out of concrete praxis, and moral principles cannot be artificially constructed. We are not suggesting a return to past patterns, but we do not create the present by erasing the past. Growth and learning must be dialectical. Moral principles demand a certain discipline—a truth we cannot forget if we wish to renew our Protestantism. Moral strength is an essential condition for meaningful living. We have learned from the revolution that morality is the most powerful weapon there is: in their hands it makes even the

251

weak strong. We need to purge our morality of pharisaism, but not of its valuable principles. We must not pull up the wheat with the tares.

Our faith, moreover, is deeply spiritual. In a society such as ours, with great spiritual values but with too much stress laid at times on the rational and the scientific, *spirituality* acquires great significance. What happens in society is not determined by economic forces alone: people are also motivated by subjective, spiritual forces. For example, the resistance of the people before their oppressors is a spiritual value. In the creation of new men and women, spirituality is a dimension that must not be forgotten. More than that, spirituality complements certain human values and resources that Marxism cannot always effectively tap. Even more than that, as our churches are converted, we must discover a new spirituality that will be the fruit of dialectical growth between the riches of the past and the opportunities of the present.

Pastoral theology is not a common idea in Cuban Protestantism. When we do speak of it, we do so with reference to activity centered on the pastor, the paternalistic care for a congregation. As Julio de Santa Ana reminds us in his book, *Por las sendas del mundo caminando hacia el Reino*, the central importance that has been given to the role of the pastor in pastoral care goes against the Reformation principle of the priesthood of all believers.

We need to evolve a Protestant pastoral care based on the priesthood of all believers and the diversity of gifts in the ministry of the church. Pastoral care has been one of the strengths of Protestantism, but it has been neglected. It needs to be revived, not with a concentration on the clergy, but through the participation of all in the growth of all.

It needs, too, to be pastoral work not aimed exclusively at strengthening the institution, but giving priority to people's sense of mission and participation. It is "pastoral care in grace": as we are faithful to our mission, we shall be blessed by grace as God's people. If there is anything we should learn from the missionary movement, it is its sense of mission.

We cannot think of Protestants without their *Bible*. How they use or interpret it is another matter! But we need to recover the Reformation principle of Scripture. Bible study needs to be more highly developed in the life of our congregations—not reading the Bible alone, but interpreting it as a community. A new reading of the Bible is imperative for the church.

The principle of *sola fide* has been a determining factor in our development as a community of believers. Faith has motivated and sustained us through all these years. It is not the security of those who wish to be left to die in peace; it is the breath of life of those who wish to fight for a new world. Faith is the liberating hope that impels us toward a future full of promise.

We are at times discouraged and feel that as Christians we have lost our *raison d'être*. But discouragement is diametrically opposed to faith. It is thus imperative that we should turn again to the faith that breaks down walls of division, that increases hope, gives us courage to fight for justice, and always enables us to glimpse the new day dawning. It is faith that gives us the political will to go forward. To recover faith is to recover hope in life.

Heritage and Responsibility in Latin America

JULIO DE SANTA ANA *(Methodist, Uruguay)*

Our Heritage

Although the Methodist movement originated in England, its emergence in Latin America cannot be explained without reference to its transmission by way of the United States. This is not to belittle the influence of original Methodism and especially its founder, John Wesley. It is necessary, however, to recognize that the development of Methodism in North America brought innovations not wholly consistent with Wesley's thought.

Among the characteristics that repeatedly appear in the evolution of North American Methodism, we must mention *first* its preoccupation with furthering the evangelistic task, principally conceived of as preaching the Christian message with a resulting increase in the number of believers. Here Methodism in the U.S. was fully consistent with the practice and spirit of Wesley.

Second, Methodism in the U.S., despite favoring independence (in radical divergence from Wesley), was characterized by the dominance of conservative positions on social and political questions, at least until the beginning of our century.

Emphasis on the salvation and sanctification of individuals led most members of Methodist churches in the U.S. to maintain a distance from the great social questions. Although they were in favor of independence, Methodists were not enthusiastic fighters for the liberty of their country.[1] Here Meth-

1. Cf. Richard M. Cameron, ed., *Methodism and Society in Historical Perspective*, vol. 1 (Nashville: Abingdon, 1961), p. 90. This conservative position flourishes even today among certain sectors of North American

odism in the U.S. was again faithful to the profoundly conservative orientation of its founder.

Third, again coherent with Wesley, this social and political conservatism did not lead, thank God, to support for slavery. On this question the majority of Methodists took a frankly abolitionist position. However, as feelings intensified during the first six decades of the nineteenth century, the Methodist church did split over the issue of slavery. The most important point here is that Methodism came to certain parts of Latin America through sectors of the U.S. church that diverged from Wesley and the official abolitionist position of the church on slavery.[2]

Fourth, Methodism in the U.S. *accepted in practice the dominant and established order of things.*

This adhesion to the status quo was seen during the Civil War in the way in which Northern Methodism and Southern Methodism each adhered, uncritically, to the position of the society where it lived.

This means that generally the position of Methodists in the U.S. was one of full support to the dominant forms, institutions, and structures of civil society. This is consistent with Wesley's elitist concept of power.[3] Within the framework of the transition from a rural to an urban industrial society, the class contradictions became clearer, the tensions increased between owners of the means of production and salaried workers, with attendant social problems. In that moment North American Methodists became aware (although in minority sectors) that their church was better equipped to serve a society expanding in search of new frontiers (toward the West) than an urban society.

Methodism. For example, Jessup, a Methodist layman, had a major role in the creation of the Institute for Religion and Democracy, a clearly conservative and antipopular organization, founded in the beginning of the eighties, closely tied to the Reagan administration.

2. The Methodists from the United States who settled in the region of Piracicaba and Americana, in the State of São Paulo (Brazil), came out of these sectors.

3. Cameron says about this: "Wesley's position, anomalous as it was, was so positively held that it set the tone of the political thinking in all the Methodist societies. He rallied the societies so well to the support of the Crown that he was charged, wrongly, to be sure, with seeking the political reward he was several times offered, but as often refused" (*Methodism and Society*, p. 44).

Fifth, and this is a fundamental point, Methodism's great force is based on its emphasis on the *religious experience*. For Wesley, experience is similar to sentiment, subjectivity, individual confirmation of what the Scriptures affirm.

No longer does social, economic, and political history witness to the acts of God. Rather, each individual's conscience does. The result, then, is inevitable: Methodism cannot escape being an *inner religion*. The reduction of Christian faith to subjective terms is inevitable, even though Wesley had not wished this to happen.

Inner religion—Wesley is very aware of this—can lead to a betrayal of Christianity.[4] Nevertheless, Wesley's ethic has at center (individual) temptations, the search for moral excellence, personal regeneration that ought to be seen in good citizenship. The social problems that concerned Wesley (alcoholism, slavery, war), and on which he assumed intransigent positions, were approached principally from an individualistic perspective.

To recapitulate, the North American Methodism that decisively influenced our own Latin American Methodism is a result of the combination of *civil religion* and that type of *individual piety* that emphasizes the private, subjective dimension of religion.

Our Heritage Critiqued by Our Context

As Latin Americans, we not only belong to the Methodist church but we concretely belong to Latin America. The elements of the Latin American situation are just as strong, if not stronger, than those of any religious tradition imported from other contexts.

We must now affirm that our present Latin American situation is not greatly in accord with Methodist tradition. The concerns and expectations of today's Latin Americans are not met adequately by the proposals of its message. In other words, the repetition of this message is not good news, is not an evangel (a gospel) in Latin America today.

No one who is truly Latin American in this time of

4. *Wesley's Standard Sermons* (London: Epworth Press, 1921), vol. 1, pp. 388-89, "About the Sermon of Our Lord on the Mount."

struggle for democracy and for a better quality of life for all, this time of effort to eradicate poverty, of attempts at self-determination, of confrontation with transnational capital that crushes and kills many of our brothers and sisters, can say this message is sufficient. This prescribed combination of individual pietism and civil religion will not make Methodism relevant in Latin America. Much more is required.[5]

That the majority of Protestantism in the U.S. adheres to the practice of civil religion serves to legitimize one of the greatest projects of domination in the whole sweep of history. This poses a serious problem: the captivity of the church. A church imprisoned by powers other than those of the triune God is a symptom of something even more serious from a theological point of view: the captivity of the Word of God.

A Protestantism that is faithful to its origins lives intensely in tension with the powers of this world, which try to keep the Word of God in submission. An "unreformed Protestantism" has not freed itself to be faithful to the Word of God. The situation that characterizes much of Latin American Protestantism, which we call *civil religion,* is a manifestation of this captivity. This is not meant as a disqualifying judgment. We must change this aspect of our heritage. The question is: *How?*

Above all, it seems to us that the liberty of God's people, this tremendous manifestation of the Holy Spirit in history, always becomes real through the expression of a prophetic faith.

Today we have a structural understanding of reality: there are systems, organizations, orders of things—in a word, structures that influence and condition our decisions and acts. The social sciences help us penetrate the dense opacity of reality and appreciate how these interrelationships take place. Thus we are able to discern their causes.

In Latin America, for example—as, indeed, in other parts of the world—we are once again recognizing the fundamental fact of biblical culture: the importance of systems to which his-

5. This explains why, little by little, some sectors of the Methodist churches in Latin America have sought greater participation in their respective realities. It is necessary to recognize, however, that it is extremely difficult to break with traditional forms and the tropical Methodists, adepts of "the old-time religion" show a great virulence in face of attempts at renovation.

torical facts are linked. Beginning with this, the premise of Jesus becomes very clear—a premise that, unfortunately, neither Wesley nor nineteenth-century North American Methodism saw clearly—that the kingdom of God is not "inner" but historic.

According to Jesus, the kingdom belongs to the poor. This declaration is pregnant with decisive consequences for Latin American Protestants, most of whom are not poor and do not act in solidarity with the poor. Here we begin to see our responsibility.

To present the gospel in Latin America today, in a continent in which the majority are poor, to announce the good news to these poor, means denouncing that which oppresses them, resisting those factors which oppress them, and taking risks in the struggle against those factors. This will lead us to assume our historic responsibilities. We must not permit ourselves to seek to escape through the mechanisms of spirituality, moralism, or metaphysics.

So, again, *how?* For a message to be believed, the form of its communication must take into consideration the human condition of those to whom the notice is given. We live in a cultural situation in which the practice of suspicion is practically a fundamental rule of life. We are children of nineteenth-century masters of suspicion: Marx, Nietzsche, and Freud. We are so distrustful of any message presented to us. For us to believe, the message must take on substance, be verified and proven. Words are not enough. This is much more true for the poor: if the words full of promises were actualized, the structures that impoverish them would be overthrown.

The beginning of knowledge is not reason but "a kind of *intuition,*" a direct vision of "spiritual realities."[6]

I believe that *metanoia,* as used in the New Testament, implies a radical reformulation of the use of reason. It means thinking that begins with the resurrection and not with the law (St. Paul), with the poor rather than with power (Gospel of Mark, Letter of James). This inversion in the use of reason not

6. John Wesley, "The Finality of the Coming of Christ," in vol. 6 of *The Works of the Revd. John Wesley, A.M., with the last corrections of the author,* 3d ed. (London: Wesleyan-Methodist Book Room, 1829-1831), pp. 274-75.

only gives attention to the message; it *believes* the message because it has content, because it is not just a discourse but a *power* (that of the kingdom) that is made manifest in facts, in historic practice that makes it possible to *verify* the message.

The message is convincing when it acquires concrete substance through the practical witness *(martyria)* of the believers. Only this *practical witness*, true historic expression of the substance of faith, can lead those who have been steeped in an anachronistic anthropology and theology to assume the responsibilities demanded by the present situation.

Recognition of this is an unconditional demand of the here and now in Latin America. It must be expressed in overcoming the schemes of civil religion, combined with private and individual piety (pietism), which we received from North America. It must be expressed in rejecting schemes drawn from behavior that withdraws from historic processes, in a conservative indifference that is not evangelical.

Latin American Protestantism is capable of taking this step. The issue is not one of words but of another type of language: communication sensitive to the expectations and struggles of the poor, the heirs of the kingdom. It calls for a message and action that is not in complicity with the rich.

Today we must transcend bourgeois liberalism. *It is necessary to move from the elites to the popular classes.*

The church of Jesus Christ is called to be the "laboratory of the Kingdom, the place where the cosmic reach of expiation becomes visible in the search for and the acceptance of faith."[7] How can we succeed in giving expression to this "cosmic reach of expiation" without participating in the struggles that expiate and purify the world of injustice from which the poor suffer? The poor are the most beloved of God, the citizens of the kingdom.

7. José Míguez Bonino, *Metodismo: releitura latino-americana* (Piracicaba: Editora Unimep/Fac. Teol. da Igreja Metodista no Brasil, 1982), pp. 51-52.

The Building of the Kingdom:
The Practice of Evangelization

A new order, inaugurated by Jesus Christ, was made manifest primarily through powerful works that convinced the people it was coming into being. Jesus' cure of the blind, lame, paralytics, and others, the purification of the demon-possessed, the feeding of the multitudes, along with his other actions, were the substance that demonstrated to the people the presence of the kingdom. For them this was good news, an evangel. In Jesus' practice, to evangelize and to build the kingdom go together.

Today, Latin American followers of Jesus should announce the presence of the new order in Latin American society[8]. It is to renew its ties not only to Wesley but to Jesus. This goes far beyond *civil religion* and *pietism*. It means seeking to participate in God's mission: justice, liberation, peace, joy, discipline, and—above all—love of the least and the weakest. At the same time it means resisting the evils that make the poor suffer, and those who cause and administer these evils.

In this way, the presentation of the good news to the poor is at the same time a radical demand for the conversion of the powerful, the rich. *The gospel is the announcement—and above all the practice that verifies and gives substance to the announcement—of that which the poor want to happen,* but which they have not even had the courage to imagine becoming reality.

The gospel is to tell the Nicaraguans they can live in justice, peace, and liberty without fear of the threat of the Reagan administration. It is to say there will be no more disappearances in El Salvador, no torture in Chile or Uruguay, no drug mafia in Bolivia. It is to say there will be water in the Brazilian northeast, and more jobs for all.

The gospel is to communicate that life is beautiful, is enjoyable, and we can share it. We cannot live it without love.

The poor want these things, but there are those who oppose their having access to them. The great value of Jesus, even

---

8. See in *La Tradición Protestante en La Teología Latinoamericana*, ed. José Duque (San José: DEI, 1983), pp. 127-204—the chapters by Zacarias Mamani, Anibal Guzmán, Emilio Castro, Jacinto Ordóñez, Elias Boaventura, and Samuel Calvo.

before the resurrection, was his having the courage to bring to the surface those conflicts which the poor did not have the courage to reveal.

The gospel is also to manifest that to which the poor aspire but which they lack: power. Not the power of the strong, of arms, of capital, of technological control, of the centralization of information, and of alliances with the powerful and arrogant. Sooner or later, this type of power will be among those things defeated by history. Our reference is to the power of the kingdom.

To evangelize, give good news, is beyond all this: it is to open the doors so the poor can celebrate life. Is there anything the poor want more than to sing, jump, and dance when something makes them happy? They even do it ritually in the great popular celebrations, including Carnival! The celebration feeds the liturgy. The liturgical sacrifices to which our rituals refer cannot and should not be disembodied. They only acquire a dimension of reality for the people when the church lives them along with the poor.

The joy of Easter comes only with sacrifice. The hopes of Latin America are neither insignificant nor cheap. The cross and—I dare say it despite Wesley—Christ's descent into hell are the steps that lead to the tomorrow of the resurrection.

If we wish above everything else that the kingdom should come, if we know how to evaluate the signs of the kingdom, the joy of the celebration is a foretaste of the "celestial banquet" of which Jesus spoke.

This is evangelization and it is our responsibility: to live Easter, not only at the level of sacrifice and solidarity with the people but also on the level of the anticipatory celebration of the kingdom of God, the republic of the poor.

PART III
EVANGELIZATION AND ECUMENICAL VISION

Toward a Church in Solidarity with the Poor

VICTORIO ARAYA   *(Methodist, Costa Rica)*

The anti-life of the poor is so inhuman that it calls into question the way we live and reflect on our faith.[1] Both in church and society, old certainties collapse. New, rich questions arise. The fundamental attitude essential for the mission of the church is one of seeking.

The Christian church throughout history and in the fulfillment of its mission has faced many varied historic challenges. This is the inevitable consequence of fidelity to Christ, of following him in the way of radical obedience, and of the announcement of the good news of the kingdom.

The challenge of the poor requires that we become a *church in solidarity with the poor*.[2] This is the way we can be faithful today. This option, which begins with a prophetic reading of the "signs of the times," has its roots in the gospel of the kingdom.

The Option of Solidarity with the Poor: A *Protestant* Demand

The criterion of the life and mission of the church begins with its fundamental option for Jesus Christ, who announced the imminence of the kingdom of God. Jesus defined the significance of his messianic practice in the following way:

1. Cf. Julio de Santa Ana, *Good News to the Poor: The Challenge of the Poor in the History of the Church* (Geneva: World Council of Churches, 1977).

2. Cf. WCC/CCPD, *Hacia una Iglesia solidaria con los pobres* (Lima: CCPD/CELADEC, 1980).

> The Spirit of the Lord is upon me because he has anointed me to preach the *gospel to the poor;* he has sent me to proclaim release to the captives and recovery of sight to the blind, to restore to liberty the oppressed, to proclaim the acceptable year of the Lord. (Luke 4:18-19)

The center and measure of our faith makes it very clear on which side he was found: in an active solidarity-identity with the conquered, the humiliated, the poor and oppressed of history.

The Swiss theologian, Karl Barth, expressed this in opportune words:

> God always takes His stand unconditionally and passionately on this side and on this side alone (the threatened innocent, the oppressed poor, the widows, orphans and aliens): against the lofty and on behalf of the lowly; against those who already enjoy right and privilege and on behalf of those who are denied it and deprived of it.[3]

If what we have said is correct—and the biblical evidence is extraordinarily clear on this point—we discover *no* excuse possible with regard to solidarity with the poor. For the church the consequence is obvious: in this world and in this history there is an unequivocal way to be with Jesus Christ. That way is to be alongside those with whom he identified himself: the little ones, the poor and oppressed; "whenever you did it to one of the least, you did it to me" (Matt. 25:40).

Jesus characterized the poor in two ways.[4]

1. The poor are *those who are despised by society*. They are the sinners, the publicans, the prostitutes (Mark 2:6; Matt. 11:19; 21:32; Luke 15:1), the simple ones (Matt. 11:25), the little ones (Mark 9:2; Matt. 10:42; 18:10, 14), the least (Matt. 25:40-45), those who are in despised professions (Matt. 21:31; Luke 18:11). In this sense, the poor are those who are defamed, those held in low esteem, the uneducated and the ignorant. The poor are the despised. They are those for whom the dominant religiosity does not represent hope, but condemnation.

2. The poor are *those undergoing some kind of real oppres-*

3. Karl Barth, *Church Dogmatics* (New York: Scribner's, 1957), II/I, p. 386.

4. Cf. Jon Sobrino, *Jesus in Latin America* (Maryknoll, N.Y.: Orbis, 1987), pp. 140-41.

sion, that is, those who have a need in line with Isaiah 61:1. They are those who suffer, the starving and the thirsty, the naked, the strangers, the sick and imprisoned, those who are hungry, who cry, who are crushed under some weight.

The poor, to whom the good news of the coming kingdom is directed, are for Jesus those who are in some kind of misery, those despised and socially discriminated against. This manner of approaching the kingdom was the cause of the scandal surrounding Jesus (Matt. 11:6).

The Option for Solidarity with the Poor: A Demand of Our *Methodist* Tradition

The Methodist church originated in England in the middle of the eighteenth century (the century of the Enlightenment) in the midst of profound convulsions of the nascent industrial revolution.[5] It was not born at the margins of these convulsions or above them. It came to birth linked to the working-class movement (the rising industrial proletariat) and as a church of working-class people. This is the human matrix of Methodism.[6]

---

5. Cf. Franz Hinkelammert, "Condiciones económico-sociales del Metodismo en la Inglaterra del siglo XVIII," in *La tradición protestante en la Teología latinoamericana,* ed. José Duque (San José: DEI, 1983), pp. 21ff.

6. J. Míguez Bonino wrote: "Wesley and his preachers set up their platforms at dawn at the entrance to the coal mines of Cardiff, next to the doors of the steel industries of Birmingham, or the textile mills of Liverpool. The audience was the rising industrial proletariat, who knew the hell of a day's work without limits; premature death, malnutrition and rickets . . . and did not know any heaven other than the tavern, where they for two pence got enough opium of the Thum for the weekend. These were the people who by the thousands received and accepted the message. The anti-Methodist writings of the times contained ample references to characterizations such as these—whose parallels sound strangely familiar— 'ragged band,' 'miserable worms,' 'pretentious rabble.' The Duchess of Buckingham made a comment about Methodist preaching, 'It is monstrous to say to the people that our heart is as sinful as that of these human ruins who drag themselves along the ground. The preachers of Wesley are stonemasons, guards, weavers, carpenters, bakers. This is the human matrix of Methodism.'" (Cf. "Nossa fé e nosso tempo," *Cuadernos de Cristianismo y Sociedad* 1/4 [1974]: 2-3.)

John Wesley was politically conservative (a monarchist who did not accept the revolution of emancipation of North America). By his insertion of Methodism into the world of working-class people, however, it has been said, in exaggeration, that the "British proletariat owes more to Wesley than to Marx."[7]

The Methodist church was not born in the heat of a speculative theological controversy. It was the product of a profound revival, that is, as the search for a new way of walking in the Spirit (orthopraxis) and of living the demands of the gospel in the life of *total holiness* ("of heart and life").

What is significant in this experience of the Spirit is the firm conviction that the search for holiness passes, inescapably, through one's neighbor (against any temptation to a privatized escape, more appropriate to mystical religions than to the historic-prophetic religion of the Bible). This is what gives rise to the workers' efforts to do good in the midst of the misery of the world: the struggle against slavery, concern for education, health, and for every type of beneficial initiative.

Today, from the experience of the poor of the earth, we know the poor as the neighbor *par excellence*. A saint is not one who is different from or separated from, but in *solidarity* with, *identified* with, the world of the other. Thus, holiness would consist in maintaining the "yes" of the God of history to the kingdom of justice and life and the "no" of God to a world of sin and oppression that must be transformed.

The Option of Solidarity with the Poor: A Demand for a *Prophetic Reading* of the "Signs of the Times"

Recent years have been characterized by the growing presence, real and demanding, of the world of the other: the poor, the marginalized, the humiliated of history. Those who were previously absent are now beginning to make their presence felt. They speak their piece.

---

7. Cited by L. J. Hobshawn, *Rebeldes primitivos* (Barcelona: Ariel, n.d.), p. 195. Cf. Elsa Tamez, "Wesley as Read by the Poor," in *The Future of the Methodist Theological Traditions*, ed. M. Douglas Meeks (Nashville: Abingdon, 1985), pp. 67-84.

The International Ecumenical Congress of Theology (CIET), meeting in São Paulo in 1980, expressed it in this way:

> The situation of suffering, misery, and exploitation of the great majorities, concentrated especially but not exclusively, in the so-called Third World, is as evident as it is unjust.
>
> Despite this, the most important historic process in our time is initiated by these same people as *protagonists*, by the "condemned of the earth."
>
> In the context of the Third World, the emerging popular classes give impulse to social movements and, through their struggles, forge a more lucid awareness of global society and of themselves.
>
> These popular social movements are expressions of much more than a simple economic demand. *In the terms in which they are expressed today they have to do with the new fact of the massive irruption of the poor in every society.*[8]

In this historic irruption of the poor, the church faces a profound challenge. There is something much more radical involved than just a circumstantial challenge or the perception (sensitive-analytical) of the hard reality of the poor. In the historic irruption of the poor, we live the judgment of the Word of God.

Never before have we heard so clearly the Word of God, which comes to us through the cry of millions of the poor of the earth, the true "condemned of the earth." We live in a time of grace and of demanding ecclesial conversion that is at the same time the source of a renewed spiritual experience: the spirituality of solidarity with the poor and of encounter with the Christ who appears to us in the suffering face of the poor.

The Poor: A Necessary Clarification

The ecclesial commitment of solidarity with the poor calls for a clear definition of who are the poor and what are the historic causes of their oppression.

The perception of the misery of the poor majority, the

---

8. Cf. Teólogos del Tercer Mundo, *La irrupción del pobre en la sociedad y en la Iglesia*, Final documents of CIET (Bilbao: Desclée, 1982), Numbers 6-9.

injustice of their situation and of the growing deterioration of their conditions, makes obvious the necessity to know what causes anti-life poverty. There is, therefore, a socioanalytic rationality that is the inevitable mediation of the Christian option for the poor.

Poverty Is Destructive

Poverty is neither innocent nor neutral. Poverty is deadly. Material poverty means that life is threatened, impeded, and historically destroyed, because the primary sources of the real life of the poor are threatened by the permanent nonsatisfaction of their basic necessities: work, bread, housing, health. It is a question of "life annihilated slowly by oppressive structures, or rapidly and violently by repressive structures" (Jon Sobrino). Poverty expresses the true death-loving nature of an institutionalized system. These structures are built on the death of the poor and work to the advantage of the few. Their benefits, then, are at the expense of the growing poverty of the impoverished majorities.

With the perception of the true nature of poverty, the Christian will first feel "ethical and prophetic indignation": "God does not wish poverty"; "things cannot continue as they are"; "it is an objective situation of sin." Poverty contradicts the creative design of the Divine as it strips God's creatures of human dignity as children of God. "It is the fruit of a great injustice which cries out to the heavens like the blood of Abel assassinated by Cain" (Gen. 4:10, CIET).

Poverty Is Structural

Poverty is not something "accidental" or casual; it is not the product of an insufficiency of natural resources, or even worse, the result of a blind and inexorable fate. The existence of the poor is not due to the "laziness" of the poor, to their "inferiority," "lack of education," or "lack of opportunity." Rather, there is a concrete cause; poverty is the result of economic, social, and political situations and structures. The poor, then, are the *product* of an unjust system structured for the benefit of the few. The poor, stripped of the fruit of their labor, are members of a social class that is exploited openly or subtly by another social class.[9]

The Poor Are a Collective Subject

The option for the poor leads us to understand that they cannot be separated from the social class to which they belong. There are no isolated poor. Each belongs to social groups, races, cultures, gender, and therefore constitutes a historically determined collective subject. This collective character of subject-poor (as opposed to the poor as object) is what makes the option for the poor difficult and *conflictive*. It is not enough that we become aware of the situation of poverty; we must go beyond that. Poverty that is destructive of life cannot be alleviated piecemeal. It is a totality against which we must fight totally.

The Poor Introduce Us into the World of Politics

"Everything is politics, but politics is not everything."

(Emanuel Mounier)

If poverty is a material, destructive, structural reality against which it is necessary to struggle, if the poor do not exist individually but as a collective subject, an option for the poor inescapably obligates one to enter into the world of politics and into its rationale. This option gives a different value to politics: not a partisan, sectarian dimension, but a global one. It takes in and demandingly conditions the collective behavior of every human accomplishment.

The political dimension of Christian love is found in the search for the common good and in the establishment of the right to life of the poor majority. There is no such thing as spontaneous love. Love of the oppressed demands a political rationale that makes it possible, dialectically, to retain its evangelical nature while being efficient, in terms of the kingdom of God, as a political commitment.

9. Cf. Gustavo Gutiérrez, *La fuerza histórica de los pobres* (Lima: CEP, 1979), pp. 79-80; *A força histórica dos pobres* (Petrópolis: Ed. Vozes, 1981).

The praxis of love is translated *today* into an effort to transform the social order that marginalizes poverty. We are faced with injustice and the misery of the majority in the so-called Third World. In this historic situation, the option for the poor and solidarity with them inevitably takes on a conflictive character. The terrain of politics today implies confrontations between human groups and social classes with opposing interests. To opt for the poor assumes enemies. Nevertheless, the gospel commands us to love the enemy.

Evangelization as Solidarity with the Poor

The ecclesial praxis in solidarity with the poor is a loving praxis. It has to do basically with giving concrete form in history to that original theological word, "love one another," so that the love of God may dwell with us and take on credibility. Karl Rahner expressed this in a radical way: "Only in the midst of an unconditional solidarity with the condemned of the earth can we dare to speak of the love of God toward us."[10] Consequently, the community of faith is called, as an expression of its true sense and purpose, to a praxis of listening, welcoming, and serving the poor. Briefly this means a praxis on several levels:

- *Listening to the poor:* listening to their questioning word which reveals to us the inhuman character of their misery and oppression, the strength of their hope, and their yearning for liberation.
- *Welcoming the poor:* welcoming "the uninvited to the banquet" in their worth and dignity as human persons, as the presence of God in history.
- *Service to the poor:* "to go directly to the poor" in concrete gestures of effective love, that is, effective assistance to the liberation of the poor.

The poverty of the poor is not an appeal to a generous action to alleviate it, but a demand for the transformation of their situation. Action that is generous in the nature of relief is

10. *Sacramentum mundi,* vol. 1, ed. K. Rahner (Barcelona: Herder, n.d.), p. 125.

directed toward the poor, but without supporting them as the active subject of the process of the transformation of their situation. Who lives and suffers the consequences of oppression more intensely than the poor themselves? Who is better prepared to capture the urgency for liberation?

It is possible that up to this point we are all in agreement. The complexity arises when we face the necessary historic mediations of the praxis of love. Christian love of neighbor does *not* have in itself the criteria for its historic realization. In addition, the church, because it is located in history, is shot through with social conflict. It is not possible to ignore the serious differences of opinion and practice that exist.

In this connection I would like to propose a vision of the contribution of the church to the hope, the life, and the liberation of the poor of our countries. Of course this vision is not the only one nor is it an isolated one. We believe it has its roots in the gospel and that there is nothing better in our Christian tradition.

If there is *only one way of being with Jesus Christ* (i.e., in an option for those whom God chose unconditionally and passionately, placing the Divine always at their side), then following Jesus demands an incarnation in the world of the poor in defense of their threatened life.

It is not up to the church to manage history. It is not the task of the church to lead the processes of liberation. The church does not found a party or popular organizations, nor take a partisan line. What can and ought we to do? With its incarnation in the world of the poor ("from underneath"), the church in solidarity with the poor has a mission of *active defense of the right of the poor to life.*

This praxis of solidarity requires a capacity for the discernment of two well defined moments:

1. The negative moment of **denunciation-unmasking:** prophetic denunciation of the oppressive-repressive *structures* that, slowly or violently, deprive the poor majority of life. It means unmasking the historic *causes* of oppression (socioanalytical discernment of the mechanisms that give rise to the historical and social situation).

Ecclesially, the situation of the poor cannot be reduced to the level of simple opinions. The supposed impossibility of scientific understanding through a serious, historic, structural analysis of the most determining aspects of the misery of the poor is one of the most effective ideological mechanisms of the system of domination.

This moment of unmasking means denouncing the abstract spiritualization of poverty.[11] On the other hand, it is necessary to pay attention (judgment and discernment) to the deformed images of God and the gospel, imprisoned within the dominating ideology. This makes theology "a religious superstructure" at the service of the preservation and sacralization of unjust economic structures responsible for the anti-life of the poor. In Latin America, for example, it is necessary to struggle less against lack of belief than against the adaptation of the liberating message of the gospel to the interests of the powerful and their practices of domination.

2. The positive moment of **affirmation-accompaniment-announcement-celebration**. This has to do with going directly to the poor in active defense of their modest hope, their cry: "I want to live!" This is the moment of confessing that the church really believes in the God of life. The defense of the poor implies:[12]

a. *Being the voice of the voiceless.* The defense of the poor demands the affirmation that their reality is actual, their aspirations are just, and their struggles are being silenced. The church announces the God of the poor as the God who makes covenant with them and is the chief defender of their cause.[13]

b. *Accompanying the poor in their just struggles for liberation.* It is the active continuation of the incarnation of the church in the world of the poor. This incarnation does not take place once and for all. Each concrete incarnation demands new incarnations in the specific reality of each given moment. This accompaniment implies defending, facilitating, and encouraging

11. Cf. Elsa Tamez, *Bible of the Oppressed,* trans. Matthew J. O'Connell (Maryknoll, N.Y.: Orbis, 1982).

12. Cf. Jon Sobrino, "El aporte de la Iglesia a la esperanza de los pobres," *II Congresso de Teologiá y Pobreza: Misión Abierta* 4, 5 (1982): 123-27.

13. Cf. Victório Araya, *God of the Poor: The Mystery of God in Latin American Theology* (Maryknoll, N.Y.: Orbis, 1987).

the decision and capacity for mobilization and organization of the poor, in the formulation of their own historic liberating project.

c. *Imbuing the Christian spirit in them as persons and as a people in their struggles.* This is done in the conviction that when they are armed with this spirit they will be stronger to struggle. "This means warning them of their limitations and criticizing their errors and sins, to improve them as a people" (J. Sobrino).

d. *Contributing,* beginning in the faith and hope of the church, *to the maintenance of a live and active hope of the poor* in their most difficult moments. The processes of liberation are hard. In the midst of pain and suffering, the radical nearness of the liberating God, who is also the crucified God, helps to avoid despair. To know dialectically how to maintain this nearness enables them to persist with unbreakable hope.

e. *Celebrating life with the depth that grows out of faith* (the praxis of celebration). Beginning with the gesture of solidarity in defense of the threatened life of the poor, the church celebrates with joy the saving action of the God of life, the fullness of life, which is manifest through the liberation (death and resurrection) of Jesus Christ.

The culminating point of the ecclesial praxis of celebration is the eucharist. The Lord's Supper has a constitutive dialectic of *memory* (paschal) and *liberty* (openness to the future). This memory is not fixed on the past but is a necessary condition for its presence in the service of the future. This memory is not a sad and nostalgic remembrance of times that have passed (*in illo tempore*) but an opening full of hope and joy and creative liberty in face of the future.

In the breaking of bread, the bread that is lacking on the tables of the poor of the earth, the Spirit recognizes the presence of the life of the Resurrected One. It is a life that recreates life; a life that guarantees that sin, oppression, and death will be destroyed forever.

This is not a naive, evasive joy, the fruit of a lack of awareness of the daily reality of anti-life and suffering. It is a subversive joy that vanquishes a world of oppression. It is a paschal joy that passes through suffering and death, but expresses profound confidence based on the liberating love of the Father whose ultimate word is life for all, and hope for the crucified of history.

Ecumenism Beginning with the Poor

The practice of solidarity with the poor demands and promotes Christian solidarity between churches. The defense of the poor takes time and resources dedicated to the defense of their life. Therefore, the defense of the poor demands and promotes solidarity between churches, those of the "center" and those of the "periphery"; between the "missionary" and the "mission field" and among the diverse Christian churches in a process of reciprocal support.

On the historic, ecclesial, theological plane (in the practice of the love of justice and hope) solidarity with the poor means eliminating the abysmal social differences, acting in a concrete and creative way on behalf of the poor in a transformation of the reality of oppression and anti-life into a reality of liberation and comradeship.

God's kingdom is breaking out in our midst. That good news is announced through a transformed reality: in the communion of solidarity, in loving participation in the earth, and in the sharing of bread. We are experiencing "new heavens and a new earth . . . filled with delight" (Isa. 65:17-25).

Calvinism and Ecumenism

ZWINGLIO M. DIAS   *(Presbyterian, Brazil)*

On July 10, 1983, in the city of Vitória, state of Espírito Santo, a new ecclesiastical structure was organized: the United Presbyterian Church of Brazil. In the last eighteen years they had separated (or were separated) from the Presbyterian Church of Brazil because of the ideological struggle within the structural matrix of Brazilian Presbyterianism. With about ten thousand members, the United Presbyterian Church of Brazil intends to be an open, fraternal, ecumenical church, engaged in the cause of the Brazilian people as demanded by the gospel.

> As the Scriptures narrate the events in the life of Israel they teach that God, though never having abandoned his Churches, sometimes destroys the political order established (in them).
>
> Consequently, we should not believe that God is so tied to persons that the Church can never be defeated, that is, that the persons who preside over it can never abandon the truth.
>
> However, the Church is still there. That is, God still has the Church, although hidden, and preserves it miraculously. But we should not think from this that they are worthy of any honor. On the contrary, they are more detestable because, instead of begetting sons and daughters for God, they beget them for devils and idols. (John Calvin)

Introduction

It is a historic step to constitute a church that is open, pluralist, free—and at the same time faithful to its historic heritage and sensitive to the reality of the Brazilian people, to whom we are sent as witnesses and instruments of the gospel of Christ.

277

Therefore, we should see this moment in our history as an opportunity to reflect on ourselves, on what we have been until now, on what we are at this moment. It can also be a moment of preparation and planning for what we intend to be in the midst of Brazilian Protestantism.

The contribution of Presbyterianism to the common struggle of various Brazilian churches comes into effect as a witness to unity in dealing with the very serious problems that affect our people.

The decision to adopt the name "United Presbyterian Church" represents a new stage in the process of renewal and realization of the Reformed tradition among us, and should be seen as an advance and deepening of the meaning of mission in our context. In this regard, I would like to recall our history and draw some conclusions that, even though tentative, may be useful for our reflection and action from this point on.

I would like to focus on some elements of Calvinism, based on my somewhat limited experience. These elements seem important in this hour in which we are challenged to give leadership to an ecclesiological reconstruction, beginning from our deepest roots, to give effectiveness to our presence in the ecumenical dialogue that is demanded by the present social, political, economic, and religious situation of our people.

I would like to reflect, first of all, on what I shall call the "necessary separation" that was imposed on us, that perhaps many of us unconsciously provoked.

Second, it is my intention to think of a theological and ecclesiological reconstruction, that is, to ask, What church do we want to constitute? How can our Calvinist heritage help us? Can we say that Brazilian Presbyterianism has been truly, until now, Calvinist? Is it not possible that the filter of the North American experience, with a refraction imposed by totally other historic circumstances, may have seriously belittled the Calvinist ecclesial purpose? Is a *Brazilian* Presbyterianism possible?

Finally, I want to reflect on the ecclesiology we have assumed until now. What do we mean when we speak of the autonomous local church and the national church? What concept of *ekklesia* are we articulating? Are we not being challenged to begin to think now of an ecumenism *ad intra*, that is, among us, interecclesial? Can this ecumenism be the basis for an ecumenism *ad extra* that would take in not only churches but all human groupings? This is the true totality of the *oikoumene,* "the whole inhabited world."

Reasons for the Present Separation

Presbyterianism has already gone through five or six schisms in the course of its history in Brazil. There were many and varied reasons for the formation of new churches, beginning with the church established by the work of North American missionaries in the middle of the past century.

The local churches and presbyteries, which had been marginalized by the Brazilian Presbyterian Church, always nourished the hope of a change in the cadres of authority. In the majority of cases, the motives that led to the removal of pastors, churches, and councils were of the strictly political-administrative order, involving no profound theological debate to justify such measures.

It is evident that in the background of the assumed positions, which led to fear in the power holders, were basic biblical, theological reasons. Yet these were never seriously dealt with by those who carried out the repressive policies of power. It is true that they said they were the guardians of the tradition, the truth, and the doctrinal purity of the church, but at no moment were they able to run the risk of a real debate. They merely used these affirmations in a demagogic and opportunistic way.

This was, I believe, the precise reason for the hope of a change in the internal leadership that encouraged many. At the heart of this political game, there were, in my view, some underlying, determining factors; I do not know whether they have yet been overcome or moved toward a new theological-pastoral perspective:

1. The issue of the role of the Presbyterian church within Brazilian society.
2. The issue of the adequacy of the theological proposal of Presbyterianism in effect among us. With regard to the Presbyterian Church of Brazil, it is evident that, although a global institution, it did not go beyond the perspective of the mis-

sionaries. It did not put down deep roots in the national culture.

3. The inability of the ecclesiastical structures to perceive their own limits and to recognize the ecclesial legitimacy of Catholicism, and oftentimes of other Protestant denominations, closed them to a genuine ecumenical practice.

These three issues, pastoral and missiological, theological and ecclesiological, are fundamental for the church we propose to be.

The structural fragility of the Presbyterian Church of Brazil, revealed in its theological insecurity, its imprisonment to the values and aspirations of the middle class, and its belligerent attitude toward Catholicism (and in a lesser degree to some other Protestants), led it to a closed stance in the face of society, and to an attitude of self-protection that eliminated the possibilities of internal discussion.

On the other hand, the conflicts were not always generated by theological positioning and ecclesiastical/political projects. Rather, I would say, some of the attitudes and actions of many of us—though we had the best of intentions, the hope of renewing the church and creating the conditions for an effective incarnation of the church in our suffering reality—were assuming a disastrous pedagogy without taking into consideration the fragile preparation of many pastors and members of the church. This sharpened the divergencies and strengthened the position of the power holders, rather than opening spaces where the ecclesiastical atmosphere could be really aired out.

We lacked, and still lack, a consistent theological vision of the church as the body of Christ in the world. In this aspect we are not very Calvinist, debtors more to the individualistic salvationism of North American Puritanism than to the ecclesiology of the Geneva Reformer.

Toward a Theological Reconstruction

Traditionally Calvinism has been seen as deterministic, with salvation by election at the whim of God while human effort counts for nothing. With such strong emphasis on the sovereignty of

God, how do we simultaneously take an option for the poor? Is this not a theological problem for Calvinists?

To me it is not a problem, because I think that the central affirmation of Calvinism—the sovereignty of God revealed in Jesus Christ—is a picture, a mirror, for human existence. All action, all situations should be transformed to conform to the Project of Jesus, God's option for the poor, which is the kingdom of God. In this sense, I think there is a new interpretation of Calvin for today.

Calvin's central affirmation of the sovereignty of God means that there is no absolute human sovereignty. All that we do is relative, precarious, and must be in perpetual change—constantly improving. We build history in the moment that we are transforming reality, all institutions and relations. All is in the process of transformation, of improvement. Nothing that humans do is final.

In this perspective, Calvinism has a contribution to make today in the ecumenical dialogue: to help other traditions rediscover the centrality of God in Jesus Christ in the new situation in which we are living.

Calvinism's distinctiveness is in these two points, opposite sides of the same coin: the absolute sovereignty of God and the precariousness of all human achievements. The necessity for the improvement of life in all senses is a permanent necessity as God is permanent. All human efforts in the improvement of life are seen as provisional and necessary in the light of the absolute sovereignty of God.

Is there a distinctiveness in Calvinism? Wesley, like many others, understood it to be a challenge to his Arminianism. But this was two centuries after Calvin and was a distortion he suffered at the hands of his own followers. They reduced his theology to a determinism.

Predestination as a central theme is inadequate. It was a logical consequence of Calvin's thought, but he was not sure himself how to incorporate it in a true perspective. It is not central in Calvinism, but has become a kind of creed. This is a false perspective, but was the theological and ecclesiastical struggle of the moment.

The Christian option for the poor, solidarity with the struggle for life, fits quite logically with Calvin's doctrine of the sovereignty of God as revealed in Jesus Christ and reflected in human effort. Geneva, for example, was transformed into a kind of refuge city for all persons persecuted during the Reformation. In this sense we can say that Calvin started what today we call the defense of human rights. He also made an option for the poor, in the sense of understanding the poor as a challenge for the wealthy. For him, the poor are God's challenge to the rich.

This gives us a basis for rereading Calvin's theology in contemporary situations. He created a very strong mission of social action in the churches—housing for the homeless, support for the poor. Naturally, this was done in the sociotheological terms of the sixteenth century. It was an effort, however, to connect socioeconomic realities with a theological interpretation of life.

The sixteenth century was at a point of transition from feudalism to a capitalist society. Calvin made a very important contribution because he perceived that the world (Europe) was changing. The old structures were finished and could not be recovered. He was looking to the future, trying to see what would happen. In this sense he was very different from Luther, who had a strong nostalgia for the fourteenth century. He wanted to recover the past. He hated the new world and the things that were beginning to happen. Calvin, however, tried to reinterpret in that moment what was going on. Perhaps he was wrong in some of his conclusions, but he tried to face the new situations. In this sense, he is very important for us today, because normally in the church we try to repeat the past. We are afraid of the future, therefore afraid to face the questions of the present. We want to wait to see what God is saying to us. Then we respond to "today" fifteen years too late.

Calvin did not fear to make errors. He started from the premise that human beings always make errors. We are sinners, permanently. What we do is wrong. We have to make decisions now, not years too late. This is a very important contribution to us today.

Toward an Ecclesiological Reconstruction

The filter of religious ideas formed in the United States and imposed on the development of Presbyterianism sacrificed the corporate vision of the church as a community in favor of Puritan individualism. Thus our ecclesiology has always been weak. We have nourished a vision of Christ independent of the church as *communio sanctorum*.

The Calvinist tradition has not always been faithful to the thought of the Reformer—for various reasons. One was the fact that Calvin went through changes in his own historical practice, both as a religious official of the city of Geneva and later in adaptation to the social and cultural conditions of other people. While the central elements of his thought took on substance in constitutions and doctrinal structures, the truth is that they did not always take on life in the concrete experiences of the churches.

This was very significant in the definition of the mission of the church. Note that the kind of preaching and the evangelization that predominated, and still does predominate, in the Presbyterian churches has nothing to do with original Calvinism. For example, the salvationist emphasis that intoxicates our churches is foreign to the best tradition of the Reformer. In his perspective, the communitarian life was essential to the manifestation and realization of the gifts of Christ. Salvation, although personal, came about through participation in the body of Christ, so that the church became a fundamental, salvific instrument. The watchword of medieval Christianity—there is no salvation outside the church—was built into Calvin's ecclesiology. His concern to reestablish ministerial orders within the local community, which in present Presbyterianism consists of Pastor, Presbyter, and Deacon, was an effort to recover the practice of the primitive church.

With this, Calvin sought the recreation of a community life where the faithful could, in fact, be incorporated by ecclesial practice into the body of Christ, manifesting themselves to the world as an effective sign of the kingdom, through mutual sharing of all the gifts and graces developed in the practice of communitarian experience.

For the Genevan Reformer, union with Christ necessarily implied the living together of all the members. This *makes them into and shows them to be* the church. Therefore, he affirms the communitarian dimension of salvation when he writes that human beings are justified and sanctified through incorporation into Christ. He says: "In fact, Christ did not achieve salvation for this or that person, but for his people; we receive it when we become part of this people, through faith."

For Calvin, the saving word is ecclesial: it is deposited in the church and announced to us through the ministry. It is simultaneously promise and calling: it offers salvation and calls the church. Faith, that by which we accept Christ, is also ecclesial.

The article about the communion of the saints, according to Calvin, was introduced into the Creed to express with great clarity the unity that exists between the members of the church and to indicate that the gifts of God redound to the common good of all. The sharing of these blessings does not exclude private property, or the diversity of gifts affirmed by Paul (1 Cor. 12 and Rom. 12:3-8). It means that the faithful share among themselves the blessings of *body* and of *spirit* in a benign and loving form, in just measure and in accordance with needs.

This assumes the unity of the community. I am greatly impressed with Calvin's use of the image of the body, which Paul used to describe the prevailing relations in the church. Plurality of functions and ordination for the common good are two characteristics of the church that forms "the mystical body of Christ." The union of each believer with Christ constitutes the ultimate root of bodily unity of the church and the communitarian unity of its members. Calvin says: "The saints are added to the company of Christ so they may share among themselves the benefits which God has given them."

Calvin does not think of ecclesial union as the result of a decision by the elect to join together in order to develop a specific task to inaugurate the kingdom. Rather, he affirms that Christ himself—because of human inability—creates among believers a mystic unity that takes on concrete form as organic and visible community. Consequently, those who are organically united collaborate with their respective gifts for the good of the whole body. Thus, to be a member of the body is not the consequence of a decision to collaborate. On the contrary, because we are members of Christ, we are obligated to keep visible before us this communion we have in Christ.

So the task of building the kingdom is a communitarian task. Extrapolating for our day, I would say that it is an ecumenical task, one that involves everything and everyone, in one form or another, linked to the enterprise of the construction of the kingdom. Calvin is profoundly impressed with the idea that the Christian, as a consequence of his union with Christ, cannot have a purely individual existence, because the task of building the kingdom is essentially a communitarian task. He said, among other things: "All of the possibilities of which the pious is possessed will be possibilities for *his brothers and sisters* and he should not seek any private advantage, but rather all efforts should orient his work and life toward building up the common life of the church."

In our journey to be faithful to the aspirations, desires, necessities, and dreams of our people, there is implied a double task: an honest reexamination of our heritage in its practices, ideas, and values and, on the other hand, an articulation of all this in the light of the national historical reality of which we are necessarily a part.

To be able to carry this out, we need to relativize our importance as an institution. If we intend to be ecumenical, we must assume the necessity of a genuine coming together among ourselves to the benefit of our people.

To say this implies an effort to discover the profile of our ecclesial identity. It is not enough to determine for ourselves that we are Calvinists, authentic Presbyterians, open, progressive, ecumenical. Our ecclesial practice, that is, what we do as local communities, needs to respond in some way to this theoretical statement we have made.

If we believe in the value of our heritage, if it constitutes part of our contribution to the interecclesial dialogue, we need to know it in depth. We need the courage to make corrections in our historic course, and the humility to recognize its limits, to accept the values of other traditions as equally valid and meaningful.

How can we be ecumenical among ourselves? What are the positive elements that unite us as Presbyterians?

What "preferential option" will we take with regard to the global struggle of the Brazilian people?

The Struggle for Human Rights:
An Ecumenical Event

LYSÃNEAS MACIEL *(Presbyterian, Brazil)*

In the midst of the most repressive moments of the Brazilian military dictatorship, as a Christian member of Congress, I was then, as now, profoundly concerned for the task of the church, especially with regard to the guarding of human rights.

I was raised in a home and church that preached the priesthood of all believers, that is, the responsibility of each person before God, his conscience, and his neighbor. When the church proposes to carry out its task, to try by all possible means to defend human rights, we cannot fail to report with sadness how such declarations often become insignificant in the face of the declared or hidden interests of those who hold the power.

The Christian church—and why not say Congress also—vacillates too long with regard to a defined action, not only in condemning oppression, but also in helping the oppressed. Those who think there is excessive insistence on this subject need to remember that what is more important than formulating rights is guaranteeing them in practice. When political sham writes into the basic charter of a country all the prerogatives that are indispensable to a free life, but does not give them the means of adequate application, dictatorship is virtually established.

The Christian churches with a pietistic formation contribute to this omission with regard to the safeguarding of human rights. I remember what the Protestant pastor, Dietrich Bonhoeffer, said just before he was sacrificed by the Nazi regime:

> The church confesses that it has been present at the arbitrary use of brute force, at the bodily and psychological suffering of uncounted innocent people, oppression, hate and assassination without raising its voice. . . . The church confesses that

286

it has looked on, mute, at the deprivation and exploitation inflicted on the poor, and the enrichment and corruption of the powerful. The church confesses that it has been guilty before numberless people, whose lives were destroyed through slander, spying, infamy.

I tie the behavior of the Brazilian church to that of Congress, because the Christian churches in their pietism contributed to a state of affairs that denied human rights to its citizens. They often do not perceive when they assist in the sacralization of injustice, saying it is the will of God to save the nation from dangers to which it is exposed.

When a Christian church tries to reach the oppressed classes, it does so allowing the dominant ideology to remain in control. But let us not talk about the peace professed by governments, but about a different kind of peace—coming from a mature and human political action. Let us talk about a peace that comes from a profound understanding of the inalienable rights of the person. This peace is not achieved through a rigidity of structures, but through a constant and permanent opening to new ideas and new constructs.

Nothing—other than terror—can maintain a static and sacralized regime. It is humans who are sacred. In this sense they should be the goal of all political action.

The frequently offered suggestion of "patience"—the advice of those who want to keep the power—is almost always given by those sectors tied to the establishment, who have forgotten that they are supposed to represent people who are poor and suffering: people who for this reason are in a hurry. Those who speak for the poor, whether they be of the church or the political world, must never be silent or "patient."

I have in mind the technocrats for whom persons are just numbers, economic groups for whom people are only consumers. I am thinking of religious and secular hierarchies which arrogate to themselves the right to be the moral guardians of others. Only the people can decide how much and when they are happy.

Just as the world changes, the forces and motivations that prepared and maintain it must also inevitably change in one way or another. From my own upbringing I would prefer this change to come about peacefully, but because of the justified skepticism I have regarding those who are insane with power I am not hopeful that this is possible.

The danger of a society that gives too much prestige to technological conquest is already clear. In the search for development there is no justification for suppressing individual liberties in any degree. Persons either are or are not free. Any kind of limitation degrades personality, principally the personality of youth in formation. In response to the rationalization that restrictions to human freedom are necessary to maintain the peace, the Bible says: "They have cured, superficially, the wounds of my people, saying, 'Peace, peace'; when there is no peace. . . .They wait hopefully for peace, and nothing good comes; it is the time for healing, and behold the terror" (Jer. 8:11, 15). Peace that is built for one group, even if it is the majority, is a decoy.

The modern world is full of illustrations of how misleading this is. Look at the situation in the Soviet Union. Without entering into the merits of the whole question, it is enough to point out that some do not have freedom to manifest their discontent. Contemporary history has shown that there has not been peace where there is suppression of basic liberties. Many other countries are similar to the Soviet Union. Yesterday the justification was to reestablish democratic guarantees; today it is to maintain them.

Repression in the name of "order" is a constantly repeated falsehood but today it does not fool anyone. We must remember that order itself is a social construct, and if each majority judges itself to have the right of suppressing responses to its "order," the political problem will never find a solution. What happens is a unilateral insistence on an "order" imposed by a supposed majority. I insist on this term *supposed* because under these circumstances the electoral process does not authorize anyone to say there is a consensus. There is an electoral fiction in which the decision-making process, the choice of leaders, does not have even a minimal representation of the people.

Whenever a group that holds power invokes order, one needs to examine its motivations. The defense of order is nothing but a rationalization. It is curious that, when dealing with dissent, leftist governments, such as the Soviet Union, invoke the same arguments as right-wing fascist governments, such as Brazil under military domination.

Once the provisional aspect of social constructs is understood (their being provisional does not make them irrelevant), we should not fall into the error of their sacralization.

The Prophetic Mission of the Church

We need to think about the church as an institution.

What happens when the individuals who make up the church relate subserviently to those who govern? The church is almost always late in its pronouncements. Often it is committed to attitudes opposite to the interests of the oppressed and poor. This institutional church concerns us. I long for a living church, one committed to the real needs of a people and a nation; that is, a prophetic church. And I believe it is appearing. Its nature will distinguish it from the institutional church that has abandoned the purposes of Christ himself, and disgraced itself.

If we begin with Christian concerns and attitudes, it is impossible to escape clear action, committed to the total extension of the human being. The political struggle is clear for all those who understand what Christ said. In his preaching and activities, one thing is unequivocal: his indifference to the institutional church. In the end it was the ecclesiastical institution that conspired for his imprisonment and was essentially the group that insisted on his death.

The question comes to us in more than symbolic form. The institution killed Christ when it tried to make static that which is essentially dynamic, that which is alive.

I am not a theologian, and even less a futurologist, but I am interested in the evolution and participation of the church in the political process—something that ought to take place without delay, so that it not be absent in the future from the relevant concerns of our era.

The character of persons and the nature of institutions are clearly revealed in the moment of crisis. The public evisceration to which both church and national political figures were subjected during the repressive era in Brazil made clear the subservience of one and the commitments of the other.

The tragic element in our churches is that because of our formation we are unprepared to verify the root of these violations of rights. We are not prepared to analyse the true origin of terror, almost always falsely identifying it as the desperation of the oppressed. We seem unable to discover the origins of terror in the established system that maintains itself by oppression and constant fear.

The Old Testament example of a prophetic church has been abandoned. A sweet, docile Christ is useful to ecclesiastics whose names are linked with constituted "respectability." When this happens the church loses its real function, and becomes— in the words of Dostoevsky—"a courtesan of power."

A comparison of the United Nations' Universal Declaration of Human Rights with the biblical text makes clear the dimensions of the responsibility of the church in the face of any threats to the humanity of human beings. I read this declaration, with relevant biblical texts and statements of church bodies, before the Congress in 1973, at the height of the repression in Brazil. I did this in the name of the National Conference of Catholic Bishops, the Episcopal Church of Brazil, the Methodist Church, the Pentecostal Evangelical Church, the Presbyterian Mission, and the World Council of Churches.

The social transformations and successive crises our society has gone through have clearly shown the necessity of a new formation of the basic elements of our beliefs. At present they are impregnated with a naive and complacent vision of the "principalities and powers of this world."

A proselytizing evangelism, which defines its success in terms of "Protestantizing Latin America," may produce a kind of euphoria. To be faithful to the gospel and the profound needs of our continent, however, it is necessary to transform society by the establishment of justice and equality for all people.

The New Ecumenism: Justice for All

Feeling these necessities, and imbued with an indispensable ardor for the fulfillment of this mission, we, Latin American Protestants, tried to deal with our difficulties in a way tied to the kind of Protestantism we inherited. We spent years trying to coordinate our many theological convictions. The most advanced sectors of our church modified their preaching.

Although this advance was indispensable, today we know it was not enough. We succeeded in breaking with some traditions and condemning the errors of the traditional focus, but we did not discover the best way of doing it.

For some of us, more devoted and desirous of rehabilitating a past filled with omissions, immobility, and even triumphalism, it was hard to see that the struggle could not take place only at the theological level. Even speaking of the necessity of structural transformations, in a certain sense our activities were limited to modifying the traditional formulations with others we thought to be more correct.

Neither logic nor internal consistency in a formal declaration is going to transform the human being; rather, transformation will be the result of a well-defined and coherent practice in the search for justice among all people.

It was not a question, we began to perceive, of carrying to the world our particular interpretation of reality, but rather of allowing that reality—tragic and alien—to penetrate into the innermost part of our churches. This would allow us to correct our activities, our foci, and even our distortions.

The greatest legitimacy of the theology of liberation does not come from the clarity of its elaborations but from a new formulation that reflects the reality that is discovered through an effective participation in society as a whole, especially assimilated from the perspective of the oppressed. This coming together of reality and theoretical formulation is indispensable to overcoming a world-church dichotomy.

There is an aspect we believe has been a serious concern to sincere Christian sectors, anxious to assimilate our reality: the loss of our identity, of our specific spiritual contribution. Identity in the form of noncommitment is the opposite of action. Isolation and timid and purist withdrawal lead to a neurotic, cowardly, and accommodating lack of character.

If we turn our eyes to the actions of the Lord of history, we will see that his message is imbued with daring and commitment. He does not isolate himself in order to maintain values in the name of tradition. It can even be said that he did not have any great appreciation of them. He lived freely with everyone and always combated injustice. He denounced the powerful and condemned the connivance of the institutional church. His identity was due precisely to the fact that he condemned and fought abuses. The objectives proposed for his ministry never isolated him from other human beings. Thus, fulfillment of his law must be understood as involvement in the life of humanity, above all in that of the marginalized and oppressed.

The maintenance of our identity comes about through the specificity of our option and the clarity of our commitment, and not from a prudent isolation. The situation of poverty, injustice, and exploitation is increasingly more tragic, to the degree that we retreat because of our conservative aspirations. We must remember that the realization of a more relevant attitude requires a sharper criticism of our ecumenical attempts.

The most important ecumenical achievements of our time have come about through groups who understand a concrete struggle on behalf of the oppressed. Once more it has been confirmed that a greater and more important struggle lessens the superficial differences in creeds and concepts.

On the other hand, we do need to observe that the groups which have tried to resolve the problems only through conversations and consultations have not been able to achieve anything beyond "ecumenical marriage." And this has been considered progress in overcoming divisions.

It seems to us that times have changed. Today we understand that one cannot flee when he or she observes in critical form the struggle for liberty and against oppression. When we debated whether or not we should participate in political struggles, we discovered that we were inept and alienated and, even more serious, that we were collaborating with oppression by our indifference and omission.

By what methodology can we define the ways in which the churches participate in the struggle, that is, their participation on behalf of justice, even to the extent of breaking with the dominant structures? Instead of keeping so quiet, asking the question as to what is the Christian manner of carrying out politics, would it not be more positive to verify how God acts through very visible signs, despite the vacillations of ecclesiastical structures? It seems to us, furthermore, that it is more important to assume concrete commitments in relation to the oppressed than to draw out theological analysis.

And we have to take into account that Christianity, in essence, is only for the life of the future and the future of life.

The suffering, mistreated, and marginalized people in whose name Christians try to speak, the people to whom so far only the wounds of Christ have been presented, long for the very body of Christ, clean and resurrected, in order to search for a new society, today, not tomorrow.

A New Protestant Understanding of Afro-Brazilian Religions

JOÃO DIAS DE ARAÚJO   *(Presbyterian, Brazil)*

Brazilian Protestantism, since its beginning, has been confronted by the presence of the black person in Brazilian society.

In 1886 a young Presbyterian pastor, Eduardo Carlos Pereira, published a small volume, *The Christian Religion and Its Relations with Slavery*. It was an attack on the slavery that had been installed in Brazil from the beginning of colonization.

The theological implications of the status of the black in today's world are now being addressed from perspectives new to Protestants (and Catholics as well) by such persons as Joaquim Beato, Rubem Alves, Antonio Olimpio de Sant'ana, and others. I would like to summarize briefly these new factors, specifically in Protestantism.

Acknowledgment

The existence of the black question in Brazilian society as a reality must be acknowledged in theological circles. Long hidden, it is a demand that must be dealt with without illusions. We do not accept the widely proclaimed thesis of the existence of a "racial democracy." Rather, Christians must be critical of the continual manifestations of racial discrimination.

In the main, the churches live out of a "white theology," forgetting that they live in a country where miscegenation has created a "colored" population. Our theology was imported from Europe and the United States. The first missionaries, as well as those here today, were drawn from "white" parishes and seminaries.

Two factors combined to produce a white mentality in

Protestant churches. First is our social heritage—we are a country that maintained slavery for almost three centuries. Second, we were evangelized by white North American and European missionaries who were, in the majority, racists. This can be illustrated by research done with missionaries in Brazil from the southern part of the United States to discover their attitude toward the U.S. civil rights movement. Out of a hundred surveyed, only two favored the objectives of the movement.

White Protestants are called to acknowledge their need for a "black theology." The church's life is on the margin of present-day culture. Blacks are marginalized within the churches. It is essential to recognize this is as theological heresy.

In this decade, the syncretism of Afro-Brazilian religion has surfaced. Always present, and known to be present, this faith expression was declared illegal by the government. The churches regarded it as paganism. Now with its widespread acceptance, Catholic and Protestant theologians are making a liberating assessment of it.

Such a recent reversal of attitude does not provide any written theological documents. What is becoming clear is that Afro-Brazilian syncretisms are culturally very important to the black population. Centuries of slavery, suppression, and oppression tend to destroy the self-image of those systematically discriminated against. However, in religious practices rooted in Africa, blacks bridge the centuries of suffering and find a self to express.

Brazilian Protestants are beginning to join Brazilian blacks in their affirmation of Afro-Brazilian religion as a way they have of asserting their black identity.

Support

Protestant theologians are beginning to support the struggles of blacks for their autonomy, and for all rights that have been denied them.

Racial discrimination, in the churches and in the society, is an impediment to effective participation of all citizens in the full humanity of a democratic society. It cannot be said that in the general membership of local churches the cause of the blacks has majority support. An even smaller minority affirms the reassessment of Afro-Brazilian religions. "When blacks join our churches they begin a process of becoming white in their mentality," observed one black pastor.

Rev. Eduardo Carlos Pereira's nineteenth-century attack against slavery created tensions within the church. One North American missionary threatened to write a book in defense of slavery. In that period the abolitionist campaign was led by intellectuals, Masons, and students—not by rank and file church members.

Today theologians are giving support to movements for the emancipation of the blacks in Brazil. We believe these struggles should be taken up by all Christians. Churches that do not support these struggles begin from the false premise that Christians should not stimulate conflict between social classes. This same point of view is taken in relation to the struggles of all other marginalized groups. It is a false premise because it is contrary to the teachings and practice of Jesus Christ, who placed himself at the side of the ill, the poor, the Samaritan, and all marginalized persons. It is also false because it defends the thesis that the victim of oppression can never rise against the oppressor. Those who help the oppressed are accused of being subversive.

Theologians have tried to attack the hypocrisy of the so-called racial democracy, which is accepted by the conservative elite in church and civil society. This thesis is one more smoke screen clouding a vision of the blacks' problem. Its effect is to discourage their struggles. In order for the Brazilian black to emerge from this social and economic marginalization, a new mentality is needed in all segments of society, especially among white Protestants.

The new attitude toward Afro-Brazilian religions offers Christians, white and black, the opportunity to declare solidarity with the black identity movement.

Positive Appreciation

Protestant theologians have a new, positive appreciation of the religious elements the blacks bring to Brazilian spirituality.

We must no longer consider the Afro-Brazilian religions

as "low spiritism" or "manifestations of the devil." The slaves who were sold to colonial Brazil brought with them their beliefs in the divinities (orixás). This African religion spread throughout Brazil, mixing with popular Catholicism and indigenous animism to form a unique Brazilian syncretism.

Christian theologians are replacing inherited attitudes with a more profound appreciation of this phenomon. To be in solidarity with the blacks' struggle for the rights of their humanity calls for affirmation of the religious expression of their African identity. Further, one cannot understand Brazilian religiosity without the contribution of its African elements.

There is a significant difference between the experience of the blacks taken to the United States and those brought to Brazil. Here they were obliged to camouflage their cults and saints with Christian names in order to survive the inquisitorial atmosphere of the Portuguese colonizers, but they did not convert to Christianity. A well-known Brazilian anthropologist declared, "The catechism was an illusion." The blacks never abandoned their African beliefs, so their religion was preserved as the bed from which seed began to sprout in all regions of Brazil.

Not all marginalization is based on race. The impoverishment of the majority results from class, sexist, social, economic, political, and numerous other elements. The oppressed poor organize themselves to demand full humanity. In all of these the central motivating force is spirituality. In cultures that include Indians there is a parallel effort to affirm the liberating elements of their spirituality.

The affirmation of Afro-Brazilian popular religiosity links Christians of all colors and classes with all other popular movements and the religiosity of all marginalized peoples. This is the current agenda of the church in Brazil with regard to the reality of the blacks in our culture today.

Pentecostal Theology in the Context of the Struggle for Life

JUAN SEPÚLVEDA   *(Pentecostal, Chile)*

Chilean Pentecostalism[1] arose at the beginning of the century as a result of a schism within the Chilean Methodist church (1910). The schism came about because the Methodist church was not able to accept or understand a "spiritual revival" movement that was developing in the churches.

Even though the dissident group theologically claimed the theme of the Holy Spirit, it may be said that the conflict was not principally *doctrinal* or *theological*. It was, rather, about religious practices and ways of living and celebrating the faith. Considering the fact that the dissident group was made up of humble folk, we may say that the two central axes of the conflict were:

- The conflict between a religiosity centered in the objectivity of dogma, in which faith consisted in the formal, conscious, and rational acceptance of doctrine; and a religiosity which gave priority to the subjective experience of God, in which faith is a response to a kind of possession of the being by the Divine One.
- The conflict between a religion mediated by specialists of a cultured class (a specialized clergy) and by an enlightened culture; and a religion in which the poor people have direct access

---

1. In the context of this chapter it seemed fundamental to distinguish between Chilean or "creole" Pentecostalism, born of a national schism and from its origin absolutely independent of foreign missions, and "imported Pentecostalism," especially from the United States which since about 1945 began its work in Chile, depending on foreign sources. The sociological, cultural, and theological differences between both types are notable. Our interest is in "creole" Pentecostalism, which is without doubt the majority.

to God, and in which the relationship with the sacred can be communicated legitimately in the language of the culture itself, and in popular language.

The fact that it was a church made up of poor people with a popular ministry meant the Pentecostal movement had a wide acceptance in the popular sector, particularly among people of unstable employment, small artisans, poor peasants, rural migrants. Pentecostalism became the *preferred religious expression of the sector that had been excluded from society.*

In this chapter we propose to study Pentecostal "theology" in the context of the struggle for life among these sectors. For greater clarity we will distinguish three moments or phases in the struggle.

Pentecostal Theology in the Context of Social Exclusion (1910–1960)

The profile of Chilean Pentecostal thought began to take shape in the epoch of its greatest growth, which coincides with the period of crisis and exclusion suffered by the nonworking poor (rural and urban subproletariat). Such a theology was articulated with the Methodist theological heritage as a starting point, faced with the reality of crisis, and with the popular religiosity and culture of those who were converted to Pentecostalism.

In this nonsystematic "theology" we are able to identify at least some themes.

A Manichaeistic Vision of the World

Perhaps the central characteristic of Pentecostal thought is its dualistic or Manichaean vision of the world: all reality is marked by the opposition between the *spiritual* dimension, the place of the divine presence and the source of all good; and the *material,* marked by the sign of sin and therefore the source of all evil. The opposition between spirit and matter is represented cosmologically in the opposition between heaven and earth, and sociologically in the opposition between the church and the world. So we arrive at the following scheme:

Spirit	vs	Matter
Heaven		Earth
Church		World
Believer		Unbeliever
God		Devil
Good		Evil
Soul		Body

All the concepts in the right-hand column are considered negative. They represent, if not sin itself, the occasion for sin. The right Christian conduct will be to *separate oneself*, as much as possible, from the world, from the body, from unbelievers, and so forth.

The term *Manichaeism* refers to the cosmological and anthropological dualism that runs through all Pentecostal theology. There is a permanent risk of *contagion* with the norms of the life of the world. The only way to neutralize the danger is by the religious community's totalitarian claim on the free time of the convert, and the demand of a passive ethic that proclaims total separation from the world.

When a Pentecostal says, "This world offers nothing, only perdition," he is not making a dogmatic statement but simply giving form to his own experience: the world in which he has lived is a world of misery. To the degree that the causes of this situation are not transparent, it is seen to be permanent: it is not that this world *might be* evil, it *is* evil. All one can do is wait for better days in the kingdom of God.

Anthropological Determinism and Pessimism

The Spirit/Matter duality is translated anthropologically into the Soul/Body opposition. Two characteristics of the Pentecostal view of the human being are explained by this dualism.

Anthropological Pessimism

In Pentecostal preaching there is nothing good to be said about the human being. Almost all discourse about persons is veiled by the discourse about *sin*, based explicitly on Genesis 3, hiding the "positive anthropology" of Genesis 1 and 2. "Original sin," often related to the sexual and understood as something "contagious" by biological inheritance, becomes the fundamental mark of human existence.

The human "image and likeness" of God is annulled by sin, reducing persons to slaves to the desires of the flesh. This is the reason for absolute human powerlessness in the struggle against evil: there is nothing good one can do before God.

Anthropological Determinism

The practices and language of Pentecostal members in their most typical expressions reflect a determinism of human behavior, of socioeconomic situation or placement in the class structure, and even of personal health. This determination can come from internal factors: passion, impulses of the flesh—with a strong sexual connotation—expressed in the Pauline term *concupiscence*. These impulses, which come from human carnality, appear as something that goes beyond the will and tends to dominate the human ego. They act through the senses, especially vision.

But the human appears to be fundamentally determined by external forces: the principalities and powers. If they are of a negative character, they are considered "demons" or "evil spirits." If they are positive forces, they are called the "Holy Spirit."

This gives one the impression that the relationship between internal factors (impulses of the flesh) and external determinism is this: to the degree to which human beings are incapable of dominating their internal impulses with the will through the exercise of ascetic attitudes, they tend to be dominated by evil spirits. Nevertheless, domination of the desires of the flesh is possible, but only under the influence of the Holy Spirit. The human will plays a secondary role, opened to the Holy Spirit through ascetic practice.

The Power of the Holy Spirit

Faced with the reality of human powerlessness in the conflict with evil in the world, and in the body itself, the power of the Holy Spirit breaks in. The baptism of the Holy Spirit is the effective mediation of the saving power of the living God. This is the definitive aspect of the Pentecostal movement.

Moreover, the baptism of the Holy Spirit is the *motive force* of the evangelizing actions of the church:

> When the Holy Spirit recently fell with power, the baptized persons, boys or girls, men or women, felt compelled to go out into the streets to preach in a loud voice, to go to their friends and neighbors, to travel to other places, with the single objective of calling them to repentance and to make them know by their witness that this sublime experience was a privilege within reach of every person today, just as in the days of the apostles.[2]

Chilean Pentecostalism has not developed a *doctrine* of the Holy Spirit and therefore is not very clear whether the baptism of the Holy Spirit is a saving experience in itself or only a step on the road to sanctification. There is no scheme of *stages* in Chilean Pentecostalism as there is in North American Pentecostalism. In general it may be said that the baptism of the Holy Spirit is not confused with *conversion* but is a kind of special power to overcome evil and to motivate witnessing.

Neither has Chilean Pentecostalism formalized the theme of the manifestations of the Holy Spirit. While in North American Pentecostalism glossolalia (speaking in tongues) is recognized as the unique, initial manifestation of the Holy Spirit in the person, Chilean Pentecostalism recognizes multiple manifestations of the presence of the Spirit—from angelic tongues to simple joy, dance, visions, and so on. Even more, the verification of the experience is sought not so much in external signs as in a changed life (the fruits of the Spirit). The authenticity of the spiritual experience is recognized in the changed life and in the certainty of pardon.

The deepest significance of the experience of the Holy Spirit for the poor and those excluded from society is the certainty of the live presence of an accepting God. Through the Holy Spirit, God is directly accessible to the poor without the need of mediation. Thus, the experience of the Holy Spirit destroys the historic separation between "qualified agents of religion" and "believing people." Now all the people, even the

2. Willis Hoover, *Historia del avivamiento pentecostal en Chile (1931)* (Valparaiso: Imprenta Excelsior, 1948), p. 43.

simplest, are legitimate bearers of the good news, to the degree to which they have experienced it in their lives.[3]

The Bible as Mediation between the Believer and Reality

In face of the appropriation of the Bible by the "professionals" of religion (theologians, hierarchy), the mediation of the Spirit gives the Bible back to the people. This is of greatest importance when we consider that the majority of Pentecostal believers come from a pre-Vatican Catholicism, when the Bible was not accessible to the laity and the Mass was said in Latin. This fact converts Pentecostalism into a form of *religious revolution*. Now each believer can have a Bible, read it, understand it through the inspiration of the Holy Spirit, and preach it to others, without the need of any special preparation. The inspiration of the Spirit allows for a correct interpretation of the Bible. At the same time, the Bible is the criterion for discerning the authenticity of the experience of the Holy Spirit:

> One must stress the boundary separating the Pentecostalists' spiritualism from surrounding forms of spiritualisms, that is, that their pneumatology is rooted in the Bible. Their whole understanding of the Spirit rests upon their reading of the Bible . . . whatever the liberties taken in regard to the Bible in the name of the Spirit, Pentecostalist prophecies or revelations have never had more than relative or temporary validity and were not treated as a new Revelation, complementary to the Holy Scriptures.[4]

Therefore, the experience of the Holy Spirit and the reading of the Bible are very closely linked. While the Spirit guides the reading, the Bible makes it possible to discern "the Spirit." Therefore, there is no absolutely free interpretation.

While traditional Protestant preaching is marked by an analysis of the text, in Pentecostalism preaching consists of a

3. This analysis has been deepened by the Brazilian, Francisco Cartaxo Rolim, "Pentecostime et Sociéte au Brésil," *Social Compass*, 26/2-3 (1979): 345-72.

4. Christian Lalive d'Epinay, *Haven of the Masses: A Study of the Pentecostal Movement in Chile* (London: Lutterworth, 1969), pp. 195-96.

kind of reproduction of the text, in which the biblical text and the witness of the experience of the preacher come together. The Bible furnishes a language not only for the Pentecostal experience but for the life of the believer. Thus the Bible becomes a *mediation* between the person and reality: all reality is seen through the "lens" of the Bible.

For the Pentecostal, the Bible's place is like that of "myth" in popular religiosity: it gives meaning to the world and to the life of the believer. The Bible is transformed into the language of excluded people whose word and voice have no place in society. This new language, even though it may be the object of ridicule, makes it possible to speak to God, the owner of the universe, and has a tremendous appeal for all those who lack a language for their life.

A "Militant Church"

There is no clearly developed Pentecostal "ecclesiological model." The "way of being church" of Pentecostals has been built out of their rupture and continuity with the models they have known: the Methodist and the Catholic.

If we wish to find a term to define the Pentecostal ecclesiology, it would be: a "militant church."

Belonging to the Pentecostal community is always mediated by *conversion*, by a personal and voluntary decision. One is a member of the church only if he or she is converted. On the other hand, a convert who ceases to "militate," to participate in the life of the community, and abandons the duties of evangelization, in reality has "gone astray" or "lost the way."

A parish structure is unthinkable. Only those are "church" who participate in all the worship and activities of the church community, above all if they fulfill the inescapable mission of evangelism.

The *militant* character of Pentecostal churches is expressed in two seemingly contradictory facts: to be, on the one hand, a *voluntary community*, while, on the other hand, to be a *totalitarian community* in which the faithful should subordinate personal, individual interests to those of the community of faith, which begins to govern all of life. Even private life is regulated by the Pentecostal community.

If we look in the history of the church for "ecclesiologi-cal models" to which Pentecostal ecclesiology can be compared, we find the so-called radical reformed or Anabaptist. Franklin Littell lifts up two fundamental points in the Anabaptist concept of the church, which can be the hermeneutical key of almost all forms of "radical ecclesiology":

> 1) The church must be a voluntary association, taking its spirit and discipline from those who intentionally belong to its fellowship.
> 2) The church must follow the guide lines of the New Testament as to confession of faith and organizational pattern.[5]

In the case of Pentecostalism, these two points are at the center of ecclesial practice. We could mention a series of points of contact between Anabaptist and Pentecostal ecclesiology, such as the emphasis on discipline, the rejection of infant baptism, the insistence on the *holiness* of the church in the sense of being *separated from the world*, a separation that must be shown in the concrete differences that distinguish the members of the community from the people of "the world."

1. Both in Pentecostal preaching and in the preaching (and writing) of the "radical reformed," there is a severe criticism of all forms of *Christendom*, that is to say, of those models in which the church is closely tied with the "secular power," making use of it even for "religious" ends. It is a protest against all forms of "official religion."

2. In both cases, even though the historic circumstances are very different, they are the religion of social sectors subject to permanent instability and endemic misery. This implies a permanent opposition of these religious expressions to the "powerful."

Out of the experience of religious and social *opposition*, the *separation* from the world and the *persecution* of the community by the world come to be the true marks of a "militant church," according to this ecclesiological model. They form the Pentecostal "theology" that arose from the experience of poor believers, those excluded from society, who in an era of prolonged crisis had to live in deep misery and social deterioration.

In a world they experienced as truly *evil*, with neither fu-

5. Franklin Littell, *The Anabaptist View of the Church: A Study in the Origins of Sectarian Protestantism* (Boston: Starr King, 1958), p. 46.

ture nor hope—in short, a world *without meaning*—the Pentecostal community, with its affirmation of its experience of the transforming presence of God mediated by the Holy Spirit, with its hope of a better world in which there will be no suffering, with a community that welcomes and shares with all the "weary and heavy laden," offers a great alternative for life and hope in a *"micro-cosmos" of meaning*.

Hopes of change at this stage are found exclusively in the workers' world, the organized proletariat, and the middle class. The Pentecostal experience has a hope that, although otherworldly, redeems the faithful from an anonymous and shattered life.

Christian Lalive d'Epinay discovers a synthesis of this "theology" of the excluded one in a framed print that adorns the pulpit of many Pentecostal churches:

> An imposing polychrome print constitutes the principal ornament of Pentecostal churches. In it one sees a rough sea whose waves break against a rocky island. On this little corner of threatened land there rests an open Bible illuminated by a ray of the sun which comes from above, coming through black, tormented clouds. One can read the following verse: "Come unto me, all you who are weary and heavy laden and I will give you rest" (Matthew 11:28).
>
> This picture represents allegorically some of the principal lines of Pentecostal ideology. In a world of perdition and disgrace, radically "evil and perverse," there survive islands of peace: the communities of believers protected by the "power of God," by the Spirit which comes from on high. The task of the elect is to give assistance to those who refuse to hear the calling to enter the refuge of the church. It is not in any way to try to tame the agitated sea.[6]

This is the Chilean Pentecostal theology in its purest expression, which in the new phases of the life struggle of the excluded will be challenged by new conditions and on occasion will be transformed by the power of new realities.

6. Lalive d'Epinay, "Sociedad dependiente, clases populares y milenarismo," in Varios, *Dependencia y Estructura de clases en Américan Latina* (Buenos Aires: Megapolis, 1975), pp. 278-79.

Democratic Development and Pentecostal Theology (1964–1973)

What are the changes in the life struggle of the poor which challenged the Pentecostal theology that emerged from this earlier phase?

There was a process of incorporation of new sectors into the democratic life of the country. Those new sectors included the priority "clientele" of Pentecostalism: the urban marginalized and poor peasants. Christian Democracy and its "revolution with liberty" needed the support of the world of the marginalized to face the power of the left with its socialist project, which dominated the world of the worker. The presence of alternatives and hopes of change in this world constitute a strong challenge to Pentecostalism, which has fed on a reality of exclusion, proclaiming a hope of change in the "beyond."

The kind of response the church makes to these challenges is influenced by other changes that have occurred within the Protestant world itself. Two important ones are:

- The Protestant condition of being a religious minority in society has been modified among Pentecostals. It continues to be a minority but it has grown rapidly at the expense of the diminution of the majority church. This is more important if we take into account the *militant* character of Pentecostal ecclesiology as compared with a more *cultural* ecclesiology of Catholicism. It is crucial that Pentecostalism have an *awareness* of this change, which in one way or another influences its response to the challenges presented to it by society.
- The beginning of relationships with the world ecumenical movement and the administration of world-wide relief funds during the earthquakes of 1960 and 1965 gave the churches a new experience of service to persons outside the Pentecostal churches.

Some significant changes in theological thought resulted from these situations.[7]

7. It is important to see that these tendencies do not necessarily involve entire denominations. Most of the time they are present in denominations along with other viewpoints. However, the position taken by the hierarchy of a denomination is determinative for the bases. It is also im-

An "Up-to-Date" Pentecostalism?

With the appearance of new alternatives and hopes in this world, and with a Pentecostal sector that in sympathy with the new tendencies in society accepts the participation of its members in the new organizations, something changes in the dualistic vision of the world. The dualism does not disappear—since it is so deeply rooted in the Christian tradition—but the notion of the *radically negative* nature of "this world" does tend to disappear. In its place appears the idea that, though the world is unjust and foreign to the will of God, there *can and should* be changes on behalf of those who suffer. There can be a development that helps to put an end to certain social ills and thus to achieve a relative good.

Dualism survived, but not as an *opposition* (church vs. world, spirit vs. matter). There is a certain *complementary* relation of the parts (complementary dualism). Church and society are distinct realities, but both are necessary to human life. There is even a hierarchy among the parts: the church is much more important since its task is the eternal salvation of persons, but as long as we live in this world, the state (and its various expressions) is the proper organ to achieve a relative good that will make life more livable. Christians, because they know God, have the duty to participate in the task of creating better conditions for life on this earth.

The articulation of the parts of this duality that appear in this phase is approximately the following: the achievement of a certain relative well-being in this world allows for better receptivity for the message of salvation.

Very soon the anthropological dualism, and the *pessimism* that derives from it, is affected. Of course, the idea of powerlessness in the face of the reality of sin and the possibility of salvation remains. However, it is accepted that the human being can do quite a bit to achieve relatively better conditions of life in this world.

Even so, the certainty of the baptism of the Holy Spirit is

portant to consider that tendencies to change—in whatever sense—are much clearer in the urban environment. In the rural sections Pentecostalism usually maintains its traditional characteristics.

translated less into a radical rupture with this world than into a change in attitude toward it. The list of the fruits of the Spirit slowly incorporates new gifts associated with the idea of *service* and of witness through leadership among students or workers.

The *militant* character of Pentecostal ecclesiology would now be at the service of a servant church. Just as Pentecostalism was a *militantly evangelizing* community, now it will be *militantly serving*. This may be where the aspect of change is most critical and conflictive.

Pentecostal *militancy* had its affirmation in the total dedication of free time to the life and action of the church, which traditionally held *daily* worship, and in separation from the world. Now this same church gives positive value to the participation of its members in another kind of organization, which also operates in "free time." Free time must necessarily be shared among diverse activities. So the church is forced to be more permissive (less *totalitarian*) and in many cases to diminish the frequency of its worship and activities.

The foregoing inevitably results in a loss of vitality of the Pentecostal congregations, a situation that will be perceived by the older generation, perhaps with reason, as a loss or crisis of Pentecostal identity.

Toward a Pentecostal Fundamentalism?

A permissive attitude in face of pressure for social participation brings internal tensions and changes that lead an important segment to develop an explicit rejection of the participation of its members in the emerging social organizations.

For this sector, the democratization and politicization of society carried with them a serious threat to Pentecostal evangelism. In an overpoliticized society that presses for the participation of all in a multiplicity of social organizations, requires taking sides in sociopolitical conflicts, and offers hope for substantive changes in the conditions of life, people are much less receptive to hearing the Pentecostal message. They are more occupied with their happiness "here" than concerned about the "beyond."

The popular sectors begin to discover a new meaning to their existence, resolving the problem of anomie and the lack of meaning formerly solved by the Pentecostal community. Consequently, sectors of Pentecostalism not only impeded the participation of its members for reasons of ecclesiastical discipline, but also tended to reject changes in themselves and to "demonize" politics.

The more *experiential*—or existential—*dualism* of Pentecostalism in its early era is transformed into a more *ideological dualism*. While the Pentecostals of the thirties said "this world offers only perdition," today's world appears less evil, since recent legislation has favored the poorer class, democratizing access to health care and education, improving the possibility of popular consumption, and the like.

The affirmation of the "evil" nature of this world casts negative value on hopes for social change, and therefore affirms the status quo. To the demand for separation from the world, there is added with new force the demand for submission to the established authorities (inspired by Romans 13). Creole Pentecostalism is strongly influenced by foreign thought, which arrived in Chile through the "imported" Pentecostal churches (coming especially from the United States).

Ambiguity exists for other reasons: Pentecostalism's awareness that it has grown rapidly, that it has become the second largest religious force in the country, in some way translated into the awakening of new political aspirations, one expectation of which is the dream of a Protestant president who will resolve the problem of the precarious juridical character of the evangelical churches. In this way the demand for separation from the world comes to coexist with an ever-greater aspiration for social recognition of Protestants by the state.

We should emphasize the fact that, with the sharpening of the political conflict that led to the end of the government of Christian Democracy, and during the government of Popular Unity (1970–1973), this more *ideological dualism* acquired an explicit anticommunist connotation. Foreign organizations bombarded the evangelical world with anticommunist propaganda.

In this new phase of the struggle for life, important new changes were initiated in Pentecostal theology, principally affecting the cosmological dualism, giving rise in one case to a *complementary dualism* and in another to *ideological dualism*. In both cases this change will have repercussions on other aspects of Pentecostal theology.

Dictatorship, Atomization of Society, and Pentecostal Theology (1973-   )

The military dictatorship that began with the coup d'état of 1973 imposed conditions that caused a repetition of the social and political exclusion of the popular sectors. The outlawing of political, social, and labor organizations and the consequent persecution of their leaders produced a profound atomization of society. Opportunities for encounter and participation by the population disappeared, especially in the popular sectors, destroying the "social fabric" that had been woven during the last decades. In consequence, a situation of isolation has been imposed on the poor.

The dogmatic application of the model of "market economy" (Chicago School) in the early days of the military regime profoundly deteriorated the conditions of life for the popular sectors. The regime systematically destroyed social achievements that were the results of years of popular struggle. The reality of growing misery imposed on the popular sectors is characterized by unemployment, underemployment, malnutrition, and reduction of access to health care and education. There is also a generalized fear that hinders any popular effort toward organization.

In this new situation of social exclusion, one element differs from that of the thirties. There is a new awareness that things can be and in fact are different. Therefore, it will not be as easy to accept misery as a fatal and unchangeable earmark of the poor.

How will this situation influence the theology and practice of the Pentecostal churches?

Our impression is that under these new conditions no new tendencies of change in theology have been produced, but there has been a deepening of the tendencies already initiated in the previous phase.

Toward a Conservative Pentecostalism

The sector of the Pentecostal world that has seen in democratic participation a threat to evangelism and growth, sees in the military coup d'état and the destruction of democracy a new opportunity for Pentecostal advance. Also, since 1975 when the relationship between the Catholic church and the military regime profoundly deteriorated, this sector has found favorable conditions for a greater recognition from the state, and thus expects a juridical improvement for evangelical churches.

Because the state was deprived of religious support through the harsh criticisms of its violations of human rights by the Catholic Church, the state was also interested in opening contacts with the Protestants as a way of achieving support from the next most relevant religious sector.

A new type of relationship emerges, then, between a part of the Protestant world and the state. Of interest here are the theological consequences of this unprecedented phenomenon in the history of Chile. We shall point to two significant changes.

From Cosmological Dualism to Ideological Manichaeism

In the discourse of the sector just defined, traditional Pentecostal dualism comes together with the ideological Manichaeism appropriate to the military regime. The opposition between good and evil, formerly expressed as the opposition between church and the world, is now expressed in the opposition of Western, Christian society vs. international Marxism. The central affirmation of a document of support for the Pinochet regime read in a celebration on September 13, 1974, said: "The military intervention of the Armed Forces in the historic process of our country, was the response of God to the prayer of all believers who see in Marxism the maximum darkness of satanic forces."[8]

So as Marxism appears as an expression of satanic forces, "Armed Forces" appear as the divine instrument of redemption. Therefore, no longer is the world in itself the incarnation of evil. The struggle between good and evil is incarnated in the ideological struggle between East and West.

Immediately the churches openly took sides in this ideological struggle on behalf of the Christian West.

---

8. "Declaración de apoyo a la Junta de Gobierno de las iglesias evangélicas" n. 2, in *Posición Evangélica* (Santiago: Edit. Pedro Puente, 1975).

From the Separated and Persecuted Church to an "Official" Church

Two symbols clearly show a rupture in the Pentecostal ecclesiology: the building of an "Evangelical Cathedral" (in reality, the mother church of the Pentecostal Methodist Church) and the celebration of the "Protestant Te Deum."

The language itself shows that this sector has borrowed the ecclesiological model of the historic opponent of the Pentecostal world: the Catholic church. The idea of a church separated from the world, a church persecuted by the powers of this world, disappears and is replaced by a church that aspires to be an *official religion*.

We believe that only time will tell which of these tendencies of change in the Pentecostal world will become its future. What seems beyond doubt is that, in the struggle for life, Pentecostalism and its "theology" has changed profoundly and has ceased to be homogeneous.

Toward a Popular Pentecostalism

The churches that had developed an attitude of openness to the participation of their membership in social organizations are now under the pressure of the reality imposed by the military to develop new practices of solidarity. To the degree that the churches, especially the Catholic but also the Protestant, are practically the only spaces of community encounter not made illegal, the poor turn to them in great numbers—making them the only place where despair and suffering can be expressed in the search for a response to a situation that threatens to destroy the very identity of the poor.

Thus a number of efforts toward solidarity began to arise, to help the poor to survive in the emergency situation. The impact of this reality on theology in this stage has been much greater than previously. Now it is not merely a question of bringing theology up-to-date with social changes or of seeking greater evangelistic efficacy; it is a question of dealing with suffering that massively affects the popular sectors, including, of course, the Pentecostal faithful.

Vision of the World and Anthropology

Once again, the lines of theology that are crucially affected are the vision of the world (cosmovision) and anthropology. The military regime has duplicated social conditions in which the world is experienced as negative, evil. In other words, the conditions of the *radically negative* world reappear (the world as the scene of the advance of evil), which in the beginning may greatly strengthen the traditional *dualism of opposition.*

However, the fact that the Chilean people have lived through a different experience that shows the relative possibility of the improvement of the conditions of life *in this world,* and, on the other hand, the undeniable evidence that the new situation of suffering is caused by the actions of power groups that have taken the government by force and imposed a given type of society, leads to a process of *historicization* of evil in this world. It becomes evident that the central problem is not that the world *may be* or *is* evil, but that there are power groups in society who fight to impose their own interests and produce injustice.

The changes in Pentecostal language show the historicization of the struggle between good and evil. It is not a struggle between heaven and earth, between spirit and matter, between God and the devil, having the world only as its scene. It is the struggle between good and evil with human beings as its actors. This change in the perception of reality, and consequently of the vision of the world, is seen in the incorporation of notions such as injustice, oppression, the powerful, and so forth in daily language, prayers, and preaching.

Thus the real evil experienced in life is no longer understood as fatality, as payment for evil itself, but as the product of a social causality: the idea of the poor as the victims of the sins of others appears.

Among the Pentecostals who participate in activities of solidarity, there is a perceptible effort to understand the meaning of this reality, questioning the traditional explanations of the problem of suffering. The words of two Pentecostal women speaking about unemployment illustrates this attitude:

> I don't know, but I think if God is love, he is not going to *punish us* in such a way that our children or we ourselves suffer.

I think that when God *tests* somebody it has to be in special cases so that they believe in him, but it turns out that in the situation in which we are living, those who know God are suffering as much as those who do not. God said he came into the world so that all might have life in abundance.[9]

To the degree that there is a perception of human and social causes of evil, the idea of the inevitable or irreversible advance of evil must give way. It is possible to do something to hold it back. Changes are possible. The meaning of participation and solidarity is discovered within this possibility.

The conviction that human beings can do something also distinctly relativizes the traditional anthropological pessimism. On the other hand, the idea that we can be collaborators with God is strengthened in the perspective of the kingdom.

This last affirmation leads us to the theme of eschatology. Just as the vision of evil in the world has been historicized, so also has eschatology: the hope of the kingdom of God is increasingly tied to the need for a profound change in the way of living in this world. This linkage leads some Pentecostal sectors to take their commitment even beyond service at the local level, participating in prophetic actions and statements, criticizing the actions of the authorities in the light of the promises of God.[10]

The Reading of the Bible

The experience of suffering and social commitment has had a great influence on the reading of the Bible. In the first place, because of the need for a foundation for the new evangelical social practices, there has been a great awakening of biblical study.

Second, the Bible, which has always been the source of the language with which the Pentecostal speaks of himself, again furnished the language for speaking of the problems of suffering during these years of the dictatorship. So in the daily

9. Notes on a conversation about the problem of unemployment by women who took part in a health course (Protestant Service for Development).

10. An example of this is that the majority of the churches that are members of the "Confraternidad Cristiana de Iglesias," an ecumenical organization that has maintained, since 1982, a critical posture toward the military regime, are Pentecostals.

language of Pentecostals we find abundant reference to the Exodus, the Babylonian Exile, the Psalms of Lamentation, Job, and many other passages as a way of referring to the very experience of the individual or the people.

There is a much more historic and less spiritualized reading of reality, and at the same time a greater capacity for dialogue between life and the biblical message. We believe there is a reciprocal relationship between this change and the change of the cosmovision and anthropology.

In part, the more historic vision of reality that we discovered above furnishes new keys for reading the Bible: injustice, oppression, despair—each ending with its opposite: justice, liberation, hope. But at the same time this new vision of reality is reenforced by this new reading of the Bible.

The Ecclesiological Model

The most notable change in the ecclesiological aspect is the lessening and almost total disappearance of the relation of opposition between the church and community. The traditional Pentecostal ecclesiology affirmed the difference, separation, and opposition between the congregation and the world. The contact between the two was only for evangelism through which the Pentecostal called "the Gentile" to conversion, to abandon the world, and to join the church. Now, the encounter between the congregation and the neighbors through experiences of solidarity has produced a new form of meeting, a new type of relationship.

Another change is a broadening of the spectrum of the mission of the church. While in traditional Pentecostalism the mission is reduced to the work of evangelism, now there are new dimensions also recognized as the mission of the church: service and what we may call the "teaching ministry."

This also implies a diversification of the "gifts" or "spiritual ministries." Both changes sharpen the crisis of the "militant church."

Pentecostal Spirituality: Identity Crisis?

These changes have made significant differences in Pentecostal spirituality. Since the centrality of the baptism of the Holy Spirit

316

has been the most definitive aspect of Pentecostalism, the crisis of spirituality has been translated into a crisis of Pentecostal *identity*.

It is not that the Pentecostal churches that have enrolled in the movements for change have lost their emphasis on the subjective dimensions of the religious experience. The problem is that Pentecostal identity traditionally has been associated with and almost reduced to the *outer manifestations* of the life of the Spirit: glossolalia and the dance, prophecy, and collective ecstacy in Pentecostal worship. This experience of festive worship was obviously nourished by the daily frequency of worship and by the unavailability to the popular classes of other channels of expression of their subjectivity. Now with a more diversified vision of the church, with greater opportunity for participation in other bodies, with the diminished frequency of worship and a more analytical study of the Bible, the weight and frequency of outer manifestations of the Holy Spirit have diminished. In other words, worship has changed.

The current understanding of the gifts of the Spirit is associated less with ecstatic expressions than with new *ministries*, gifts of teaching, serving, and the like. In Pentecostal discourse today there is a certain movement from the gifts of the Spirit to the "fruits of the Spirit" (Gal. 5:22). Basically, this means that the verification of the authenticity of the spiritual experience is sought less in outer manifestations than in the way of life.

This changed perception often comes through as a crisis of identity. Can it be that we are no longer Pentecostals? This is especially a crisis for the older members of the church who remember the worship from the time of their conversion.

How is Pentecostal identity being reelaborated in this context? The truth is that there is no systematic reflection on the problem. Arising out of our ongoing dialogue are clues which help us to answer the question, *What does it mean to be a Pentecostal?*

- To be Pentecostal is above all to have a personal experience of God. God cannot be known only through the study of the Bible or by the experience of others. God must be lived.
- Experience of God, through the Spirit, is directly accessible to the poor and the excluded for whom conversion represents a

dignifying change: "from ignorant to powerful," "from a humble person a giant appears."

- The experience of the Spirit is shown in a new *freedom*. This freedom means the loss of fear and is expressed in facing up to any person or group, at any social or cultural level. It also means freedom to express feelings without fear of prejudice or cultural repression. And in a context of oppression, such as the present one, it means freedom to speak the truth without fear.
- The Pentecostal experience is verified in a change of life-style. Such change is expressed in a new *sensitivity* toward others (the problems of others are *felt* as if God were speaking through such problems), in an attitude of more *confident* life, and in a life of *hope*, in spite of the signs of death that are present in the world.

It is notable that for this group, the experience of Pentecostal spirituality described in these terms is not the exclusive property of the churches that call themselves Pentecostal. It is an experience that can be given to any church open to the action of the Spirit, because "the Spirit blows where it wishes." The richness and contribution of the Pentecostal movement would be in having rediscovered this dimension of religious experience, opening the door to a revitalization of all Christian churches who themselves open their doors to the experience.

Toward an Ecumenical Pastoral

FEDERICO PAGURA   (Methodist, Argentina)

Recently, while reading *La tradición protestante en la teología latinoamericana,* I came upon the words of the Primitive Methodist local preacher of Alford, who said:

> I believe that the day is not far off in which God will send to his church apostles and prophets worthy of it, who will visit the poor aged ones and will seek to know how they succeed in living on three shillings a week which they receive from the parish to pay for the charcoal and the light, and besides this feed themselves and subsist; apostles and prophets who will protest such cruelty and will preach with matchless vigor the Word of God.[1]

I ask myself, then, very seriously, if this dream is not beginning to become a reality in our own continent. Christians of the most diverse confessions are beginning to awaken to the reality that has been hidden from us, or to which we had become accustomed in the midst of our "spiritual exercises."

I ask myself if this same clamor does not begin to be heard in the land of our mother churches. They are situated in the center of sumptuous opulence, and the most awe-inspiring technological advances, but also in the center of an insane arms race, of the most cynical imperialism, of a galloping moral and psychological decadence, and of a growing mass of unemployed. Do we not see there also the signs of the awakening of a radical and prophetic gospel, the only hope for a nation otherwise condemned to self-destruction?

If this happens, then in the words of the preacher of Alford there will be multiplied in our own midst apostles, proph-

1. Edited by José Duque (San José, Costa Rica: Departamento Ecuménico de Investigaciones, 1983).

ets, and martyrs, "and they shall preach with matchless vigor the Word of God."

In relation to an ecumenical pastoral, I dare only to lift up some elements we cannot ignore:

1. There is an evident crisis in all confessional pastorals practiced on our continent, even in the most "successful" denominations, those characterized by aggressive proselytizing. The alienating effects produced by sectarian pastoral practices, which do not engage in the struggles of the oppressed, deserve condemnation as harsh as that placed on the lips of Jesus: "Alas for you, scribes and Pharisees, you hypocrites! You who travel over sea and land to make a single proselyte, and when you have him you make him twice as fit for hell as you are" (Matt. 23:15).

Perhaps we should recognize here that some of the most promising signs are to be seen in a renewed Catholicism expressed in the base communities so influential in rural and urban sectors of the poor population.

2. In the search for a Protestant pastoral that responds to this moment in our continent, we should keep in mind Dr. Míguez Bonino's accurate observation that

> a good part of the confessionalism that is being reborn with vigor in our time is part of the search for an identity that permits us to resist the changes and perplexities of the present moment, a memory which frees us from creating a project.[2]

3. For the same reason, confessional reflection should not be taken to be more than a way station on the road that leads to the recuperation of a Protestant, prophetic, popular, and relevant pastoral. It is, as Míguez Bonino says, "a call to a reinterpretation of history which frees us of the blockages and allows us to participate in these changes, a memory which evokes a challenge and a mission."[3]

Latin Americans of all confessional families are challenged to participate in the search for an ecumenical pastoral that takes seriously the following considerations:

a. The people whom we have been called to serve: the

---

2. "Was Methodism a Liberating Movement?" in *Luta Pela Vida e Evangelização* (São Paulo: Edições Paulinas, 1985), pp. 24-25.

3. Ibid.

Latin American people, with their greatness and their misery, with their frustrations and their hopes.

b. The particular project that challenges us at this moment in history: dependency or real independence; oppression or integral liberation. Here we Christians cannot avoid the epithets of "naive" or "smart" Christians, which come from Paulo Freire in his valuable study "The Churches, Education and the Process of Human Liberation in History": "Either they transform their naivete into 'smartness' consciously assuming in this way the ideology of domination or else they become committed to the true search for the liberation of the oppressed as one of them."[4]

c. The ONE church that, more than by agreements at an elitist level of administrators, is being born from the people, their sufferings, struggles, frustrations, hopes—something that the Conference of Latin American Roman Catholic Bishops at Medellín (1968) affirmed:

> We are on the threshold of a new epoch in the history of our continent. It appears to be a time full of zeal for full emancipation, of liberation from every form of servitude, of personal maturity and of collective integration. In these signs we perceive the first indications of the painful birth of a new civilization. And we cannot fail to see in this . . . an obvious sign of the Spirit who leads the history . . . of peoples.[5]

d. A renewed and relevant concept of evangelization, of conversion, of the new human being, of life committed as demanded by this moment in the crucial history of our continent. As Cardinal Pironio says, "We have a continent which is baptized, but only superficially evangelized. It is urgent that faith be illuminated, matured and committed to life."[6]

e. A renewed, authentic concept of piety, of true worship and its relation to service and, even more, to political commit-

---

4. Ibid., p. 5.

5. Second General Conference of Latin American Bishops, *The Church in the Present-Day Transformation of Latin America in the Light of the Council*, vol. 2: *Conclusions* (Washington: U.S. Catholic Conference, 1973), p. 35.

6. Mons. Eduardo Pironio, *La Iglesia que nace entre nosotros*, p. 75. See also Lesslie Newbigin, "Context and Conversion," in *Mission y evangelizatión. Una afirmación ecuménica* (Geneva: CMI, n.d.).

ment. Frei Beto (Brazil) deals with the subject in great depth in *A oração na ação*. Leonardo Boff (Brazil) sets the problem in very clear terms when he writes in "Mistica e ação política":

> The problem is not simply the prayer-action relationship but prayer-liberation, that is, prayer-political, social, historic, transforming action. Correctly formulated, the question is put in terms of Mysticism and Politics.

f. Intimately related to this question: given the gravity of the problems that affect our Latin American peoples today, has not the moment arrived for the church in its ecumenical dimension to assume a clear and more concrete political commitment? A commitment that, even if it scandalizes and shakes the "principalities and powers" of this world, will give back to the church of God a credibility and authority it has been losing? The populist, socialist, radical current of North American Methodism is worth attention, as described by Robert Craig, in "Methodism, Popular Struggles and Social Change—The U.S. Case," a chapter in the volume I mentioned at the outset.[7]

Some years ago in an important assembly of our Argentina Methodist Church, Míguez Bonino brought the dilemma up-to-date in the following terms:

> The question, "church and socialism" has been debated in Christian thought for more than a half century now. I believe we have arrived at a point at which the decision to be with Jesus and therefore with those with whom he identified himself demands a clear answer. I believe a responsible choice against imperialism and capitalism can only become concrete if we have the courage to say we seek a socialist order. . . .
>
> This option means concretely the subordination of the economic to the social—in counterposition to the materialist economics of capitalism.[8]

g. The increasing rediscovery of the eschatological values of the revelation, which have served not only as the base for the contemporary witness of our Latin American martyrs but also as a "motor force of salvation history" and the inspiration

---

7. *La tradición protestante en la teología latinoamericana*, pp. 31-61.
8. *Nuestra fe y nuestro tiempo*, pp. 19-20.

for a theology of hope. This openness to the future can survive, even in the midst of paralyzing fears of militarism, of the arms race, and of a nuclear apocalypse. In the words of Gustavo Gutiérrez:

> The recovery of an historic vision centered on the future and animated by the hope that Christ will lead everything to its complete fulfillment puts in a different light the new human whom the present action seeks to create.[9]

The eschatological perspective is inevitable in our theological understanding of the unity of the church in our time. We live in a permanent tension between eschatological unity (Eph. 4) and the historic conflict in which our churches participate.

Furthermore, the eschatological affirmation is essential, for two reasons: (1) because it relativizes the conflict, just as do the provisional forms of unity we try to establish in history, and (2) because it defines the content of an authentic Christian unity. We look for the manifestation of our Lord Jesus Christ *(parousia)*, the coming of his kingdom: "new heavens and a new earth in which justice dwells" (2 Pet. 3:13; Isa. 65:17-25). Therefore we have nothing less than this as the final goal of the Christian church and the human community, as the vision that maintains a dynamic missionary and prophetic life of the people of God, and as the permanent pressure of the *eschaton* on history, propelling it in the direction of the kingdom, the direction of the *shalom* of God.

Finally, I believe that, beginning with an ecumenical pastoral that takes these elements into consideration and walks together with others of different confessional roots, we will discover that we are in condition not only to offer the ministry that people need and demand in these hours but also to extend our witness with humility, clarity, and firmness. And we shall see the broader ecumenical family: that of our brothers and sisters of other regions of the Third World, companions in poverty and hope; and that of our brothers and sisters of the First and Second Worlds, with their multiple privileges but also with their visible or hidden burdens of guilt and fears.

9. *Hacia una teología de la liberación*, p. 76. See "Eschatology and Politics," chapter 11 in Gutiérrez's book, *A Theology of Liberation* (Maryknoll, N.Y.: Orbis, 1973), pp. 213-50.

FEDERICO PAGURA

Miguel d'Escoto, priest and foreign minister of Nicaragua, gives the parable of the Good Samaritan a new meaning in these times in his land:

> God catches us on the road with unforeseeable and surprising events. Above all in the wounded neighbor, in God's and our wounded people. Suddenly then I find myself in a situation where I must get down off the animal on which I am riding and take care of my wounded people, leaving my usual missionary activity. I had to follow the example, not of the priest but of the good Samaritan. My fidelity to Christ and my love of the people, which are not different things but the same faith and the same love, the same cross, obligated me to this.[10]

I offer you my brotherly embrace in the love of Christ who sustains us, impels us, and fills us with hope by his resurrection and victory.

---

10. *Ministers of God, Ministers of the People* (Maryknoll, N.Y.: Orbis, 1983).

A SERMON

The Question of the Children— Still the Same

NANCY CARDOSO PEREIRA (Methodist, Brazil)

"But . . . where is the lamb for the sacrifice?"

The question is repeated in different forms, from the mouths of different children, in different moments in history, in different places in the world.

Isaac's question to Abraham extends to the whole patriarchal society, its customs, and its relationships with other cultures that accepted child sacrifice, among other practices, as a form of pleasing the gods, calming their wrath, achieving their favor, and justifying their domination.

Isaac's question denounces an experience of God, a form of knowing God, which admits infanticide . . . a perception of God built on relationships of domination, among them the domination and sacrifice of children.

"But . . . where is the lamb for the sacrifice?"

Isaac's question is the expression of the poorest of the poor—the children—asking for justice. The question refers to the promise of God to Abraham: the promise of land, of sons and daughters, and of blessings. In order for the promise to become real, it was necessary to break with the infanticide of that time, to break with what had been the experience of God until then. It was necessary to affirm a God who defends the life of boys and girls—a God who offers something else in sacrifice rather than boys and girls, the guarantee of the promise of the realization of life.

"But . . . where is the lamb for the sacrifice?"

This might have been the same desperate and silent question of the many children sacrificed by the Pharaoh in Egypt at the time of the oppression and slavery of the people of Israel—the systematic extermination of children as a form of social control and maintenance of power structures. The well-known strategy of the powerful was to torture the fathers and mothers to the point of forcing them to reject their sons and daughters (Exod. 1:22ff.; Matt. 2:13ff.).

"But . . . where is the lamb for the sacrifice?"

This same tearful question was raised by the children persecuted by the indiscrimate fury of Herod, who was tormented by the possibility of a child who might be the liberating Messiah. The same question was heard in the clamor and lamentations of mothers weeping for their children, mothers who could not be consoled because their children were dead (Jer. 31:15; Matt. 2:18).

"But . . . where is the lamb for the sacrifice?"

This cry is heard until Jesus calls the child and places it in the midst of his disciples and says that of such is the kingdom of God; until Jesus warns that if anyone harms one of these "it is better that a mill stone were hanged around his neck and he were cast over a precipice."

Jesus not only rejects and denounces a society and a religion that accepts and coexists with infanticide, with the domination and exploitation of boys and girls, but he also proposes and announces the reign of God that belongs to the child. In his announcement of the reign of God, Jesus makes it quite clear that boys and girls are the criterion and the measure for participation in it: "Whoever does not become as one of the least of these will not enter into the Kingdom."

Jesus proposes a new community with new relationships where the child has a privileged place. It is a community that not only rejects child sacrifice but is necessarily built on consideration for the very least. For this new community, Jesus offers himself as the lamb for the sacrifice. God offers the Divine self in sacrifice in place of the poor whom God loves, like a mother and a father, so that nevermore need they be sacrificed. In this community, the disquieting question of Isaac does not exist. The community is built on the death and resurrection of Jesus; it is already living the concrete sign of liberation; it is always present and always moving forward in the reign of God.

The challenge that comes to us is to hear the question that comes from the boys and girls of the whole world, especially in the different realities of the Third World.

The challenge that comes to us is to hear and understand that, like Isaac, they cry out for justice, they question the structures in which they live. They ask us about the lamb who is going to be sacrificed.

New ears and eyes are needed to hear, understand, and take seriously the truth that in the voice of the very least is the strongest denunciation of the present economic/political system and the most radical demand for transformation and liberation.

The challenge that comes to us is to hear, understand, take seriously, and commit ourselves to the voice of children who express themselves in various ways, in various organizations, with various proposals for transformation. We do not have to be the voice of the children. We do not have to formulate the question for them.

The challenge that comes to us is to commit ourselves to their question and to sacrifice what really needs to be sacrificed—that which threatens life.

Eyes and ears committed to the struggle for justice are needed, if we are to offer something other than children in sacrifice.

In Brazil today, millions of children are systematically sacrificed by the economic and political structures that respond to the interests of international capitalism.

They are sacrificed in the streets of the great cities where they live abandoned and vulnerable to every type of exploitation and injustice.

They are sacrificed by an inefficient and elitist system of health care that condemns thousands of children to stillbirth and infant mortality, and thousands of poor women to die in childbirth.

They are sacrificed by hunger and malnutrition that create very high indices of infant mortality.

They are sacrificed in the rural and urban areas as unskilled workers without fair pay or any kind of protection or security.

They are sacrificed by a land-holding system that concentrates the land in the hands of the few, destroys the viability of peasant families, and demands a constant and chaotic migration where all suffer, especially the small ones.

These are the sacrificed, marginalized boys and girls who today organize themselves as men and women in the struggle for life and justice. They question and denounce the powerful who maintain their power by the sacrifice of generations. They are determined that the present political, economic, and social system be sacrificed. They propose the construction of a new community, with new relationships between men and women, children and adults, capital and labor, knowledge and power. They denounce religious structures that justify and sustain the powerful in their operations. They denounce an individualistic religiosity that conceives of a god who accepts the sacrifice of millions of children. They denounce and break with this piety. In place of this experience of God they demand another.

This has been the challenge lived by Christian men and women in Brazil; to hear, understand, take seriously, and commit themselves to the question raised by millions of marginalized boys and girls. This demands of the churches themselves, and of Brazilian—and every other—society, commitment to and defense of life, and the decision to sacrifice what really needs to be sacrificed in our structures.

Because the kingdom of God is of the children.

Because it is necessary to learn from them.

Because it is necessary to be like them in order to belong to God's kingdom.

The challenge is to convert our structures and our programs with children so that the voices of millions of poor boys and girls in our country may be heard in our Protestant communities. And that we may be capable of committing ourselves to projects designed to free children from exploitation and to support their human development.

This is also the challenge to the Brazilian and international ecumenical community.

This is the challenge to the church everywhere.

This is the challenge to all women and men of good will.

"But . . . where is the lamb for the sacrifice?"